Faith
For
Souls

My husband and I were fortunate to have William Burgess as our pastor for several years.

We met when he came to our home and introduced my husband to Christ. I spent 14 years praying for Wes to embrace Jesus. Our lives will never be the same after this significant event. I am so grateful that William put it all in a book!

Faith For Souls can convict, embolden, encourage, and transform your interactions with others.

I passionately recommend this book. It has the power to revolutionize your life.

Loretta Walker
MA/Receptionist | Broken Arrow, OK

You must devour this book! Bill Burgess genuinely is a man of God! He has done a great job revealing the Father's heart concerning soul winning. This is God's message to the world. It will never get old.

I absolutely love this book. It's written to inspire you to learn and to experience Jesus' words for yourself to *'go into all the world and preach the Gospel.'* You will laugh and cry at Pastor Bill's many stories and be changed. Faith will come to believe that a *'man that wins souls is wise'* and that you are that man.

His words are profoundly touching and encouraging as he explains how to become a soul winner, an ambassador of Christ. How different would your life be if you said, *'Here am I, Lord, send me?'* For me, my life and heart will never be the same.

Amber Wright
Associate Pastor
Walnut Grove Church | Broken Arrow, OK
Principal ACE School
Retired

As you read, you discover William's passion for winning the lost is infectious. Every believer should experience the joy of leading people to the Lord. This book shows the simplicity of sharing the Gospel. As you read the testimonies, you will laugh, cry, and be inspired to share your salvation story with others. So get ready to be moved, encouraged, and stirred to share Jesus!

Pastor Fred Benzel
Grace Life Church | Lincoln, CA

Brother William (Bill) Burgess and I have known each other for almost thirty years. He possesses God's heart and a clear vision for the lost. On his behalf, I was privileged to organize Pastors & Leaders Seminars and a monumental ten-day Evangelistic Crusade in Srikakulam, India. It's commendable how he resolutely relies on God.

When confronted with problems getting police clearances for the crusade, he remained steadfast in his faith and refused to bribe the authorities. Hundreds of individuals embraced Christ and experienced remarkable healings, some through the laying on of hands and others through prayer alone. People in the region are still discussing the crusade.

Brother Bill wrote *Faith For Souls* after years of winning souls. This handbook is essential for any devoted Christian seeking to bring people to Christ. William recounts his first-hand encounters while witnessing for Christ. By reading this book, one can learn the art of winning souls *through faith*.

Brother Melchizedek
Bible Teacher, Author, *Grace Realities—
Where Sin Has No Dominion*
Visakhapatnam, Andra Pradesh, India

The real-life stories in *Faith For Souls* are captivating and motivate me to aspire to be more like Jesus.

William's love for people and sensitivity to the Holy Spirit to minister to others provokes you to want to reach out. I see so much passion and love shown in his everyday journey to be used by God. It is so compelling . . . it's like he makes it so easy, how Jesus wants it to be. Anyone can do things out of their own strength. But the depth of his life and time spent with God makes communicating with others natural and compassionate. This is what Jesus wants for all of us.

Reading *Faith For Souls* made me slow down, watch, and listen to the Holy Spirit so that I might be more available to be sensitive to the needs of others, especially the lost. Too often, believers can just be 'busy with life.' *Faith For Souls* will help you focus on what is dear to Jesus' heart: the precious lives of people around us every day.

This work is invaluable.

Pastor Beth Wilson
West Coast Life Church | Murrieta, California

William H. Burgess was my pastor for several years before I became a pastor. I believe Bill's passion for winning lost souls to Christ he received from our Lord Jesus Christ. I know of his love for people and his boldness to witness. Bill prays regularly for the lost, asking the Lord for divine appointments *'to lead one more person to Christ.'* He has gone to many nations preaching the Gospel of Jesus Christ.

While attending his church, he trained my wife and me to lead the lost into a personal relationship with Jesus Christ. We received *Faith For Souls*, the confidence to witness to people, and how to give a reason we believe in Christ. This revelation that he received from the Lord of the Harvest will provide you with a new fire for the harvest of souls for the Kingdom of God. *Faith For Souls* is a comprehensive guide to sharing the gospel with others. I have enjoyed reading the stories of real people coming to Christ. His book is hard to put down. So inspiring.

You will learn how the Lord will enable you to win the soul winner's crown. William provides clear, concise instructions on starting conversations about faith, overcoming objections, and praying for those open to hearing about Jesus. He shares many adventures he and others have experienced as Jesus worked through them to win souls to Christ. An essential resource for anyone who wants to make a difference by sharing the love of Christ.

This book is deserving of my highest recommendation. If you want to strengthen your faith and have a meaningful impact on the world, I recommend reading *Faith For Souls: Supernatural Transformation To Win Souls To Christ*. This resource is indispensable for those seeking to bring others to Christ. It will enable you to bring many more souls to heaven!

Pastor Michael Burdick
Fredericksburg Victory Fellowship
Fredericksburg, TX

Bill Burgess has profoundly affected my ministry to the lost not once but twice. In the early 1990s, he guided me to accept Jesus as my Lord and Savior. *Faith For Souls* is the second.

I am compelled to reach the lost and understand the pressing nature of the current moment. The reader will find this book profoundly significant, particularly today.

Harry Roberts
Director, Human Resources
(for a Fortune 500 electronics corporation)
[*My dear brother Harry has entered his heavenly home, cheering us on to win souls!*]

Faith For Souls

SUPERNATURAL TRANSFORMATION TO WIN SOULS TO CHRIST

by

William H. Burgess

WORD & SPIRIT
PUBLISHING

The design, content, editorial accuracy, and views expressed or implied in this work are those of the author.

No part of this publication may be reproduced, stored in a retrieval system, or transmitted by any means—electronic, mechanical, photocopy, recording, or otherwise—without the prior permission of the copyright holder, except as provided by USA copyright law.

Unless otherwise indicated, all Scripture quotes are from the *New King James Version* of the Bible. © 1982 by Thomas Nelson, Inc. All rights reserved.

Scripture quotations marked KJV are from the *King James Version*. Copyright in Great Britain, the British Dominion, and Possessions Copyright in Philippine Islands Assigned 1964 to the Zondervan Publishing House. Copyright © 1964, 1972 by Zondervan Publishing House. Used by Permission.

Scripture quotations marked AMPC are from the *Amplified Bible*, Classic Edition. Copyright © 1954, 1958, 1962, 1964, 1965, 1987 by The Lockman Foundation. Used by permission. (www.lockman.org)

Scripture quotations marked NLT are from the *Holy Bible, New Living Translation*. Copyright © 1996, 2004, 2007, 2013 by Tyndale House Foundation. Used by permission of Tyndale House Publishers, Inc., Carol Stream, Illinois, 60188. All rights reserved.

Scripture quotations marked MSG are from *The Message*. Copyright © by Eugene H. Peterson 1993, 1994, 1995, 1996, 2000, 2001, 2002. Used by permission of Tyndale House Publishers, Inc.

Scripture quotations marked BSB are from the *Berean Study Bible*—public domain. April 30, 2023.

Scripture quotations marked BLB are from the *Berean Literal Bible*—public domain. April 30, 2023.

Scripture quotations marked WUEST are from *Wuest's Expanded Translation of the Greek New Testament* by Kenneth S. Wuest. Copyright © 1956 by William B. Eerdmans Publishing Company.

Scripture quotations marked NIV are from *The Holy Bible: New International Version*®. NIV®. Copyright © 1973, 1978, 1984 by Biblica. All rights reserved worldwide.

Scripture quotations marked TPT are from *The Passion Translation*® Copyright © 2017, 2018 by Passion & Fire Ministries, Inc. Used by permission. All rights reserved. ThePassionTranslation.com

Scripture quotations marked ESV are from *The Holy Bible, English Standard Version*. Copyright © 2001 by Crossway, a publishing ministry of Good News Publishing. Used by Permission. All rights reserved.

Scripture quotations marked YLT are from the *Young's Literal Translation*—public domain.

Scripture quotations from *The Englishman's Greek New Testament: An Interlinear Translation*. Copyright © 1970, 1976 by Zondervan Publishing House.

Unless otherwise indicated, all Greek word definitions are from *Thayer's Greek Lexicon*—public domain.

Unless otherwise indicated, all Hebrew word definitions are from the *Brown, Driver, Briggs, Gesenius Lexicon*—public domain.

All other copyrighted materials are the intellectual property of their respective owners and are included for educational purposes only.

Faith For Souls
Copyright © 2025 by William H. Burgess
ISBN: 978-1-685730-68-0

Published by Word and Spirit Publishing
P.O. Box 701403
Tulsa, Oklahoma 74170
wordandspiritpublishing.com

Printed in the United States of America. All rights reserved under International Copyright Law. Content and/or cover may not be reproduced in whole or in part in any form without the expressed written consent of the Publisher.

Dedication

To those who have gone before, sharing Christ and living the Gospel. Because of them, we now know Jesus as our Lord. And we are able to . . . reach yet one more.

I have sent you out to harvest a field that you haven't planted, where many others have labored long and hard before you. And now you are privileged to profit from their labors and reap the harvest.

—**John 4:38 TPT**

Contents

Foreword	Pastor Stephen Fraser	xiii
Preface	William H. Burgess	xv
Author's Note		xx
Introduction	William H. Burgess	xxi
Chapter 1	The Purpose of Our Faith?	1
Chapter 2	What Are You Going to Do?	21
Chapter 3	1,800 Saved in Eight Days	31
Chapter 4	Faith For Souls	43
Chapter 5	Handling the Religious	61
Chapter 6	Witnessing Jesus-Style	79
Chapter 7	Divine Appointments	101
Chapter 8	Closing the Witness	115
Chapter 9	As Much As in Me Is	133
Chapter 10	Spirit & Soul: Renewing the Mind	159
Chapter 11	What Gospel Do You Have?	177
Chapter 12	I Don't Believe in Atheists	199
Chapter 13	Bold, Not Brash	223
Chapter 14	Just Minding My Own Business	237
Chapter 15	It's Hard Here	261
Chapter 16	Creativity of the Creator	277
Chapter 17	Power from on High	291
Conclusion		315
My Prayer for You		325
Prayer of Salvation		328
Bibliography		334
Appendix: The BULLET		342
About the Author		345
Faith For Souls Series: Book 2		347

Foreword

Following my call as an evangelist and completing Bible school in 1992, I was fortunate to collaborate with the accomplished soul winner, William H. Burgess. His remarkable love for people affected me the most during those two years. He longed for all people to meet His Savior, Jesus Christ. I discovered that this love and passion were more than just human compassion: they were the Lord's hand upon his life.

One moment remains etched in my memory. Sitting in his parked car, William shared, as his custom was, some of his soul winning stories. I was refreshed and strengthened as he shared how God had anointed him with a special anointing of the Father's love.

Then, in an instant, as I turned my head to look up at him again, his face transfigured before my eyes. I no longer saw William Burgess; instead, I saw the face of Jesus in place of his. I will never forget that.

There used to be a group of us at his church who would playfully chant, *'If Pastor Bill can't get 'em saved, nobody can.'*

The pages of *Faith For Souls* will ignite your faith to share Jesus with the lost. Soul winning is made easy as faith replaces fear and complacency. Get ready to go on a journey that will reveal truth to you and impart the love of the Master Himself—a love that casts our fear and makes us fishers of men.

Faith For Souls

The publication of this book could not be timelier. Unsurprisingly, it was delayed from completion for over twenty years. I say this for a couple of reasons. First, many churches have lost their zeal to shine as lights to a very lost and dying world. Another positive reason is that revival tremors are felt in colleges, sports events, and many unusual places.

Faith For Souls: Supernatural Transformation To Win Souls To Christ is an instruction manual that provides training for such an army. I pray this book transforms your life and will go viral throughout the church world.

May *Faith For Souls* empower, train, equip, and mobilize ordinary men and women to fight in this End-Time battle we now face.

Pastor Stephen Fraser
Author, Evangelist
Founding Pastor
Life of Faith Bible Church | Louisville, KY

Preface

*T*wo things constantly beat in my heart. *First*, that every person I meet or know—acquaintance, family, or friend—would come to know Jesus. There is nothing more important in life than *I might know Him* (Philippians 3:10) and that everyone I meet would know Him, too.

> *Now, even though I am free from the obligations to others, I joyfully make myself a servant to all in order to win as many converts as possible.*
>
> *I became 'weak' to the weak to win the weak. I have adapted to the culture of every place I've gone so that I could more easily win people to Christ.*
>
> 1 Corinthians 9:19,22 TPT

My wife Shirley and I constantly ask God for *divine appointments* so that one more person may come to Christ.

Just Yesterday a Soul Came to Christ

We had stopped at The Home Depot (one of my favorite stores) to get a few things after the Sunday morning church service. Upon checking out, I gave the cashier one of my **The BULLET** tracks[1] (see Appendix).

Faith For Souls

Stepping outside, two more employees were standing by the entrance. I had one more *BULLET* in my pocket. I gave it to the older man, *'When you have time, check this out. I wrote this.'* He took the tract.

Shirley was waiting in the car. We were parked close to the front of the lot. I unloaded the rock salt and was just about to shut the trunk when one of these guys spoke, standing behind me. It was the younger of the two; he was only 19 years old. He had the tract in his hand and pointed to the second page. At first, I thought he might argue. But he wanted to thank me. *'Thank you for this. I am going through a lot. I feel like this is God talking to me.'*

This surprised me, but I was delighted. He then told me he was in a hard place. (I will call him *Sam* for now.)

Sam told me that his older brother had OD'd (overdosed) and died last May (this was September). I told him I was so sorry. I could feel his pain.

> *'Have you asked Jesus into your heart?'* I interjected. *'I try every day.'* Sam responded.
>
> *'It is like getting married. You can have a great girl. You can be engaged for a long time. But until you say, "I do," you're not married.'* I shared another analogy.
>
> *'Sam, it's like a lamp. Let's say your grandmother left you a beautiful lamp. You turn it on—but it does not work. So, you change the light bulb, but it still won't light up. Then your friend says, "Hey, it is not plugged in."'*
>
> *'Sam, sin has tripped the chord. We have all sinned. We are all "unplugged from God."'*
>
> *'Jesus plugs us back in.'*

I said to Sam, *'Let's do it right now.'* He prayed right there by the open trunk of my car. *'Congratulations!'* I asked if he had a Bible and if he had tried to read it. *'Yes, but it was hard to get much out of it.'*

'Sam, now that is all going to change.' And then I showed him John 1:12:

> But as many as received Him, to them He gave the right to become the children of God, to those who believe on His name.
>
> John 1:12 KJV

'Now, you are a son of God. God will talk to you through His Word. It will be different.' I instructed him to read the Gospel of John. He nodded.

We exchanged phone numbers and began texting one another. (I am following up with my *new little brother*).

The *Second* Beat

With everything within me, I yearn for *the whole* body of Christ to be free. Winning souls is effortless and exhilarating, but that was not where I began. Wrapped up in my life, I was not paying attention to those around me daily who were going to hell.

But God stopped me. He asked me a question. *'How will you reach people with the Gospel of Jesus on your campus this last semester of college?'* I wept. I repented. Then I began. I had no clue what I was doing and with no apparent fruit.

This book is about my journey. It will set you free. You will win souls everywhere at a moment's notice. Why? Because by *this revelation*, **Faith For Souls**, Jesus, the Master Soul Winner, will come alive in your life. Read it. Be changed. Experience the delight by bringing in *your* harvest.

And then together, we will each hear Him say, when we look into His eyes,

'Well done, thou good and faithful servant.'

Matthew 25:21

Conclusion

Let me tell you about the three classes or categories of Christians when witnessing or sharing your faith.

First, there are the *'Lit Up Actively Soulwinning'* Christians. You are free of encumbrance and fear and go about *'leaving a trail of casualties on the devil everywhere you go, people saved, healed, and delivered.'* You will love **Faith For Souls**. Laugh, gain new insights, and get even more fired up to win the lost!

Second, the *'I love the Lord Christians, and want all my friends, family, and neighbors to come to Christ.'* Sometimes, you have been effective as a witness. Other times, your heart has ached, yearning that you could do so much more. You have been faithful in your walk, but it is time to get in. Put on your seat belt—you are about to go for a ride! **Faith For Souls** will light you up!

Third, there are those *'CIA Christians like me.'* You love the Lord, but almost no one in the outside world (the unsaved) knows 'you are one of them' (a Born Again child of God). You need help! Maybe, like me, you can live your life daily and never think about the lost all around you heading for an eternity in hell. You do not even notice. And to be honest, this topic is almost assaultive to you. *'But that is someone else's job.'* The problem is that this is not true, according to Jesus.

Preface

Let me make you an offer. Just take this book in, read it, and let God birth the soul winner from within that Christ designed you to be. **Faith For Soul**s will set you free!

> *But I promise you this—the Holy Spirit will come upon you, and you will be seized with power. You will be my messengers to Jerusalem, throughout Judea, the distant provinces—even to the remotest places on earth!*
>
> Acts 1:8 TPT

William H. Burgess
Pastor & Evangelist

P.S. Friend, if you have never accepted Jesus as your personal Lord and Savior, I invite you to do it now. There is no greater joy and peace than to know that if your life were to end, you would be in the presence of the loving God of the universe forever.

Please take a moment and turn to the PRAYER OF SALVATION at the back of the book.

Author's Note

All events and circumstances are as I experienced them. However, because of the duration of these events, some of which occurred so many years ago, the names of some individuals have been changed because I no longer have contact with them or to provide anonymity to those who would desire it.

Introduction

*S*ome scriptures stand out to each of us. Some are *life scriptures*, others are *directional (guidance) scriptures*, and others become *mandates for our lives*.

A *life scripture* for me are these two verses of Proverbs. I especially like *Young's Literal Translation* here:

> *In the fear of Jehovah [is] strong confidence, And to His sons there is a refuge.*
>
> *The fear of Jehovah [is] a fountain of life, To turn aside from snares of death.*
>
> Proverbs 14:26-27 YLT

The Lord spoke to me about *the fear of the Lord*. I was leaving India on my seventh trip. God had poured out His love and grace. He made way for us to sponsor the construction of three church buildings and freshwater wells in India and do the dedication for each. Salvations, deliverances, and healings. These things only happened because I had listened and obeyed His voice this time. He had told me:

> *And you must wait in My Presence. You cannot do this if you do not wait in and upon My Presence.*

The Fear of the Lord

As I was about to board the plane, the Lord defined *the fear of the Lord* to me. He spoke within:

The Fear of The LORD (Isaiah 11:2) is the complete submission to God, the exalting of God, and total un-reliance upon ourselves. It is the ultimate dependence upon the absolute supremacy of God.

When I have held to this, I have done well. I have seen God's wonders. God wants that for you.

Our Spirit, God's Treasure House

For me, a directional or *guidance scripture* would be Matthew 13:52.

He said to them, Therefore every teacher and interpreter of the Sacred Writings who has been instructed about and trained for the kingdom of heaven and has become a disciple is like a householder who brings forth out of his storehouse treasure that is new and [treasure that is] old [the fresh as well as the familiar].

Matthew 13:52 AMPC

Regarding winning the lost to Christ, God has built a *treasure house* in my spirit. He has taken me from that *CIA Christian*—who had no guts and no will to share the Gospel—to one who can empower believers everywhere I have traveled. This is truly God's grace.

I recognized this *treasure house* when I obeyed and addressed the penning of **Faith For Souls**. The book has become a reference manual for soul winning—much more than I originally planned. Your heart will grow full of faith.

Introduction

Believing in Me, You Will Do the Same

Blessed with a minimal church heritage, one with little indoctrination, *I did not know*. I did not know you could not just believe the Bible. I did not know that miracles had passed away. It blessed me to be ignorant. Believing that I could do the same things as Jesus was life-altering. Now I know.

> *Most assuredly, I say to you, he who believes in Me, the works that I do he will do also; and greater works than these he will do, because I go to My Father.*
>
> John 14:12

This has become a *mandate for my life*. It is my directive to help you, and all believers, learn who you are in Christ so that you can understand how to do what you were created to do and who you were created to be. God made us to be *witnesses to Jesus Christ*.

A Brief Introduction

Through a secular public university, working on my master's degree, I was required to draft a poem entitled *I Am From . . .* You know how sometimes we look over our shoulders and observe things about ourselves, sometimes things we have not seen? This poem did that. Look over my shoulder with me. I have so much hope inside. May I share it with you? I know God will do wonders in your life. Let me help you.

I Am From . . .

I am from a kind man and a good woman.
From love, belief, devotion.
All else fails, but not love.
I feel it yet.

Faith For Souls

I am from a tall man of action.
And a red-headed woman of reflection.
She is an artist like me.
He is a champion for others.
I have hope.
I am from laughter and good memories.
Where who I am is accepted
Where being artistic
It is different, but good.
I am from Italy, a hospital where no one spoke English.
From my father's laughter, as he
Translated to my mom, she said,
'Push lady, Push!'
I am from checkered tablecloths and red wine.
A gondola ride, the boat almost tipping
All wanting to see the 'Piccolo bambino!'
Fat American baby boy.
I am from countless hours on planes, buses, taxis & cars.
From foreign streets, with brothers' hearts beautiful.
Comradeship. Love. Devotion.
Quest for God.
I am from miracles.
A birth not expected. A hand, now mine
Upon eyes that are blind.
Now, 'it is bright, it is very bright!'
Husband contented. My mind blown!
Inside, I'm screaming,
'Can this life be mine?'
I am from faraway places.
The streets of Bombay reek of decay.
Earnest faces, eager eyes, asking,
'How do you like our city?'

Introduction

My heart speaks truth of what I could.
'The people are wonderful.'
I am from Wonders.
A deaf who can hear.
Beautiful child beaming.
Mom's eyes glisten with gratitude you can feel,
'Who am I? I am just flesh.'
I am spirit, soul & flesh, yes,
But someone who is more.
Oh, how wonderful the human.
Color, race, age are no more.
Beautiful, beautiful people.
Each in their way, all is so precious.
How can they see there is more hope?
There is a better way.

The Book Itself

Looking to begin an illustrated fictional evangelistic story, my mind was set. But I had yet to obey. Having traversed the United States, five continents, and seventy mission trips, preaching and doing personal soul winning, my book **Faith For Souls** sat twenty-five years unfinished. Now was the time. The Lord made it clear—*you must get this revelation I gave you to the masses before you do anything else.*

As I began, the book grew. Then some more. Then more. It is now a series of books to win souls to Christ. I give you the wealth the Lord has invested in my life now. It is full of examples and real-life testimonies. (I read my own stories, *and* I am amazed!)

Faith for Souls – Book 1

The first three chapters reveal transformation results, leaping from fear to **Faith For Souls**. Chapter 1 *The Purpose of Our Faith?* asks, what is God's real plan—and are we aligning with it? Chapter 2 *What Are You Going to Do?* God's question began this adventure, and I was NOT looking for it! Chapter 3 *1,800 Saved in Eight Days!* tells of a revival of personal soul winning at an African church. This can happen here. And it must.

Chapter 4, *Faith For Souls*, is my testimony. I began effortlessly winning people to Christ with no work or plan of my own. Chapters 5 through 8 give breadth to this revelation, covering the topics of *Handling Intimidation* (Chapter 5), *Witnessing Jesus Style* (Chapter 6), *Divine Appointments* (Chapter 7), and *Closing the Witness* (Chapter 8).

Chapter 9 *As Much As in Me Is*, and Chapter 10 *Spirit & Soul: Renewing the Mind*, target who you see yourself to be and how to align with how God sees you. What He thinks is what counts.

Chapter 11 *What Gospel Do You Have?* expounds upon the Gospel of grace, as opposed to one of works. We cannot begin by grace, but then try to work our way home. Chapter 12 *I Don't Believe in Atheists*, addresses what God says about it—no man can deny His existence. Believing His Word deflates intimidation and fear.

Chapter 13 *Bold, Not Brash*, shows how and why we must be bold, not rude. Chapter 14, *Just Minding My Own Business*, discusses God's partnership: the Gospel and miracles. This is a promise and removes the pressure. When we spread the message of His Gospel, God will confirm it.

Chapter 15 *It's Hard Here*, is a myth buster. So many excuses why it won't work here, or for me, to share my faith are not true. I prove it by the Word and by example. Chapter 16 *Creativity of the Creator* is all

Introduction

about glorious freedom and spontaneity by the Spirit that makes soul winning easy and fun!

Chapter 17 *Power from on High* outlines the biblical basis and necessity for the Baptism of the Holy Ghost. I share glorious outpourings I have been privileged to witness, beginning with my own.

Conclusion and *My Prayer for You*, impart my love and faith for you to succeed in the Kingdom of God, to do what we were all created to be, *the light* in this world.

Now, let's begin.

Let Jesus give you what He gave me: **Faith For Souls: Supernatural Transformation To Win Souls To Christ. [Book 1]**

William H. Burgess
Pastor & Evangelist

To receive notification of new book publications, speaking engagements, and artwork, please sign in to our website: *WilliamBurgessCreations.com* or *WilliamBurgessCreations.world*, or scan the QR code below.

Christ purposed to bestow on mankind the very conditions of His own life and being, and to give to man through the gifts of the Spirit and the Gift of the Spirit, the same blessed ministry to the world that He Himself had enjoyed and exercised.[1]

—**John G. Lake**

*For the Son of man is come to seek
and to save that which was lost.*

—**Luke 19:10 KJV**

CHAPTER 1

The Purpose of Our Faith?

Jesus knew why He was here. To bring humanity back to God. One purpose. Only one. Everything He did had one goal—*to seek and save that which was lost.*

He gave His disciples a directive: *'Follow Me.'* Jesus tells us the same.

Then He said to them, 'Follow Me, and I will make you fishers of men.'

Matthew 4:19

Pretty clear. Then how do we miss it? Why do we wonder what our purpose in life is all about?

Every Part of Life Counts

The Christian life is rich. What an incredible adventure! We live by faith (Hebrews 11:1-6). We follow our Master. The Bible is God's Word and our road map. God speaks to us through His Word about every area of life. He wants and expects us to follow both His Word and His Spirit. Many things are important. Yet one, and only *one purpose*, is central to our existence.

Many Things are Important

So, what is the purpose of our faith? To buy that car or afford to send a child to college? The Word of God does say, *'But my God shall supply all your need according to his riches in glory by Christ Jesus'* (Philippians 4:19). I have stood upon that promise many times, and probably so have you. But is the primary purpose of our faith to have God help us with a school test, for a church Christmas program to go smoothly, or even for protection on a trip through an unknown place? All valid requests. These are important.

The Lord knows what is necessary to live. He cares. His perspective differs from ours. In Saint Matthew's Gospel, we read Jesus' words:

These things dominate the thoughts of unbelievers, but your heavenly Father already knows all your needs.

Seek the Kingdom of God above all else, and live righteously, and he will give you everything you need.

Matthew 6:32-33 NLT

I can hear the love in His voice. The Father does not want you to go without. But what is seeking the Kingdom of God? According to Jesus, this is the *highest purpose* of our faith.

By faith, we receive God's promises (Romans 4:16-25). Therefore, using our faith to obtain the Kingdom of God is the highest purpose of faith. We must do this *above all else*. So, what is it to seek the Kingdom of God and His righteousness?

First, We Must Know Him

The first purpose of our faith is to know God. I like the *Amplified Bible's* (Classic Edition) expression for faith (from 2 Timothy 3:15):

The Purpose of Our Faith?

'salvation which comes through faith in Christ Jesus [through the leaning of the entire human personality on God in Christ Jesus in absolute trust and confidence in His power, wisdom, and goodness].' God wants us to lean into Him for everything, especially with our heart and soul. He loves us. He saved us by sending His only Son to a brutal death on that hideous cross. Jesus paid for all your failings, sin, and disobedience. Too good to comprehend, but He did. Can you even imagine sending your child to die for someone else? I cannot. Yet He did.

> *For He* (God the Father) *made Him* (Jesus, the Son of God) *who knew no sin* (of His own) *to be sin for us, that we might become the righteousness of God in Him.*
>
> 2 Corinthians 5:21 (parenthesis mine)

> *For God so loved the world that He gave His only begotten Son, that whoever believes in Him should not perish but have everlasting life.*
>
> John 3:16

Salvation by Faith

You and I receive God's terms for salvation only by faith (Ephesians 2:8-9). We must put our absolute trust and confidence in the resurrected Christ alone to save us. Faith does this.

> *But without faith, it is impossible to please Him, for he who comes to God must believe that He is and that He is a rewarder of those who diligently seek Him.*
>
> Hebrews 11:6

Martin Luther started the reformation of the church (16th century) by recognizing that salvation and righteousness with God are obtained through faith.

'At last meditating day and night, by the mercy of God, I began to understand that the righteousness of God is that through which the righteous live by a gift of God, namely by faith. Here I felt as if I were entirely born again and had entered paradise itself through the gates that have been flung open.'[2]

First, the purpose of our faith is to know God through His Son Jesus Christ (John 14:6; Hebrews 9:14-15).

What is the Entire Purpose?

Is this the purpose of our faith in its entirety? Why are we to know God? So, one day, we can sit in our easy chair in heaven, sip tea, and say, *'Well, I made it!'* But no, I think not. There must be something more.

The same Jesus by whom we came to know the Father desires, *no commands, 'Follow Me'* (John 1:43). Follow Him, where? For *what* purpose? There it is again, *a purpose*. Most people today do not have one. But Jesus did. He knew exactly *where* He was going and *what* He was to do. He knew *how* He was to do it and *when* it was supposed to happen.

My Purpose Is in His Purpose

As I have aligned with Him and His purpose, I, too, have a purpose. *I know what I should do and how to do it.* As I follow His leading, He is showing me *where* and *when*. How great to have a purpose in life! His plan is my plan. I count. Knowing God's plan for my life is immensely fulfilling. I have a *purpose* because I found out **His purpose**.

Please open your Bible to Luke 19:10. I want you to compare every word. Know Jesus' purpose. I want you to get it just as He spoke it. Jesus spoke of himself. He said, **'For the Son of Man is Come to Seek and to Save that Which is Lost.'**

Jesus Came to Seek and Save

Jesus came to seek the lost. He came to look for you. You were hanging on the edge of a rock jetty over the side of a cliff. The screams of the demons of hell echoed up the canyon wall, calling your name. Hell is real, folks. Jesus taught us it was. (Luke 16:19-31; Mark 9:43-48; Matthew 25:30)

The devil had a meat hook with your name on it; he was about to give that last tug when the **Good Shepherd** appeared. His beaming eyes of love sparked a hope, and you gasped, *'Jesus save me!'*

He Came to Save You

He did not lecture you on why you should not have gotten into such an evil condition. That was *not* His purpose. He did not philosophize or give theories about rescue techniques. He did not come for theory. (We have offered theories for solutions to a hurting world.) Instead, we need to make an introduction—to introduce them to our friend, the *Good Shepherd*.

Jesus came not just for moral support. *He Came to Save You!* Jesus came to reach out His strong, *nail-scarred* hand down over the cliff to grasp yours just as the rock gave way. Jesus *saved you*. He saved me. And if we are biblical, He has already saved every person who walks this planet. But regrettably, they do not know it yet. Therefore, they cannot receive it.

> *In other words, it was through the Anointed One that God was shepherding the world, not even keeping records of their transgressions, and He has entrusted to us the ministry of opening the door of reconciliation to God.*
>
> 2 Corinthians 5:19 TPT

They Need Someone

They need somebody to tell them. God needs someone to say, *'Here I am, send me'* (Isaiah 6: 8). The world must hear the Gospel.

> *How then shall they call on Him in whom they have not believed? And how shall they believe in Him of whom they have not heard? And how shall they hear without a preacher?*
>
> *And how shall they preach unless they are sent? As it is written: How beautiful are the feet of those who preach the gospel of peace, who bring glad tidings of good things!*
>
> Romans 10:14-15

Are Your Feet Beautiful?

Are your feet beautiful to God? Beautiful to those to whom you have gone with the *good news?* Mine were blood-stained. Stained with the blood of those souls I had not warned (Ezekiel 33:6).

No, I do not believe we can witness to everybody by ourselves, but I believe God has *divine appointments* all around us *daily*. But unless we have *'ears to hear what the Spirit'* is saying, we will not hear. Therefore, we will miss the opportunities God puts before us.

Oh, the deep joy of soul and spirit I have experienced by receiving *ears to hear*. What guilt and shame I suffered when the Spirit said, *'Tell this man about Me now.'* I said, *'I will go later.'* For this man, there was no later. The next day, he died of a heart attack.

Why Do We Not Share Christ?

I know you have experienced that shame with me. Do I condemn you? No. I would have to blame myself. You do not witness for Christ (most believers) for **one** reason. That one reason is that **You Are Afraid**.

The Purpose of Our Faith?

I know the excuse, *'It is not my ministry.'* Or *'I would not want to say something wrong.'* A popular one among those who claim to be *'Spirit-filled'* is, *'I do not feel **led** to a witnessing ministry (or outreach, etc.).'*

That is the spiritual equivalent of the alcoholic who says, *'I can hold my liquor. I know my limit.'* No, come on. Take an intense look deep inside your heart and soul. You are afraid. *Scared spitless.* And so was I. Few can surpass this insurmountable wall. It is the **Wall of Fear**.

I'm Not a Fearful Person

I know many believers are not fearful people. However, we have to be honest with ourselves. If we are not afraid, then why do we not act? Why are we not passionately sharing the Gospel with the lost all among us? This isn't just a suggestion; it's our job description from the Lord Jesus. Our Lord. Consider the parable of the Talents (Matthew 25:14-30). The man who did not act had a root cause, *'I was afraid,'* he tells his master (verse 25).

Paul writes to Titus (Titus 1:15-16) *'Unto the pure, all things are pure, but unto them that are defiled and unbelieving is nothing pure;'* He then states, *'They profess they know God, but in works they deny Him.'* Our works speak loudly. We can say what we will, but what do our works say? These are harsh, weighty words. I am not seeking to weigh anyone down. But lift you. However, we must be honest with ourselves.

The Root of Procrastination Is Fear

Though I possess remarkable artistic skills (I am gifted with the ability to draw and capture a likeness of anyone), I often need to work on completing the artwork. Why? After much reading, submitting to mentors, and more, I have discovered the root of my procrastination—the fear that my work will not be perfect enough. Hence, I do not do it. I hit the wall—that same wall—*the wall of fear.*

Jesus Was Intent about Resisting Fear

How many times did Jesus say, *'Do not be afraid'*? In His teaching, He said, *'Do not fear'* (Matthew 10:26, 28, 31). His Gospel message gave assurance, not fear. To Peter, James, John, and others, He said, *'Do not be afraid'* (Luke 5:10). At His transfiguration, He said, *'Arise, do not be afraid'* (Matthew 17:7). In His resurrected appearance to the disciples, Jesus greeted them with, *'Do not be afraid'* (Matthew 28:10).

To Jairus, the ruler of the synagogue, upon hearing it was too late, *'Your daughter is dead,'* Jesus responded,

> *As soon as Jesus heard the word that was spoken, He said to the ruler of the synagogue, 'Do not be afraid; only believe.'*
>
> Mark 5:36

Jesus Is Not Fear

In the Gospel of John's account of Jesus walking on water, the disciples *were terrified* (John 6:19 NLT). When Jesus responds, in the Greek word order, it says:

> *I AM not fear!*
>
> John 6:20 [Interlinear Greek[3]]

I love it! Jesus, *the I AM*, is the opposite of fear. This takes us straight into John's revelation of fear, in contrast to the love of God. We read,

> *There is no fear in love; but perfect love casts out fear, because fear involves torment. But he who fears has not been made perfect in love.*
>
> 1 John 4:18

The Purpose of Our Faith?

Preceding this, John tells us,

And we have known and believed the love that God has for us. God is love, and he who abides in love abides in God, and God in him.

1 John 4:16

God wants you and me to be free. He does not wish for us to be *tormented by fear*. He does this through the principle of *mutual exchange*.

The Principle of Mutual Exchange

Years ago, while serving as associate pastor at Church on the Move[4] in Tulsa, Oklahoma, I heard Pastor Willie George[5] often talk about the *Law (or Principle) of Mutual Exchange*. He meant that whenever God asks or commands something of us; He gives to us in return. And His return is always greater.

Look at the command to be Born Again.

Jesus answered and said to him, 'Most assuredly, I say to you, unless one is born again, he cannot see the kingdom of God.'

John 3:3

We must be born again to be *in* the kingdom of God. Or no heaven. Only damnation. We must do our part and choose Jesus. When we make Him Lord of our life, we are then Born Again. But what do *we* get?

For God so loved the world (you and me) *that He gave His only begotten Son, that whoever believes in Him should not perish but have everlasting life.*

John 3:16

Eternal Life—that is a good deal. His life is in us now. For eternity, we will be with our loving Heavenly Father, in His presence. By doing what? Our part.

Mutual Exchange and the Harvest

Jesus commands us to preach the Gospel to all the world.

And he said to them, 'As you go into all the world, preach openly the wonderful news of the gospel to the entire human race!'

Mark 16:15 TPT

Okay, that is our part. What do we get? Before I answer that, let me ask who is greater, the servant or the master? Jesus taught,

I assure you, most solemnly I tell you, a servant is not greater than his master, and no one who is sent is superior to the one who sent him.

John 13:16 AMPC

Jesus is the Master. He is Lord. We are the servants of God.

So here is the question. Who stands to receive the most significant benefit—us or God? Can we out-give God? Absolutely not. When we obey God and proclaim Christ, He will strip away fear and intimidation will leave our lives. Why is that crucial?

Because he that fears is not made perfect in love. God is love.

This Commission Is the Power of God

The Gospel is *the power* of God to the world, but also to you. To set you free.

The Purpose of Our Faith?

*I refuse to be ashamed of the wonderful message of **God's liberating power unleashed in us through Christ!** For I am thrilled to preach that everyone who believes is saved- the Jew first, and then people everywhere!*

This gospel unveils a continual revelation of God's righteousness—a perfect righteousness given to us when we believe. And it moves us from receiving life through faith, to the power of living by faith. This is what Scripture means when it says: 'We are right with God through life-giving faith!'

Romans 1:16-17 TPT (emphasis mine)

Preaching the Gospel is God's gift to release you from the heavy weight of fear. And to immerse you in His Love. *You need* to embrace this call as a gift. It is a gift, not a burden. This immersion is far-reaching.

German State-Run Counseling Center

One Sunday, I was delighted to see a couple from the German Bible School where I had preached years before. They were visiting my church. These two were young students when I taught *Faith For Souls*. Now a married couple, the man shared over lunch that his mother, who had also been a student, heard the message. She was a counselor at a German government-run family counseling center. He said the center practiced many methods, endeavoring to help people. They employed everything from Tarot Cards to zodiac readings to transcendental meditation, but not the Bible.

However, the message of *Faith For Souls* changed his mother. She broke free from fear. Over the next five years, his mother led every one of the counseling staff, including the management, to Christ. *'Now, the counselors are helping marriages and families using God's Word!'*

Faith For Souls

You Can Get over the Wall

This book is about scaling the wall! God helped me. God showed me how. If you let me, I can show you how. I have taught what the Spirit of God gave me to thousands across the United States, parts of Europe, Asia, South and Central America, and Africa. It works because God's Word is made simple for you and me. I like what Charles Capps often said, *'I do not practice what I preach. I preach what I have practicedand practiced.'*[6] He would also say, *'God's Word is easy to understand, but people have written books to help you misunderstand the Bible.'*[7] This book is not one of those. *Faith For Souls* will make it *so easy* for you to win the lost to Christ.

This book will take you to a raw, *pure form of Christianity*—a Christianity where Christ's followers are effective witnesses for Christ. It will not be perplexing. If you endure through this book, you will either love me for this invaluable Jesus-inspired revelation or hate me for pulling down The Wall. The absence of fear leaves just one thing: *Just Do It*.

Take the Challenge

Take the challenge. *Read this book*. Oh, the inexpressible joy of seeing those eyes open after a prayer. The light of heaven sparkling through. Eyes of someone you have just prayed with to accept Jesus Christ as their personal Lord, Savior, and *best friend*.

Let Jesus give you what He gave me . . . **Faith For Souls**.

PostScript-Terminology

As believers in Christ, we assume all Christians understand our speech. However, that is only sometimes the case. I will never forget a moment of misunderstanding with my mother. While home for the holidays, when attending Bible college, I used the phrase *'stand upon the*

The Purpose of Our Faith?

Word of God.' My mother grew somber. Then she asked, *'Do you put your Bible on the ground and stand upon it?'* My precious little Presbyterian mother was unfamiliar with the same terminology I used. Let me discuss a few words or phrases you will read throughout this work, so I can help prevent some misunderstanding.

Christian

To me, a Christian is a *Christ-follower*. This individual has encountered the living Christ and submitted their life to Jesus, making Him their Lord and Savior.

A person is not a Christian because they were *raised in a Christian home* or their parents were believers. Church membership, attendance, benevolent deeds of service, and even moral rigor cannot make you a Christian. Nor is a person a Christian because of their nationality or ethnicity. Everyone must personally meet Jesus and declare from the heart that He is Lord. A genuine Christian is an individual who has *received Jesus into their heart*.

> *Though you have not seen Him, you love Him; and though you do not see Him now, you believe in Him and rejoice with an inexpressible and glorious joy.*
>
> 1 Peter 1:8 BSB

Synonyms: Believer, Born Again, Child of God, Receiving Jesus, Saved

Soul winning

This book is all about *soul winning*. We are to be influencers of other people's hearts, so they may reach a point where they desire and choose to make Jesus the Lord of their life. The scripture teaches that the spirit of man is born again or reborn. But we must persuade the soul, which comprises the mind, will, emotions, and all the mental faculties, that Jesus is Lord. The New Birth or the Born Again experience is instantaneous. We become *new creatures in Christ* (2 Corinthians 5:17). Yet the decision to follow Christ is lifelong. It is a process. This journey to follow Jesus begins when we become persuaded that Jesus is the risen Lord and Savior.

A *soul winner* is a person who leads another into their own relationship with Jesus.

> *Then they said to the woman, 'Now we believe, not because of what you said, for we ourselves have heard Him and we know that this is indeed the Christ, the Savior of the world.'*
>
> John 4:42

Synonyms: Witnessing, preaching the Gospel, testifying of Christ, sharing the Good News

Lost

Jesus believed in and taught about the Kingdom of God and hell. Both are eternal. A soul will exist forever in the Presence of the God who is love, or in perpetual damnation in hell. Without Christ, we are all *lost* and bound for hell. Therefore, there is no greater urgency and more vital purpose in this life than influencing people to open their hearts to Christ and miss hell.

> *That at that time you were without Christ, being aliens from the commonwealth of Israel and strangers from the covenants of promise, having no hope and without God in the world.*
>
> *But now in Christ Jesus you who once were far off have been brought near by the blood of Christ.*
>
> Ephesians 2:12-13

Synonyms: Damned, Unbeliever, Unsaved

The Purpose of Our Faith?

Believer

A believer is a Christian. However, as one man said, 'There is an eighteen-inch difference between heaven and hell: from intellectually believing versus believing with the heart.' But in what, or in whom, do you trust to save you? Your performance, or the sacrifice of Jesus on the cross.

When the Ethiopian finance minister sought to be water-baptized,

> *Then Philip said, 'If you believe with all your heart, you may.' And he answered and said, 'I believe that Jesus Christ is the Son of God.'*
>
> Acts 8:37

Synonyms: Born Again, Child of God, Christian, New Birth, Receiving Jesus, Saved

Saved

To be *saved*, you are no longer lost. The Holy Spirit has forgiven the believer and sealed them in their heart. You are a child of God. Peace has entered your heart; heaven will be your home, and God's Spirit lives in your heart now.

> *In Him you also trusted, after you heard the word of truth, the gospel of your salvation; in whom also, having believed, you were sealed with the Holy Spirit of promise.*
>
> Ephesians 1:13

> *But as many as received Him, to them He gave the right to become children of God, to those who believe in His name.*
>
> John 1:12

Our faith in Jesus transfers God's righteousness to us and he now declares us flawless in his eyes. This means we can now enjoy true

> and lasting peace with God, all because of what our Lord Jesus, the Anointed One, has done for us.
>
> Romans 5:1 TPT

Synonyms: Believer, Born Again, Child of God, Christian, New Birth, Receiving Jesus

Unsaved

The *unsaved* do not have their names written in the Lamb's Book of Life. These are those individuals who have rejected Christ. They are irretrievably lost and damned.

> Then Death and Hades were cast into the lake of fire. This is the second death.
>
> And anyone not found written in the Book of Life was cast into the lake of fire.
>
> Revelations 20:14-15

Synonyms: Damned, Lost, Unbeliever

Witnessing

The Greek[8] word for witness is **matureo**, which means 'to testify, give evidence or bear record.' To witness or bear witness is 'to affirm that one has seen, heard, or experienced.' Our witness originates from our unique and personal relationship with the living Jesus. We are to show the love of God, which He has given us. 'We love Him because He first loved us' (1 John 4:7,11).

> Now when they saw the boldness of Peter and John, and perceived that they were uneducated and untrained men, they marveled. And they realized that they had been with Jesus.
>
> Acts 4:13

Synonyms: Preach the Gospel, Share Christ, Declare the Good News, Witness

Faith

Biblical *faith* is not blind. The Greek[9] word is **pistis**. It means *'faith, belief, trust, confidence, fidelity, faithfulness.'* In scripture, faith is trust in God's integrity, character, and nature. *The Amplified Bible* for Hebrews 11:1 is excellent:

> *Now faith is the assurance (**the confirmation**, the title deed) of the things [we] hope for, being **the proof** of things [we] do not see and the **conviction of their reality** [faith perceiving as real fact what is not revealed to the senses].*
>
> Hebrews 11:1 AMPC

We have this *'confirmation,' 'the proof,'* and *'the conviction of their reality'* because God is faithful. Faith is taking God at His Word, and He is *'not a man that He should lie'* (Numbers 23:19). What He has declared, He will perform. And God *'watches over His Word to perform it'* (Jeremiah 1:12).

Synonyms: Belief, Trust

Preach

We are to *preach* the Gospel. This is to declare, proclaim, herald, or share. We may preach before a large audience or in a personal one-on-one conversation. However, it is the content of the message that determines whether we are preaching the Gospel.

> *Now, brothers, I want to remind you of the gospel I preached to you, which you received, and in which you stand firm.*
>
> 1 Corinthians 15:1 BSB

Synonyms: Declare the Good News, Share Christ, Witness, Witnessing

Faith For Souls

Born Again

Jesus said, *'You must be born again'* (John 3). He explained that there are two births: *born of water* (natural birth) and *the Spirit* (spiritual birth). Jesus used many analogies to describe this New Birth of a man's heart. *Living water, the Bread of Life, the Light of the World, The Door, the Good Shepherd, and The Resurrection* all speak of Christ, giving a man a new life. To be *Born Again* is to have a clean conscience and be a new creature (person) on the inside.

> *Now, if anyone is enfolded into Christ, he has become an entirely new person. All that is related to the old order has vanished. Behold, everything is fresh and new.*
>
> 2 Corinthians 5:17 TPT

Synonyms: Believer, Child of God, Christian, New Birth, Receiving Jesus, Saved

Spirit Led or Led by the Spirit

The scripture says that the Holy Spirit leads God's children. After becoming Born Again, the believer in Christ has a host of gifts given to them. Assurance of salvation, or confidence of going to heaven, acceptance by God, peace with God, cleansing of the conscience, and forgiveness of sin are some of the beautiful bounties that God pours upon the child of God. Another powerful gift is the ability to be *led by the Spirit of God*. This is an internal guidance system whereby God speaks and leads your heart (or spirit). He does this by bringing remembrance of scriptures and directing the steps of a believer. This is often a very subtle *inner knowing* of what to do. Every believer must develop their ability to listen and obey God's leading. It takes practice and a humble attitude. To do so produces a fruitful and blessed life.

The Purpose of Our Faith?

For as many as are led by the Spirit of God, these are sons of God.

Romans 8:14

Synonyms: Hearing the voice of God, A leading, Impressed by the Spirit

Gospel

The *Gospel* is the ultimate expression of grace. God altruistically sacrificed His holy Son to redeem the morally corrupt human race. He requires only one thing. And that is, we must believe wholeheartedly in His Son, Jesus, and follow Him. The Gospel is the death, burial, and resurrection of Jesus Christ (1 Corinthians 15:1-4). The scripture tells us that *if we confess Jesus as Lord and believe in our hearts that God raised Him from the dead, we will be saved* (Romans 10:9). This is the gift of God. This is the Gospel.

But God demonstrates his own love for us in this: While we were still sinners, Christ died for us.

Since we have now been justified by his blood, how much more shall we be saved from God's wrath through him!

Romans 5:8-9 NIV

Synonyms: Good News, the Faith, the Living Way, the Blessed Hope, New Covenant

There is no peace in my soul until it is willing to obey the voice of God.[1]

—**Dwight L. Moody**

Our love for others is our grateful response to the love God first demonstrated to us.

—**1 John 4:19 TPT**

CHAPTER 2

What are You Going to Do?

*T*hat is what the Spirit of God said to me.

Finally, I had just registered for my last semester of classes to graduate from college. I had signed up for an almost double load to complete it. My dad constantly urged me to finish school. If the US government were to re-implement the draft in the post-Vietnam War era, he thought I could join as an officer. In that case, the likelihood of me being on the front line and getting shot would be lower.

It was a lovely sunny morning at San Jose State University in California. I had just walked out of the Student Union. *Finally, I will finish college. My dad will be relieved. I will be relieved!* Those were my thoughts.

Then, the Holy Spirit spoke within my heart. He asked a question. Have you ever noticed that God does not ask us questions because He needs to know something? Instead, he asks us to instruct and reveal our hearts.

> *What are you going to do this last semester of your college to reach people with the Gospel of Jesus Christ?*

My Heart Was Struck

The sharp point of His Word struck my heart. I found a quiet place under a shade tree and repented. Tears streamed down my cheeks as I, alone with God, reckoned with *His Purpose for my existence.*

A person may have many ideas concerning God's plan for his life, but only the designs of God's purpose will succeed in the end.

Proverbs 19:21 TPT

You and I must reckon with the fact that *we are witnesses. We are lights* to the world. (Notice in Acts 1:8, Jesus said, *'You shall be witnesses to Me.'* He did not just say, 'Go witnessing.')

You are the light of the world. A city that is set on a hill cannot be hidden.

Nor do they light a lamp and put it under a basket, but on a lampstand, and it gives light to all who are in the house.

Let your light so shine before men, that they may see your good works and glorify your Father in heaven.

Matthew 5:14-16

Where Is Your Light?

The question is, *where is your light?* On the hill, or in a hole? Mine hid in a deep, private hole where no one would bother it.

As the moment passed, I cried in repentance to God for my apathy. (God told me several years later that He would use me to confront many believers with this truth, *'... as I directly confronted you.'*) His Spirit then comforted me. I prayed to God: *'Lord, I will go out* (to witness) *one hour weekly, every Friday between 4 to 5 o'clock.'* I was sincere but also sincerely scared! How many students could be on campus at 4 p.m. Friday? Praise God: He is merciful even with our slight efforts to progress.

I went out every Friday. I kept my promise to God, and He was so gracious. I was not powerful, bold, or skilled, but now I was something I had not been before—*available*.

Not one person prayed to receive Christ throughout that entire semester. However, something significant happened. *I began to care about **the lost** all around me.*

Where is Your Love?

God's love is in your heart and mine.

Now hope does not disappoint, because the love of God has been poured out in our hearts by the Holy Spirit who was given to us.

Romans 5:5

For many, we have buried that love under many dusty things in the attic. *'I know it is up here somewhere.'* Do you remember saying words like that while trying to find something you have not used for ages?

Today, I ask the church this question: *'Do you really love?'* Jesus taught:

A new commandment I give to you, that you love one another; as I have loved you, that you also love one another.

By this all will know that you are My disciples, if you have love for one another.

John 13:34-35

Can you say, *'I am a Christian, I love the Lord,'* yet be motionless, silent, unfeeling towards people, souls slipping off into an eternity without God and without hope?

> *That at that time you were without Christ, being aliens from the commonwealth of Israel and strangers from the covenant of promise, having **no hope** and **without God** in the world.*
>
> Ephesians 2:12 (emphasis mine)

Can You Hear the Cries?

The worship leader of a church I pastored came up to me after a very moving Sunday morning service. He said,

> 'When you got up between songs and explained how you remember what it was like when you were lost, walking the busy corridors at school, people all around, yet feeling alone, so very alone—I heard it. I could hear their cries. Not your cries. **The cries of souls going to hell.** That is what you had described for so long.'

Ask God to Help You Find Your Love

Believer, *what do you hear?* Listen. *Listen again.* Still nothing? Ask God to help you find your love again. It is in there somewhere!

> *To the angel of the church of Ephesus write, 'These things says He who holds the seven stars in His right hand, who walks in the midst of the seven golden lampstands:*
>
> *I know your works, your labor, your patience, and that you cannot bear those who are evil. And have tested those who say they are apostles and are not, and have found them liars;*
>
> *and you have persevered and have patience, and have labored for My name's sake and have not become weary.*
>
> *Nevertheless, I have this against you, that **you have left your first love.***

> Remember therefore from where you have fallen; **repent and do the first works**, or else I will come to you quickly and remove your lampstand from its place—unless you repent.
>
> But this you have, that you hate the deeds of the Nicolaitans, which I also hate.
>
> He who has an ear, let him **hear what the Spirit says to the churches**. To him who overcomes I will give to eat from the tree of life, which is in the midst of the Paradise of God.'
>
> Revelations 2:1-7 (emphasis mine)

> If anyone boasts, 'I love God,' and goes right on hating his brother or sister, thinking nothing of it, he is a liar. If he won't love the person he can see, how can he love the God he can't see? The command we have from Christ is blunt: Loving God includes loving people. You've got to love both.
>
> 1 John 4:20-21 MSG

I Did Not Know How to Minister Healing

While in college, I had a friend and co-worker (from the campus donut shop) who had polio as a child (or a similar disease). I approached her one day, telling her the Lord could heal her. She graciously let me pray. We then got up and walked. She struggled as before. We prayed again, walked again, and she limped along again. Another time. Then, one more. Poor girl. I did not know how to minister healing.

Demons, I Had No Clue

Another day, I visited a friend who worked at a halfway house near the campus. The old Victorian home near the college housed residents released from either mental facilities or prison. (I called them *inmates*.)

My friend and I were chatting out on the street. While we talked, a resident came up to me. He put his face in mine and snarled, *'I am the devil.'* I looked at him and did what any self-respecting Christ-follower would do. I told the spirit, *'Get out!'* Then, with a snarl and a jeer, the man just walked off.

Some *man of God* I was.

The Lost I Did Not Know How to Reach

Later, my friend and I went to grab a burger. We had walked a few strides when I abruptly stopped and spun around. I pointed my finger in my friend's face and declared,

> *I may not know how to cast out devils, I may not know how to heal the sick, I may not know how to lead people to Christ, but* **I'm gonna find out how**!

But I Got Hungry to Learn!

There it was. Something I never had before in my Christian life—*hunger*. A yearning to follow Jesus, to be like Him, and to do what He did. Hunger to take Him at His Promise:

> *I tell you this timeless truth: The person who follows me in faith, believing in me, will do the same mighty miracles that I do—even greater miracles than these because I go to be with my Father!*
>
> John 14:12 TPT

Are You Hungry?

You have to want it. You must be hungry to follow Jesus; His way (John 14:6) is not for the fainthearted or the apathetic.

What are You Going to Do?

My wife was an administrator of a Christian school for many years. Countless times, I heard her speak of trying to help students. *'You cannot want it more than they do.'* Do you want it—to walk as Jesus did in His earthly ministry?

Jesus will help you become a *fisher of men*. You can walk in His shoes. A Christian is a follower of Christ. That is what they do: they walk in the ways of the Master. But we must go after it.

Let the Dead Bury the Dead

Why did Jesus say unusual things like *'let the dead bury the dead'* (Matthew 8:22)? The culture was different. The man may have put off Jesus' call (His invitation to follow) because he said, *'My father is old; let me wait until my father passes.*²*'* Maybe. But what I know is that Jesus wants you to follow Him **now**. No excuses.

Are you hungry? Are you willing?

I Know You Want to Win the Lost to Christ

I know you want to see people come to Christ and desire to be used by God to help make that happen. How do I know? I will prove it to you.

Before you became a *born from above* believer in Jesus Christ, your wants differed. Before receiving Christ, I did not think about reading the Bible. Did you? I was uninterested in attending church and did not consider becoming a vital member. How about you? Prayer—what was that? Did you pray much before being saved? (Maybe in a crisis.) For some, you may have been brought up in church. If you shared my wife's Catholic faith, there were numerous obligations to fulfill—but were they motivated by love and freedom or merely duty?

The Right to Become Children of God

But when you and I became children of God, things changed. I love this promise:

> *But as many as received Him (Jesus), to them He gave the right to become children of God, to those who believe in His Name.*
>
> John 1:12 (parenthesis mine)

Now, you desire to go after God. Church, Bible reading, prayer, and fellowship with other believers all became of value. We may swerve in our Christian walk from day to day, but in our heart of hearts, we love Jesus. If we are mad at a believer, we must work through it, but we still love Jesus. There is a yearning for His love. We want to see Him. We desire to please Him. It would be our greatest delight when we look into His eyes, to hear Him say to us, *'Well done, thou good and faithful servant'* (Matthew 25:21).

You Want to Please Him

Would it please Him if you were to bring even one precious soul to heaven with you? Certainly. Why? Because you love the Lord and **want others to know Him**.

Why? Because you and I are children of God. That's who we are.

A Fresh Start

Pray right now and repent for losing it—for losing your first love and your first works. Repent means to 'change direction; to think one way, and then turn to think another.'[3] In practical application, repenting means to take your eyes off yourself and put them squarely upon the Lord Jesus, who saved you. He saved you *from yourself*.

What are You Going to Do?

Pray this prayer right now with me:

Dear Heavenly Father, I love you.

I love you, Jesus. I am so grateful for you, Lord. But Lord, forgive me. I have acted as if I were ashamed of You. There are specific times I know I should have witnessed for you, Lord, and I did not. It was as if I were ashamed of you, Lord. I am so sorry. I am not ashamed of You.

I repent. Wash my heart, God. **Please give me a fresh start.** *Forgive me.*

Give me a fresh hunger *to follow You—to follow You where You lead. Help me get out of my comfort zone and go to seek and save the lost.*

In Jesus' Name. Amen.

Attitude is Everything

Remember, all God needs is our *availability*. He promises He will give us what to say (Mark 13:11). We will delve into that later. Right now, enjoy your *fresh change of **heart***. Attitude is everything.

> God does not need perfect people. He just needs people, available people.[4]
>
> **—Darryl Strawberry**

When you want what God wants, for the same reason He wants it, all of Heaven is behind you. You cannot fail![1]

—Jerry O'Dell

Behold, I am the Lord, the God of all flesh. Is there anything too hard for Me?

—Jeremiah 32:27

CHAPTER 3

1800 Saved in Eight Days!

'*1,800 Saved Within Eight Blocks in Eight Days!*' read the headline in the newsletter of the dear veteran missionary evangelist Jerry O'Dell[2], who had taken me to Africa. What a blessing. I had never taken a mission trip, yet so many were saved—most of them Muslims.

The believers were ecstatic. Revival had come to that church. The night meetings became like an indoor mass evangelic campaign. The lost and the new converts followed us to church to attend the meetings. Excitement was everywhere.

[Jerry O'Dell had been one of my instructors at Rhema Bible Training College. While pastoring my first small congregation in rural Arkansas, Jerry came twice to minister to our small church. In addition, Jerry had invited me to join him on a mission trip for several years. This was the first trip I took with Jerry.]

For Success in Business, Do God's Business

On the first day of the outreach, 200 workers came. Before this, I taught three lunch-hour sessions about 'Success in Business by the Holy Spirit.' On the last day, I gave a challenge. I announced,

> *'Now, if you aspire to be successful in your business, be about God's business—win the lost to Christ. So come to the outreach on Friday; let's evangelize this neighborhood.'*

We averaged about 300 attendees for the 'Success in Business' sessions. Nearly 200 came out to share the Gospel of Jesus at the week's end! The statistical average for a church outreach is only about 3%. We had 66 percent—that was a miracle! Hearts were expectant.

439 Born Again in One Afternoon

I preached *Faith For Souls*. I enrolled them in *'Jesus's School of Winning the Lost.'* We went out into the streets of Lagos, Nigeria and 439 were Born Again in one afternoon. Miracles were happening in the streets. [See: Mark 16:15-18; Matthew 10:7-8; Acts 6:3-8; Acts 8:5-8; Jeremiah 32:27]

A brother named Jeffery shared that as he was witnessing to an older woman, a man walked by with a heavy limp. He finished praying with the woman to receive Christ; the man limped by again. Finally, the brother spoke to the man. *'Jesus Christ can make you whole!'* He reached out and touched the man's leg, and it was instantly healed!

A Girl Who Could Not Talk

The next day was Saturday. We had about 150 workers. (Some could not attend.) We saw 400 more receive Christ! Many children accepted the Lord.

As we wrapped up for the day, Peter, my interpreter, and I stood near the road, waiting for the others. A small group of kids approached us. They explained that one girl in their group could not talk. She just grunted as if her tongue could not form the words. *'Peter, do you want*

1800 Saved in Eight Days!

to pray for her, or do you want me to?' [I meant, 'Do you want to work a miracle, or shall I?' He motioned for me to pray.]

Jesus Did Unusual Miracles

Following my spirit, I told her (Peter interpreting),

'This is unusual, but I am going to touch your tongue.'

Jesus had done many unusual things ministering to people, as in this account in the Gospel of St. Mark:

Again, departing from the region of Tyre and Sidon, He came through the midst of the region of Decapolis to the Sea of Galilee.

Then they brought to Him one who was deaf and had an impediment in his speech, and they begged Him to put His hand on him.

And He took him aside from the multitude, and put His fingers in his ears, and He spat and touched his tongue.

Then, looking up to heaven, He sighed, and said to him, 'Ephphatha,' that is, 'Be opened.'

Immediately his ears were opened, and the impediment of his tongue was loosed, and he spoke plainly.

Then He commanded them that they should tell no one; but the more He commanded them, the more widely they proclaimed it.

And they were astonished beyond measure, saying, 'He has done all things well. He makes both the deaf to hear and the mute to speak.'

Mark 7:31-37

Sometimes, God leads in unusual ways to get a person's attention so that they will react from their heart and trust God (Hebrews 11:6).

God Loosed Her Tongue

I touched her outstretched tongue, grasping it with my thumb and forefinger. *'Be loosed in Jesus' Name!'* Then, turning to Peter, I instructed him to tell her to count her numbers. She did! Peter then sang a native childhood song. She sang along! The other girls all chattered at once. Finally, Peter said, *'They are saying she could not do that before; she could not do that before!'* Praise God. God had loosed her tongue!

Did That Happen?

Heading back to the church, Peter spoke of the next step in his work, from foreman to general contractor. He was enthused about what God had told him during the 'Success in Business' sessions.

I stopped him. *'Peter, did that girl's tongue become free, and now she can talk plainly? She could not speak, but now she can?'*

'Oh yes.' He then resumed his conversation about his new business. I was in awe. I wanted to pinch myself—was it but a dream?

A Woman Pleaded for Her Deaf Child

On Monday, the third day of the outreach (resting Sunday), a woman approached while out in the neighborhood. I had just shared the Gospel of Christ with a Muslim man who received Jesus as Lord. The woman spoke to me (she spoke English). She attended the church meetings. This woman had an eleven-year-old daughter who was deaf. She asked for our help.

The woman explained that her husband was Muslim and had taken their daughter to mosques, Juju priests, and witch doctors, and had done everything he could to help her—but she remained deaf.

Surprised and unprepared to think about it, I just responded from my heart. They placed the girl in front of me. Then, remembering what Jesus had done in the scriptures (see Mark 7:31-37 above, verse 33, *'he put His fingers in his ears'*), I did the same.

Deaf Spirit, Go!

I spat on my fingertips, placed them into each of the girl's ears, and commanded, *'Deaf spirit, go! In Jesus' Name.'* The young lady was turned to face her mother behind her. I told the mom, *'You watch her face. You tell me if she can hear.'*

I snapped my fingers next to the child's right ear. Her mother's face lit up; her head nodded. She smiled. However, I could tell from the girl that she could hear. With every snap on either side of her head, the girl would twitch in that direction. We brought the girl's older brother up. The eleven-year-old was tested in front of him. Again, he affirmed. I think we tested her before another, I do not remember. But then the father came outside. Others gathered.

Upon seeing her father, the girl got still—she seemed a little intimidated. We tested the girl before for her dad, but she did not respond. She just sort of 'frozen up.' Imagine hearing when you have never done so.

We said our goodbyes and went on our way.

The Muslim Father Came to Christ

That evening was another large church service. People packed the place. The African worship was beautiful.

But what especially made the evening was the close of the service. They gave the invitation to *'Give your heart to Christ.'* I sat in wonder as

I watched the same father, his hand on his young daughter's shoulder, walking together to the front of the church. They came to give their lives to Jesus. Jesus had opened this man's daughter's ears, and he knew it.

The Lord Confirms His Word

T.L. Osborn used to say, *'Miracles are the Dinner Bell for the Gospel³.'* The scripture tells us that the Lord confirms His Word.

And they went out and preached everywhere, the Lord working with (them) and confirming the Word through the accompanying signs. Amen.

Mark 16:20 (Note: *'them'* is not in the original Greek. The Lord confirms *His Word* when we preach it.)

Family Members Came to Christ

On Monday, Tuesday, and Wednesday, the teams gathered to go out. New workers were coming each day. By the fifth day, over 1,800 were born again—confessing Jesus Christ as the Lord of their lives! We made follow-up visits on Thursday and Friday, visiting those newly saved. Not only did we affirm they had received Jesus, but additional family members prayed to receive Christ as well! Glory!

Could This Happen in My Life?

Oh, could anything this marvelous happen in my life? Absolutely, without a doubt! How? By having *Faith For Souls*. The successful harvest of souls didn't originate from the outreach on Friday. The beginning can be traced back to the Wednesday night before.

We got permission from the senior pastor of this large church (with a congregation of about 4,000) to evangelize on Tuesday afternoon. The pastor responded, 'Yes, we could take people out soul winning.' He released faith.

Seeds for Revival

At the last teaching session on Success in Business (on Wednesday), I challenged them to *'Be about God's business—win the lost to Christ, and He will bring success to your business.'* Seeds for revival had been planted.

The Lord Spoke That 2,000 Would Come to Christ

But that night (late Wednesday evening), I heard the Lord speak before I slipped into bed. I was coming out of the bathroom in my pajamas. The Lord said to me, *'2,000 will come to Christ.'* (Including an outdoor night service I preached, we reached all 2,000!) When I heard *that word*, I had a choice. I could receive it and say, *'Yes, Lord, I believe it!'* (Luke 1:38; Hebrews 13:8) Or I could doubt that God could use my labors in such a way. How could I embrace this promise? I could embrace this word that 2,000 souls would be won to Christ because, in my heart, I had *Faith For Souls*.

I Am the God of America, Too!

Flying back from Africa, reflecting upon all that had happened, God spoke to me. His voice boomed within my heart:

'I AM not the God of Nigeria only; I AM the God of America too!'

What He did there, He can and will do here or wherever you live—if we have *Faith For Souls*.

A Note About Mission Trips

Let me take a moment to talk about taking mission trips.

First, you do not have to cross the globe to affect others. Across the street will do. *All* need to hear the Gospel. I loved what T.L. Osborn would say, *'The World is your Estate!*[4] (As you will discern, T.L. Osborn was one of my most outstanding mentors. Though I only spoke a few words with him twice, I have regularly listened to his messages and read his books and literature. To this day, I can still hear his voice.)

You Do Not Need Money

Second, you do not need money for foreign missions and trips worldwide. Let me say that again. Money is **not** what you need. *What you **need** is a word from God.*

What do I mean? If you seek God, and He impresses upon your heart that you are to take such a trip, you have all you need. Why? Since He has commissioned you to go (even on a short-term trip), He has already provided two things because of *His character.*

They are the physical means to go—the provision—and His promise to go *with* you. He never lies. Because He only calls if He will also provide the way, which includes the physical provision, the grace, and the anointing to carry out the work. These are all contained in *His word of direction to you.*

Let Me Give You an Example

In my lifetime, I have made seventy mission trips abroad. Ten of those were to India, twice to Africa, German-speaking Europe, throughout much of the United Kingdom, South and Central America, and more. I crisscrossed the United States, preaching, teaching, and demonstrating *Faith For Souls* as church members and pastors, and I went out

1800 Saved in Eight Days!

into their communities. These *'God adventures'* ministering worldwide are a delight to tell.

After almost every service, believers would approach me and say, *'I want to go on a mission trip ... if I only had the money.'* In response, I would explain what I am attempting to explain here. Few understood. *How can I not need money to go?*

A Louisiana Man Got It

One young man from Louisiana named Rustin understood. Rustin was an unlikely candidate. He was the church custodian and worked a side business as a handyman. He had four children who were home schooled so he was the sole breadwinner. Life was already tight.

But after cleaning the church one evening alone, Rustin entered the sanctuary to seek God. He worshipped, prayed, and waited. Finally, Rustin asked the Lord whether he was to take a mission trip (he and I intended he would accompany me to India).

As He Waited Upon the Lord, the Lord Spoke

As he waited upon the Lord, the Lord spoke to his heart, *'Yes, you are to go with William to India.'*

The next day, he called me and shared his experience with the Holy Spirit. I gave him straightforward instructions. *Describe in a letter what you believe the Lord wants you to do.*

Rustin did this. But before he shared the letter with anyone besides his pastor, his pastor told him to wait. He (the pastor) wanted to discuss the topic with the congregation. So the pastor shared with the church what Rustin believed he was to do, and then they received an offering.

Provision Came to the Dollar

The cost of the ticket (the sole expense Rustin would have as my travel companion) was $1,536. The offering received for Rustin for India was the same amount—to the dollar!

Rustin was overseas for three weeks; his family received groceries, clothes, and cash gifts. The church even paid his salary while he was with me in India. His family had more provisions while he was not home working. Why? Because he sought the Lord—*and heard from Him*.

More Trips Followed

Rustin made two trips with me to India. On the first trip, he helped me dedicate three new churches and freshwater wells. On the second, he and my Indian counterpart, Melchizedek, served as campaign managers for a mass ten-day crusade in Srikakulam, Andhra Pradesh, India, which reached about 40,000 combined meeting attendees and 3,500 decision cards were filled out for Christ.

Rustin later worked with his other family members in various parts of the world, including Ukraine. (They still assist believers they know during the current Russian assault upon Ukraine.)

We Need a Word from God

What we need today is a *Word from God*. If we hear and trust His direction for our lives and ministries, we can accomplish much more for the Kingdom of God.

What is Faith For Souls? How Can I Get It?

'What is Faith For Souls? Can I have it? What is the process of acquiring Faith For Souls?' It didn't come naturally to me. Instead, I had *'fear'* for souls. Just the idea of witnessing made me tremble inside.

My First Experience

You should have seen me the first time I experienced witnessing. I was a freshman at California Polytechnic State University, San Luis Obispo, California. For a couple of months, I had known Jesus as Lord. Rick, a water polo teammate, had led me to Christ. Then, the Lord sent another man, Gerald, to instruct and disciple me in a Bible Study.

Gerald would sometimes show up unannounced at my dorm room to nurture a friendship. He would often take me for ice cream or ride bicycles together.

Come on. We are going Witnessing.

One afternoon, Gerald came by, and I greeted him, *'Hey man, what's happening?'* (expecting a trip to the soda shop). But he responded, *'Come on. We are going witnessing.' 'Witnessing?'* I asked hesitantly, *'What's that?'* Gerald explained we would talk to perfect strangers about God and share the Gospel of Jesus Christ. I must have turned three shades of green, then white! Utter horror shot through my chest.

But I went because of pride and not wanting to lose face before this man I admired. I did not say a word until Gerald had paved the way and proved that *'these are not hostile natives'* and that they *'would not eat us!'*

What Was I Lacking?

What was the thing I lacked? What do we all need?

A FAITH FOR SOULS

A first-hand revelation of God does not just impart something to you, it changes you. You become the revelation.[1]

—**Tommy Barnett**

Stop fearing. From this moment as characterized by what has taken place, you shall be catching men alive.

—**Luke 5:10 Wuest**

CHAPTER 4

Faith For Souls

$\mathcal{A}$fter graduating college in December, I moved from California to Oklahoma to enroll in Rhema Bible Training Center for the following school year.

By the time I arrived in Tulsa, something had changed. My *availability* and *care* to reach the lost had grown into *compassion* and an *intense yearning* to see them saved. Zeal to reach the world for Christ beat in my spirit as my heart beat in my chest.

I Made My Plan

'I know what I will do,' I determined in myself. *'I will go to the apartment manager* (where I had moved) *and win her to Christ. Then, she will give a warm approval and allow me to go to each door in the complex to present the Gospel.'*

Wrong! Yes, she listened courteously as I shared with her in between phone calls and apartment showings. But, no, I did not win her to Christ. No door-to-door for me.

Desperate to Be a Witness

I went back to my apartment, frustrated and defeated. When I climbed the stairs and shut the door, I was mad! I grabbed my Bible, opened it wide, and kneeled. I proclaimed to God, *'God, I am not leaving here until you speak to me!'* (I read aloud for an hour and a half.) Finally, His Word spoke, not about soul winning, but at least I heard His counsel. However, the stage was set. I was *desperate* to be an effective witness for Christ. My appeal was before the Almighty. Indeed, He would respond. Certainly, He would answer.

A Trail of Casualties on the Devil

Well, answer He did, through a small-framed Italian (short to my 6 foot 2 inches) from Pittsburgh, Pennsylvania. His name was Ron. Ron had been a *druggie* in high school. He had been belligerent towards Christians—shouting at them, mocking them. When Ron came to Christ, he was bold for Jesus. I like to say, *'Ron left a trail of casualties on the devil wherever he went. People were saved, healed, and delivered everywhere he went!'*

Ron became my roommate. He was a second-year Bible school student while I was in my first year. It seemed he always had some adventure to tell how God had used him to minister to others and lead many to Christ. I was glad for Ron, but I envied his success.

Envy or Rejoicing?

You know, we Christians are funny that way. We will ask the prayer group to agree with us to get a loan to buy a house, but when another brother gets a bigger home, we are envious.

The Bible teaches to *'Rejoice with them that do rejoice, and weep with them that weep'* (Romans 12:15). It seems many Christians have this backward. We weep when another gets blessed and rejoice when someone previously fortunate loses. Why? Envy. It is a terrible sin. Charles G. Finney,[2] the great American revivalist, called it a *'spirit of hell.'* He warned of envy, *'Repent deeply before God, or He will never forgive you.'* I am convinced that when we do not enthusiastically rejoice like the angels in heaven (Luke 15:10) when someone testifies of leading one to Christ, it is usually because of envy.

Thirteen Won to Christ in One Hour

That was my attitude. I wouldn't say I liked Ron's success, but I hated my failure even more. Then, one day, *the final straw broke the camel's back.* Ron shared with enthusiasm and yet with tranquility,

I was returning from school today when the Spirit of God impressed me to get off the bus. So I got off and knocked on five doors (at five houses). He said that *thirteen people accepted and received Jesus as Lord.*

I could hardly fathom it. In less than one hour, Ron had led more to Christ than I had led to Jesus in six or seven years as a Christian. He had tripled my results.

Jesus had promised, *'Follow Me, and I will make you become fishers of men.'* (Mark 1:17) He did not say, *'Come on boys, let's try our luck at fishing.'* That was me. Ron had what Jesus promised.

Ron, What Are You Doing?

So, I composed my inner feelings of contempt and inquired, *'Ron, what are you doing?'* He responded, *'Two things'* (as he held up two fingers).

First, I must tell you something on a humorous note so that you will never forget these *two things*. Ron had an annoying habit of calling me by my childhood name, Billy. Being an Italian from Pittsburg, it was more like *Beelly*. His other annoying habit was poking his finger in my chest as he preached.

'Beelly, Two Things.'

Ron said, *'Beelly, Two Things'* as that bony finger jabbed into my chest. This time, I did not care. I wanted to win souls. With my entire being, I wanted to see the lost all around me come to Christ. But I needed help, and I knew it, so I listened.

Enroll in Jesus' School of Evangelism

*Beelly, **first**, the Lord told me to enroll in His school of evangelism. He told me to enroll in Jesus' school to win the lost. I asked the Lord, 'Where is this school, Lord? Pennsylvania, Oklahoma, California, New York, across the world?' The Lord answered me, 'No, it is not a school any man has. **I am the Master Evangelist**. But, if you look to Me, I will make you a great fisher of men!'*

Ron explained how he had raised his right hand like a new citizen who pledges allegiance to our country. He said,

'Lord Jesus, I enroll in Your school of winning the lost. You are the Master Evangelist. Teach me how to win souls.'

Years after this, I *'swore in'* all those believers in *Jesus' School of Evangelism* in Lagos, Nigeria, before we won 1,800 souls to Christ.

Meditate upon Luke 5:1-11

'Second,' Ron continued, *'Meditate on* **Luke 5:1-11**.*'* That was it. But I did exactly as he instructed. When we precisely follow the instructor

Faith For Souls

who is proficient to become proficient before we try to improve it with, *'Oh, but I could do it better this way,'* we will succeed. It sounded so simple, but if that enabled Ron to be an influential soul winner, then I would do it.

Just Do What the Pro Tells You

An illustration of this occurred when my oldest son, Zac, and I took our first golf lessons. I remember thinking, *'Bill, listen closely, and just do what the golf pro tells us to do'* (nothing more, nothing less). The pro described a 360° arch when you pull back and then swing along that arch. I saw myself doing just that- and I did it. I was popping off balls flying straight 150 to 200 yards the first day. Next to me, my eighteen-year-old son was chipping the ball and saying some things I won't repeat.

Just listen. Just do.

A Decision and a Declaration

Now, the 'enrollment' took just a moment. That was a decision, a declaration given in trust to God. For indeed, without a doubt, *Jesus was and is the Master Evangelist*. After all, Jesus stopped and asked the Samaritan woman for a drink of water (John 4), which turned into a two-day revival with the whole town being saved! I would say Jesus knew what He was doing! Yet, too much of the church looks at its statistics, methods, and ideology. For instance, something commonly stated is that *'few come to Christ after 18.'* I have led as many grandparents (and great-grandparents) to Christ as teens, and I have led many youths to Christ!

Jesus did not poll the denominational records to see what was possible. No. He believed *'For with God, nothing shall be impossible'* (Luke

1:37). We have heard it often said, *'You cannot put God in a box,'* and yet we have all tried so hard to fit God in the *'box'* of our conceptions.

Meditate, Not Just Read

'Meditate on Luke 5:1-11.' Ron didn't instruct me to read or remember the commonly known story of Jesus in Peter's boat. Instead, he specifically said to *meditate*.

According to God, meditating on God's Word will cause you to succeed.

> *This Book of the Law shall not depart from your mouth, but you shall meditate in it day and night, that you may observe to do according to all that is written in it. For then you will make your way prosperous, and then you will have good success.*
>
> Joshua 1:8

> *His passion is to remain true to the Word of 'I AM,' meditating day and night on the true revelation of light. He will be standing firm like a flourishing tree planted by God's design, deeply rooted by the brooks of bliss, bearing fruit in every season of life. He is never dry, never fainting, ever blessed, ever prosperous.*
>
> Psalm 1:2-3 TPT

Observe to Do

Notice the wording of these promises. After meditating on the Word of God *'day and night,'* you will *'observe what to do.'* And then, *'you will make your way prosperous and have good success.'* The same is inferred in the analogy of the tree planted by the living water.

To meditate on the Word of God involves speaking it over and over to yourself. It is like letting the Word of God cook slowly in you like a roast in a rotisserie.

Home Made Spaghetti

Let me give an example that illustrates this beautifully. When I was a bachelor attending Bible school, I invited a bunch of guys over for dinner. I cooked spaghetti with authentic homemade sauce. I went to the market and bought the oregano, the fresh garlic cloves, and the bay leaves to be cooked from scratch (using the *Betty Crocker Cook Book*[3] my mom gave me when I moved out). As an inexperienced cook, I did not quite get everything right. I left off the last instruction. *'Let it simmer for 1½ to 2 hours.'*

We define simmer as *remaining at or just below the boiling point; about to break out, as in anger.* Simmering in cooking blends the ingredients and brings out the *full flavor.*

When the guys showed up, the spaghetti was hot, and they ate it. They were happy. (Young bachelor guys could be more discerning. They are good if it is a hot meal and free!) But I was disappointed. It did not taste any better than the sauce you can buy in a jar; it was not even as good.

Now It Was Great!

The next afternoon after church, I pulled out the pot of spaghetti sauce and put it on the stove on low heat. I cleaned, found some old photos, and forgot about the spaghetti. For an hour or two, I got immersed in old memories.

Suddenly, I remembered, *'Oh, yeah, the spaghetti sauce!'* I ran into the kitchen and checked it. The sauce was fine, simply good, and hot. I cooked some spaghetti noodles, drained them, put on the sauce, and sat down to eat. I said my blessing and took a bite. *Fantastic!* This sauce was superb! Why was it so much better? I had let it *simmer*. Believer, if you and I will do what the Lord inspired Joshua and David (Psalm 1) and will indeed allow the promises of God, one promise at a time, to *simmer* in our spirits, then suddenly, *'we would observe how to do the Word of God.'*

The Spirit of God Will Quicken

The Spirit of God will quicken (make alive) what the Holy Spirit meant when He inspired the writing of the Bible (2 Peter 1:20-21), and we will receive *that spirit and the life* contained in God's Holy Word. We should not just read words dull to our understanding and dry to our hearts.

Jesus said, *'It is the Spirit who gives life; the flesh profits nothing. The words that I speak to you are spirit, and they are life.'* (John 6:63)

I had to have the life in those words, so I meditated Luke 5:1-11. Several times through the day and night, I re-read those words over and over softly to myself. Peter's encounter with the Messiah was becoming vivid to me. As if I were in the boat. One day, I picked up another translation that gave a little more feeling than the King's English.

Luke 5:1-11 in the Wuest New Testament

The *Wuest New Testament* reads this way:

And it came to pass that while the people crowded up against him and were listening to the word of God, that He himself took His stand beside the lake of Gennesaret. And He saw two boats which had been moored along the lake. But the fishermen, having disembarked, were cleaning their nets. And having gone on board one of the boats, which was Simon's, He requested him to put out a little from the shore. And having sat down He went to teaching the crowds out of the boat. Now, when He had ceased speaking, He said to Simon, Put out into deep water and let down your nets for a catch. And answering, Simon said, Master, through the entire night having worked to the point of exhaustion, we took not even one thing. Nevertheless, at your word I will let down the nets. And having done this, they enclosed a great number of fish, and their nets were torn apart. And they made signs to their partners in the other boat to come and lend them a hand. And they came, and they filled both of the boasts so that they began to be sinking. Now Simon Peter, having seen this, fell down at Jesus' knees, saying, Depart from me at once because I am a man, a sinner, Master. For amazement took possession of him and of all who were with him because of the catch of fish which they took, and likewise also James and John, the sons of Zebedee, who were partners with Simon. And Jesus said to Simon, Stop fearing. From this moment as characterized by what has just taken place, you shall be catching men alive. And having brought the boats to the shore, having abandoned all, they followed Him as His disciples.

Luke 5:1-11 Wuest

What I Saw

Let me now put what the Spirit of God quickened to me in my own words. Peter had just about finished washing his nets and was ready to head home to rest. Laboring all night and not catching anything was discouraging.

Then, the prophet Jesus of Nazareth came. He walked right up to Peter's boat, stepped in, and asked him to push out a little from the shore so He could teach the crowds pressing upon Him. Peter was glad to have Him choose his boat. Jesus' words lifted his soul and stirred him deep within.

Certainly, He will Finish Soon.

But as the prophet continued, Peter's eyelids grew heavy. *'Surely He will finish soon,'* Peter thought. He did, but to Peter's surprise, Jesus requested to go further into the lake. *'Put out into deep waters and let down your nets for a catch.'* Peter agonized, *'Master, though the entire night having worked to the point of exhaustion, we took not even one thing. Nevertheless, at your word, I will let down the nets.'*

As the light breeze caught the sail, Peter said within:

'He may be a prophet, maybe the Messiah, but He is not an angler. He is the son of a carpenter. My father and my father's father were fishermen. Anyone would know you cannot fish in this lake in broad daylight. The fish will laugh at the nets! We tried all night. I hardly ever come back empty. I am a good fisherman.'

Jesus sat quietly at the bow, looking out over the water. Peter wondered, *'What if He knows something I don't?'*

They Reached the Dark Waters

Finally, they reached the darkened waters. Peter lowered the sail and went for his nets. *'How long will we have to wait until we can go back in?'* The boat jerked. Then again, and again. Peter lunged to the side and peered over. The water was churning! Fish! Everywhere! This was a big catch! With automatic reflex, Peter's sun-bronzed body worked like a machine. Reach, pull, lift ... bright, shining, flopping fish tossed and flipped into the boat's bottom. Reach, pull, lift ... another section of net packed full of sizeable deep-water fish! *'What a catch!'* Peter's mind

Faith For Souls

raced as he worked. *'I take it all back. But I am too busy to apologize. I must get in all the catch . . . but so many!'*

The boat filled. Peter was ecstatic. He could *'get out of debt, make his boat repairs, and have money left over with this catch!'*

Hurry! John, James!

The boat waddled under the tremendous weight. *'Oh, I had better call John and James,'* He cried, *'Hey, James, John, get out here NOW! We have a great catch! Come on! Hurry!'*

The partners leaped into their boat and quickly sailed to the site. They dropped their nests. *Boom!* The fish hit their nets, too! They shouted at one another, laughing as they hauled in the fish. More fish. *And more.* There seemed to be no end. James and John's boat wobbled under the incredible load.

'Peter,' James cried. *'The boats are sinking!'* Peter had **never** caught fish like this. No one on the lake had. When he went fishing as a boy with his father, his father had never caught fish like this. His grandfather's greatest fishing stories never equaled this catch.

[I highly recommend you watch *The Chosen* TV series. Season 1, Episode 4, entitled, *The Chosen: Jesus Calls Peter*.[4] Fabulous series. My wife and I have wept while watching the series.]

Depart from Me, Master

Then, it struck Peter. A holy shiver went down Peter's spine. He stopped and looked towards the bow of the boat. There, Jesus sat like a sovereign Lord presiding over the harvest. His eyes met Peter's. The dark eyes of this Jewish prophet glistened with the fire of God. Jesus was staring into his heart. Peter's knees dropped. His arms went limp. His head bowed down. But Peter could not let go of the Nazarene's gaze. Finally, Peter groaned out, *'Depart from me, Master. I am just a sinner.'*

Peter's left hand lifted to shield his eyes from the intensity of His stare. Then Jesus spoke directly into Peter's soul. His words, like warm fluid, struck his heart. *'And Jesus said to Simon, Stop fearing. From this moment,* **as characterized by** *what has just taken place,* **you shall be catching men alive.***'* (emphasis mine.) Those living words rang within Peter's heart so much that when he reached shore, he left all, all that great catch, to follow **The Master**.

Those Words Were Not to Peter. They Were to Me.

As I read the passage, I saw it similar to how Peter must have experienced it. Yet, those words were not to Peter. They were to me. They entered my heart in the spring of 1981 and have been echoing in the corridors of my spirit to this present day.

People Were Getting Saved

One night at about 12:30 am, a security guard just off duty, still in uniform, walked into the supermarket where I worked the night shift. He clutched a full-page newspaper advertisement. It said, *'Jesus is Coming Back!'* That was true, but it said, *'This Sunday!'* which was incorrect (Matthew 24:36). The man was severely in shock. His words were, *'What must I do to be saved?'* Right there by the registers, I prayed with him to receive Jesus.

Two Guys out at the Pool

A few weeks later, another *'catch.'* I was out by the pool at my apartment, sitting in the cool air of the early Oklahoma spring. Since I worked nights and attended Bible college in the mornings, I had little time to sleep. That made it particularly hard to stay alert to study. But the chill kept me awake. After reading for about 20-30 minutes, the Spirit interrupted, *'Ask that man over there how long he has been Born Again.'* I resisted. Not because I was afraid any longer but because I was busy. I was studying for the ministry! (Ironic! We can be so busy doing God's work that we have no time for **God's work!**)

The Holy Ghost persisted. He said, *'Ask him how long he has been Born Again.'* I protested within myself. *'Lord, I don't know that man except for coming through my check-out line at night. He is from Mexico and is in Tulsa to attend aviation school. Being a Mexican from Mexico, he most surely will be Catholic. He won't know what Born Again is.'*

The Holy Ghost spoke a third time, *'Ask that man how long he has been Born Again.'* *'All right, Lord.'* I consented, *'I will ask him how long he has been Born Again.'*

'Excuse me.' He looked up from the lounge chair. The young Mexican man next to him on the other chair woke up. I asked, *'How long have you been Born Again?'*

He responded, *'What is Born Again?'* So I shared how to receive Jesus and be saved, and they were **both Born Again!**

Another Man Came to Christ a Very Different Way

Another man came to Christ in quite an unusual way. It was Memorial Day weekend. The school year was out, and I worked earlier in the evening. At about 9:30 p.m., a businessman came through my check stand. I remember he wore green slacks, a matching vest, and a light green shirt. His collar was open, with no tie. He also wore no smile. Try as I may, he responded to nothing I said. He left. *'Oh well, another grumpy customer,'* I thought.

I went on about my work. Then, at about 10 o'clock, the phone rang. I remember the manager going behind the counter to answer the phone. The next moment, he stood behind me, saying, *'I will finish checking this woman's order. The phone call is for you.'*

That was unusual. I never received calls at work. So I went behind the counter and picked up the phone. *'Hello.'* It was the businessman. He was calling to apologize. He said, *'You were so friendly and joyful, and I was so rude. Please forgive me.'*

That's unusual! There are many disgruntled customers, but I have never had one call back to apologize! I answered, *'That's all right. I am not offended. It is just **the joy of the Lord** in me.'*

What is the Joy of The Lord?

He said, *'What is this **joy of the Lord**?'*

'Well, I can't talk right now. I am working. But if you want to come for dinner some night, I will tell you all about it.' So that man, Len, made a dinner appointment to get saved!

He came over on Monday, Memorial Day. I cooked chicken, yellow corn, and white rice. How do I remember? Len had just taken a fork full of white rice poised over his plate. He said, *'Tell me about this **joy of the Lord**.'*

That fork did not move for twenty minutes as I preached Jesus to him. Not one piece of white rice fell off his fork. Then he pushed out of his chair and got down on his knees. After that, I realized, *'I guess it is time to pray!'*

I knelt opposite him, took his hand, and led him in a prayer to confess Jesus Christ as Lord of his life! So earnest was his prayer. It was as if he drank the words right out of my spirit. He was famished for the love of God.

The Infilling of the Holy Spirit

I thought, *What else can I share with him?* The Holy Ghost reminded me of the infilling of the Spirit. So, I explained briefly and then prayed with him to receive the Baptism of the Holy Spirit. The Spirit of God gloriously immersed Len. He spoke in *a new prayer language*. Then Len wept.

You Don't Understand!

I was so thrilled. He had been Born Again and filled with the Holy Spirit. I hugged his neck and laughed and cried. Then he pushed me away and said, *'You don't understand. You don't understand!'* I did not know what he would say. Len told me the story of his life. He had been an orphan. No one had loved him. He was passed from one foster home to another. Then, in his twenties, he finally met a lady who became his wife. *'For two years, we were so happy. But then, my wife became pregnant, but she lost the baby. She was so devastated that she committed suicide. This happened three years ago, and* **I have never shed a tear***!'*

Here is Len, saved, filled with the Holy Ghost, crying like a baby, set free—all because I smiled at him over a grocery register! It is not a great technique that will *'catch men alive.'* But *the Faith of God in your heart for the souls of men* that will draw the net, bringing them to Christ.

Turn on the Living Water

I see the believer's human spirit as if it were a water pipe. Many believers have fear and unbelief in their hearts like rocks and gravel in a pipe. Water can still get through, but only as a trickle. Receiving Jesus' Word and mixing your heart's trust (faith) is like a vital breath

Faith For Souls

from God's lungs, blowing the rocks and gravel of doubt and fear right out! Then, whenever He wants, He can turn on *The Living Water* (John 7:37-38), and it will flow.

It is time to get out the rocks and gravel of fear and doubt.

Say This Prayer. Make Your Proclamation.

Say this prayer with me, trusting Him to remove the ugly debris from your spirit. I suggest you stand on your feet, raise your right hand, and proclaim this prayer as a new declaration over your life.

Dear Heavenly Father, I repent for the fear and unbelief towards Your Word. By faith, I command them to GO! **Fear, get out of my life NOW, in Jesus' Name!**

Heavenly Father, cause Your Words, Your promise that I will **catch men alive**, *to quicken in my heart. Right now,* **I am enrolling in your school, Jesus, your school to win the lost.** *I submit to you as the* **Master Evangelist, enable me** *to bring people into the Kingdom of God.*

Jesus, instruct me *and* **teach me how to win men to God by the Power of the Holy Spirit** *(Acts 1:8). I thank you, Lord, that from this moment forward, I am your student. Teach me to be effective. Give me words that reach into people's lives and touch their hearts.*

Lord, I believe you will help me catch so many, *like Peter,* **that it blows my mind.**

Lord, give me an 'overflowing, boat sinking catch of souls won to Christ, so many souls I cannot count them all.' Win them, Lord, through my life. Work through me, Lord.

And, Lord, I believe that when I stand before you, I will hear you say, **'Well done, thou good and faithful servant.'**

In Jesus' Name. Amen.

Thank Him for this change He has brought into your life.

PostScript

About ten years later, I ran into Ron. I shared with him the beautiful things the Lord had done in my life, the souls that came to Christ, and how I assisted many others in leading people to Jesus as Lord.

I told him of that day in the apartment, where he told me *two things* in a couple of minutes.

Funny, Ron did not even remember doing that. Yet, it has affected my life for decades, and I have been able to help thousands receive **Faith For Souls**.

This is the power of God and not of man.

Glory to God.

Jesus was fed up with religion. A man can be religious and not know Jesus. A man can be religious and not be born again. A man can be religious and be moral.[1]

—**Donnie Moore**

So, when they continued asking Him, He raised up and said to them, 'He who is without sin among you, let him throw a stone at her first.'

—John 8:7

CHAPTER 5

Handling the Religious

*T*he morning had dawned—the third day of the tremendous revival in Lagos, Nigeria. Workers had gathered around, ready for prayer and instruction and then to be sent out. One of the young ladies, a college student about 21 years old, raised her hand. *'May I ask a question?'* I answered, *'Yes, please, go ahead.'*

> *'The other day, when we were witnessing,'* she said, her voice soft and hesitant, *'my team of three ladies had a problem. We came up to a Muslim man wearing a turban—very austere. He said, "The Bible says women are not to teach men." We did not know what to do.'*

When Fear Raises Its Ugly Head, Cut It Off!

Let me note something essential to any team leader directing a witnessing outreach or even an evangelist in a revival. When fear raises its ugly head, you must **chop it off skillfully**, hurting no one else! Fear is one of several things that will stop a revival. Immorality, apathy, and strife are three other *'killers'* to a move of God. However, fear can be just as lethal. Because I had received the question that fear (like a contagious disease) was now exposed to all the laborers. If not dealt with correctly, we would not have won the other 1,000 to Christ!

The Holy Spirit answered within my heart. We need not to fear the confrontation of fear. We do not have that spirit. (*'For God has not given us the spirit of fear, but of power and of love and of a sound mind.'* 2 Timothy 1:7) The Lord showed me how to answer.

Men and Women Were Preachers at Pentecost

First, I had the woman open her Bible to Acts, chapter one. I had her read who was gathered together so that she might see the *'they'* of the Pentecostal outpouring on whom the Holy Ghost fell (Acts 1:12-14; 2:1-4). In Acts 1:13, we have a list of the eleven disciples. Then verse 14 reads: *'These all continued with one accord in prayer and supplication,* **with the women** *and Mary the mother of Jesus, and with his brothers.'* Note it says, *'With the women,'* I said to the young Nigerian woman. The men and women poured out into the streets when the Holy Ghost came *'like a rushing, mighty wind.'* Men *and women* flowed into the streets of Jerusalem that sunny day. The Jews gathered from the nations to celebrate Pentecost. They *were confounded because that every man heard them* (men and women) *speak in his language* (Acts 2:6). *'We hear them speaking in our own tongues the wonderful works of God'* (verse 11). [A beautiful description of what witnessing should be.] God comforted this young woman and all the workers.

How to Handle Intimidation

Then, I addressed the more prominent topic: **intimidation**. What I am about to share, I have preached hundreds of times in hundreds of churches around the globe. I call it *'Handling the Religious,'* but you could also call it *'How to Handle Intimidation'* or *'How to Rely Upon the Spirit of God.'* This message came like a breath. *'The breath'* that a group of eager evangelists needed. I have since observed that this is a message we all need.

Handling the Religious

'Turn to the Gospel of John, Chapter 8. Let us begin in verse 1,' I instructed the workers.

> *But Jesus went to the Mount of Olives. Now early in the morning He came again into the temple, and all the people came to Him: and He sat down and taught them.*
>
> *Then the scribes and Pharisees brought to Him a woman caught in adultery. And when they had set her in the midst, they said to Him, 'Teacher, this woman was caught in adultery, in the very act.*
>
> *Now Moses, in the law, commanded us that such should be stoned. But what do You say?'*
>
> *This they said, testing Him, that they might have something of which to accuse Him. But Jesus stooped down and wrote on the ground with His finger, as though He did not hear,*
>
> *So when they continued asking Him, He raised Himself up and said to them, 'He who is without sin among you, let him throw a stone at her first.'*
>
> *And again He stooped down and wrote on the ground.*
>
> *Then those who heard it, being convicted by their conscience, went out one by one, beginning with the oldest even to the last. And Jesus was left alone, and the woman standing in the midst.*
>
> *And when Jesus had raised Himself up and saw no one but the woman, He said to her, 'Woman, where are those accusers of yours? Has no one condemned you?'*
>
> *She said, 'No one, Lord.' And Jesus said to her, 'Neither do I condemn you; go and sin no more.'*
>
> John 8:1-11

What Jesus Was Facing

Let me clarify the actual situation Jesus was facing.

Point # 1: Jesus had *'all the people'* who were then following Him as His audience. The Pharisees threatened the credibility and competency of His ministry before all who looked to Him—a public threat.

Point # 2: The Pharisees were not presenting hypothetical situations but had actual physical evidence. Jesus was being put on the spot. He could not theorize. They thought, *'This time, we have him!'*

Point # 3: The Law (the Old Testament Mosaic Law) was on their side. Leviticus 20:10 states, *'And the man that commits adultery with another man's wife, he who commits adultery with his neighbor's wife, the adulterer, and the adulteress, shall surely be put to death.'* Adultery under Mosaic Law was punishable by death (stoning). Noteworthy, they omitted to accuse the male adulterer. He may have been among them!

Point # 4: Roman rule, the civil government that controlled Israel, forbade all such execution, except by the Roman court, not Jewish (John 18:31). So the Pharisees 'knew' they had Jesus *'between a rock and a hard place.'*

If Jesus allowed the stoning, the Romans would arrest him. If He tried to compromise the Law because of the Roman occupation, the scribes and Pharisees would denounce and deface Jesus as a heretic before all His followers.

The Master at Work

What was Jesus to do? Talk about intimidation! Let us now watch the *Master Himself at work!*

Look again at the passage. Verse 6 reads, *'This they said, testing Him, that they might have something of which to accuse Him. But Jesus stooped* down and wrote on the ground with His finger as though He did not hear.' Notice it says, *'as though He did not hear.'* At one of the most critical and most discrediting, intimidating moments of His public ministry, Jesus leans over and writes with His finger on the ground. **What?**

Can You Imagine Billy Graham Snapping under Pressure?

Had He lost it? Had Jesus snapped under pressure? Imagine the very respected evangelist, Billy Graham. He is preaching in front of one of his vast audiences when television cameras and news crews rush onto the platform. First, the newscaster cites some slanderous charges of financial or moral misconduct. Then, they stick the microphone in front of Reverend Graham.

'What do you say to these allegations, **Reverend** *Graham?'* What if, at that moment, Billy Graham was to stoop down, with television viewers watching nationwide, and he began tying his shoe? Everyone would think he had cracked under pressure.

Jesus' disciples feared this had happened to Him. Months of public attack had taken their toll. Finally, the prophet of Nazareth had met his match.

But no! Jesus did something none of the Pharisees had ever expected. What did He do?

Jesus Could do Nothing ... But What the Father Showed Him

Please turn to the fifth chapter of John's Gospel for our answer. Now read one of the most remarkable statements ever uttered by Jesus:

> *Then Jesus answered and said to them, Most assuredly, I say to you,* **the Son can do nothing of Himself, but what He sees the Father do**; *for whatever He does, the Son also does in like manner.*
>
> *For the Father loves the Son and shows Him all things that He Himself does; and He will show Him greater works than these, that you may marvel.*
>
> John 5:19-20 (emphasis mine)

Notice Jesus said, *'The Son* **can do** *nothing of Himself . . .'* He could do nothing of Himself. Not He *would do* nothing of Himself, or He *should do* nothing . . . but *'He could do nothing of Himself, but what He sees the Father do.'*

In verse 20, Jesus continued, *'For the Father loves the Son and shows Him all things that He Himself does.'* The secret to Jesus' life and ministry, and in overcoming intimidation, was **complete dependency upon the Spirit of God**.

Getting Heaven's Vision but Using Our Plans

How could we then expect to find success apart from our *complete* dependency upon the Father God? Yet most of us seem determined to learn the hard way. How many times have we set out to follow the leading of God but in our strength? We seek the Lord. He answers with vision (direction). Then, with glee, we grab the idea and develop our plan, asking God to bless it rather than to get *the plan from Heaven* to follow the vision we received from Heaven. Jesus did not do that. He waited on God first to *'get it straight from the mouth of God.'* Only then did He take His course of action. *'. . . for what things soever He doeth, these also doeth the Son likewise.'* John 5:19b KJV

One Fifteen-Word Sentence

When Jesus stooped down, He asked the Father how He should respond. The Father spoke to His heart. Jesus lifted Himself and ended the matter in one fifteen-word sentence, silencing every accuser. *'He who is **without sin** among you, let him **throw a stone** at her **first**'* (verse 7, emphasis mine). Not only did His words cut like a knife, but by now, the Pharisees had pushed in closer and closer as they had *'. . . continued asking Him.'* Finally, when Jesus stood up, they were face to face.

I tell you, no man on earth with vileness in his soul can withstand that gaze. As I have become more persuaded of the power of the Gospel (Romans 1:15-17), the Lord has used my eyes like His. Professing atheists have told me, *'You are very convicting.'* (That should be impossible if there is such a thing as a *true* atheist. But we will get into that later.)

The Longer We Live without Christ, the More We Know We Are Lost

Let us continue. Jesus stooped back down, breaking off His gaze. The men slipped away, but notice they left *'. . . beginning with the oldest even to the last'* (verse 9). Why? The longer we live apart from Christ, the more our consciences sink deeper into the mire of sin. Apart from Christ, age is a horrid thing. I have ministered much in nursing homes. The eldest saint is one of the most beautiful creatures on earth. But an aged infidel can be one of the most repulsive.

Note verse 9 again. *'Then those who heard it, being convicted by their conscience, went out one by one, beginning with the oldest even to the last. And Jesus was left alone, and the woman standing in the midst.'*

One by one, they left *convicted in their conscience*. How did Jesus bring such conviction and turn the tables? He spoke words from the Spirit of God toward **their hearts**. This is the key to effective witnessing.

The Gospel is from the Heart to the Heart

*The Gospel is **not** a Gospel to the head. It is a **Gospel to the heart**. The Gospel is not from the head. It is a Gospel from the heart.*

After preaching this message dozens of times, the Lord revealed something else I had not seen. Of course, by speaking that word, Jesus saved that woman's life. But by that fifteen-word sentence, He also *ministered great love* for those Pharisees. How?

Jesus burst the bubble of a false sense of self-righteousness. The first thing that needs to occur with a self-righteous man is that he must be brought to understand that *he, too,* is a **sinner**. Jesus brought that understanding.

I am sure this was a turning point in many of these religious leaders' lives that later resulted in their conversion. In Acts 6:7, we read, *'... and a great company of the priests were obedient to the faith....'*

You Can Follow the Voice of the Spirit of God

You may respond and say, *'Oh, Jesus could hear God. He could escape that mess, but I do not know how to hear God speak to me.'*

Jesus taught you do hear His voice.

*To him the doorkeeper opens, and the sheep hear his voice; and **he calls his own sheep by name** and leads them out.*

*And when he brings out his own sheep, he goes before them; and the sheep follow him, **for they know his voice**.*

Yet they will by no means follow a stranger, but will flee from him, for they do not know the voice of strangers.

John 10:3-5 (emphasis mine)

Handling the Religious

We Are His Sheep, and We Hear His Voice

And then, for emphasis, Jesus said again, *'My sheep hear My voice, and I know them, and they follow me.'* John 10:27. You not only hear the voice of the Spirit of God in your born-again spirit, but I believe you hear daily, constantly, *'This is the way, walk ye in it'* (Isaiah 30:21). Jesus is *the Way* (John 14:6). You and I could not have gotten saved without hearing and responding to His voice! Read John 6:44. *'No man can come to Me unless the Father who sent Me draws him; and I will raise him up at the last day.'* Note: *'No man can come **to Me** unless **the Father** who sent Me **draws him**.'*

Fishing at a Trout Farm

Let me illustrate this with this comical situation. Once, a friend and I went fishing at a *trout farm*. The trout are corn-fed, all swimming in a clear artificial pond. They were so dense that they appeared to run into one another. My friend snagged five trout. I had caught none.

Finally, in despair, I laid aside my pride and asked, *'What are you doing?'* The answer was simple. *'You simply pop the corn on the water quickly three times in the same spot and then, on the fourth time, let it sit. The trout will be so eager by the corn tapping, tapping, tapping, and now just floating, they will not notice the hook, and they will strike!'* So I tried it, and it worked. (By the way, I finally got seven fish, but my friend caught eight, and the largest!)

The Lord Gave Me a Trout's Eye View.

The Lord gave me a *trout's eye view* to teach me about the *'drawing of the Father.'* Unless the Spirit of God had begun to 'tap, tap, tap' at the door of our conscience, we would not notice to respond. (Consider

Revelations 3:20). This is where prayer for the lost man, the soul winner, and the Holy Spirit team together.

The Holy Spirit will 'reprove' or 'convince' the heart that *God is*, and He *is to be feared*. At age sixteen, I prayed, *'God, are you real?'* and the Spirit of **the Almighty** responded, and this atheist has never been the same since!

How Does This Apply to Defeating Intimidation?

How does this apply to overcome intimidation? Simply this: *if you do not know what to do,* **ask**! Oh, it is the *'simple things that confound the wise.' 'Do not lean to your own understanding'* (1 Corinthians 1:27; Proverbs 3:5-6). **Ask the Father.**

This process can be quicker than words. It can be a thought in our heart inquiring of God what to do, and if we attune ourselves to listen, He will answer us just as quickly.

The Blind Eyes Opened

I cannot illustrate this process any better than when the Lord told me to *'spit on the ground, make mud, put it on her eyes. Then, have her wash, and she will see.'*

This event occurred in Madras (now Madurai), India, but began during the trip to Lagos, Nigeria, the year prior.

The Vision of Blind Eyes

Before the Lagos outreach started, I had a private prayer the evening before (see Chapter 3). Bowing down in worship and with the utmost earnestness, I sought the Lord and longed for a prepared heart. Suddenly, *eyes became visible*. Eyes were visible even though mine were shut. I couldn't determine the person's age, race, or gender, but I saw their eyes. They had an unusual appearance, with a white film covering their iris, a common trait among blind individuals. In my spirit, I sensed where I would find the blind person the following day.

In leading the outreach, the Lord was gracious. I had no experience with such a large church, but I managed, coordinated, and led 200 church members. Groups of twenty left the church. My group also left to go into the neighborhoods. I found myself in just the right place. My party of three, an older woman and a college gal from the church, and I were standing in a Nigerian version of what we would call a 'government housing project' near the freeway exit. This was just what I had envisioned.

The Blind Woman Appeared

With the help of the two ladies, I conversed with three young men (18, 19, and a 21-year-old) sitting at the end of a building. Just then, a blind woman walked around the corner. She had no cane. Her hands both extended, gently waving back and forth. She was blind, but it was also apparent that this was her home, and she knew where she was going. My heart pounded in my chest as I saw her blind eyes. They were just like those I had seen during prayer the evening before.

I watched her. But then the young woman, the college student, spoke, *'Ah, that old woman, she won't receive anything.'* My heart tugged. But then I looked back at the young guys and resumed speaking to them.

I did not act.

God Gave Me a Mini Vision of What I Should Have Done

Later that night, I took time to pray. This time, the Lord did something else. He played a repeat or revision of the day's event. In this 'version,' I acted. I saw myself tell the college student, *'Ask that woman if she wants to see.'* The young lady walked over, asked the woman, and called over to me, *'Yes, she says she wants to see.'* I responded, *'Tell her, "The Man who opens the eyes of the Blind is Here."'* I recognized it was Jesus, not me, who was within me.

The woman came back over. I instructed the blind lady, *'This is unusual, but Jesus made mud with spit, put it on the eyes of the blind, and they saw. That is what we will do.'* I did. She washed. She returned with her sight.

You could argue, *'Yes, but you did not do that. You just saw yourself doing that.'*

True.

But the story still needs to be finished.

God is so patient. He is so kind. He is the ultimate teacher and nurturer of our lives. I was learning to hear. That pleased the Father. I was making progress. Step out. Try. He will also be patient with you.

Another Blind Lady

One year later, I was on another journey, this time to India (my first of ten trips). Again, I was traveling with the same senior evangelist.

I thought we could follow our approach in Nigeria, but I was devastated to learn that foreigners were prohibited from publicly expressing their religious beliefs. That afternoon, alone in my room, I cried as I prayed. Then, finally, the Lord spoke to me about several things. First, concerning street outreach, He impressed upon me that taking a few Bible school students and talking with people on the streets would not be a problem.

Bible School Students and I Preached the Gospel

The following day, I went with two students, Kumar and Lushano. Kumar could speak English and proper Tamil. Lushano understood educated Tamil and spoke 'street Tamil.' (I needed both guys to help me communicate.) We talked to several small groups. I made my Gospel message simple (to translate twice!) First, I asked the people, *'Why did God send His Son?'* I shared my favorite miracle: when Jesus raised the widow's dead son and returned him into her arms—such compassion (Luke 7:12-16). Next, I told them of Jesus spitting on the ground, making mud, and putting it on the eyes of the blind. I then repeated, *'But why did God send His Son to the earth?'* Then, with arms stretched out, I told them, *'To die for you, for me. To die for our wrongs. Our sins. The things that separate us all from a Holy God—the Maker of heaven and earth.'*

Many of these sweet people responded and received God's Son, Jesus, as their Lord and Savior.

My Wife Is Blind

In one such group, an older man spoke to me (via the interpreters) right after we had prayed together to receive Christ. He stated, *'My wife is blind'* (she was standing just over to the side of the group near the wall).

'Well?' The little crowd looked on. I knew the older man's logic, and it was correct. *'I have received your Jesus. He opened the eyes of the blind. My wife's eyes are blind. Please open her eyes as Jesus did.'*

Jesus Christ Is Not in Retirement

How can we proclaim the whole person and work and divinity of Jesus Christ and then retreat to say, *'He has gone into semi-retirement and is no longer doing miracles?'* What a religious façade! Either He is the GREAT I AM, or we Christians are wasting our time following Him.

Working miracles ... and believing in miracles are two different things. *It takes the working of the Spirit to produce miracles; therefore, knowing how to respond to His every leading is of absolute importance.* (See Galatians 3:5; Romans 8:14)

Lord, What Do You Want Me to Do?

The man's pleading eyes continued asking. From the depths of my soul, I said, *'Lord, what do you want me to do?'* Another way to say it: **'HELP!'**

As quickly as I breathed out the thought, like an 'inhale,' He said, *'Do you remember what I showed you (to do) last year in Lagos?'*

I got it.

This Is Unusual, But I Am Going to Put Mud on Your Eyes

I spoke to the woman. Kumar interpreted. Then Lushano interpreted it into *street* Tamil. I told the little woman (I am 6 foot 2 inches, and she was maybe only 4 foot 10 inches), *'Now, this is unusual. But Jesus spit on the ground, made mud, and put it on the eyes of the blind. They washed. And they saw.* **That is what we are going to do.**'

The words flowed out of my mouth as if performing miracles was second nature. I squatted down and looked at the ground. The ground was gritty, hard to make mud. I also observed that most of the people were barefoot. Not *'feeling the Spirit'* of which some ministers speak. I felt normal, my heart was calm.

Spitting on the ground, I made a little gritty mud. When I stood, the woman's face was tilted back. She was expectant—perhaps more than me. I applied the mud. I squatted and got some more. As I finished applying the mud with relief, I uttered, *'Go wash.'*

Handling the Religious

A Man behind Offered a Pail of Water

But, to my chagrin, a man behind me reached out a pail of water. (A common occurrence on the streets in India. People will 'set up shop' to sell hot tea by the road with just a small bucket of water and a burner. 'British style, of course, with sugar and milk.')

They placed the bucket in the woman's hands.

Me, I panicked. Feeling frozen, I asked the Lord again, *'What if nothing happens?'* Upon this, I heard the Lord laugh! His voice spoke with tender amusement, *'You're in this so far. Why don't you watch and see?'* I thought, *'Cute God, real cute. My spit is on this woman's eyes, and nothing has happened yet. What more can I do?'* Nothing, of course. That was the point. But what else could I do but **watch** and **see**?

Peter Understood the Working Miracles

Peter understood the working of miracles. **You do what you are told to do; He does the miracles.**

> So, when Peter saw it, he responded to the people: 'Men of Israel, why do you marvel at this? Or **why look so intently at us**, as though **by our own power or godliness** we had made this man walk?'
>
> 'And **His name, through faith in His name, has made this man strong**, whom you see and know. Yes, the faith which comes through Him has given him this perfect soundness in the presence of you all.'
>
> Acts 3:12 & 16 (emphasis mine)

He alone is the miracle worker. Our part is to be dependent. Listen, act upon His voice, and *expect* God to do His work. As long as you keep that straight, you will be all right!

It's Very Bright! It's Very Bright!

The woman washed. Kumar, Lushano, and I asked her, 'What has happened?' The little woman responded, 'It's bright. It's very bright!' I told her, 'Your eyes are getting used to the light. If you had been in a dark cave for several days, your eyes would have to adjust to the light.' So we told her we would give her a moment.

We walked down the street a short distance and spoke to another small group.

Then we returned to the woman.

God Had Opened Her Eyes!

By this time, the excitement was high. Kumar jumped right in. He addressed the woman. Raising two fingers before her, he asked what she saw. Looking at me with shock, Kumar said, 'She sees TWO! She sees two!' He then held up four fingers, but put his hand an inch from her nose. Then, perplexed, he said, 'She sees five?'

I grasped Kumar's forearm and pulled it back. 'Kumar, I cannot even see that close.' He then asked her again. Finally, he exhaled and said, 'She sees Four!' **God has opened her eyes!**

Inside, I was screaming!

In the group stood a taller man with his arms crossed. He had a very content look on his face as if he were saying, *'This should happen every day.'*

That afternoon, when I got to my hotel room, I screamed aloud, 'God, you opened the eyes of the Blind!'

You Can Hear the Spirit of God

We are capable of hearing the Spirit of God. But we need to acknowledge Jesus' words about us, even if they refer to us as dull sheep. Speak what Jesus has said over your life:

*'**I hear the Good Shepherd.** He calls me by name and leads me forth. He goes before me and I follow Him, for **I know His voice**.'*

(From John 10:3-4)

When we seek the Father's guidance, no matter how difficult the situation, He will lead us to *triumph*! (2 Corinthians 2:14). We will not be intimidated. *God never is.*

PostScript

God did something dear for me on that day in Nigeria.

On the third day of the outreach, I welcomed the church workers who had come to evangelize. *'The angels rejoice over one that is won to Christ!* (Luke 15:10) *And we have seen 839 brought to Christ in these two days!'* Just then, I had a mini vision. It appeared as a flash. I saw my father standing with two angels on either side. My dad was a big man—6 foot 5 inches tall. The angels on either side were about 8 to 9 feet tall. My dad was yelling, jumping up, slapping the back of the angels, shouting, *'That's my boy down there!'* He was hollering as he did at a San Francisco 49ers Game (as if the players down on the field could hear him way up in the stands), embarrassing my mom, brother, and me.

One month before my trip to Africa, my father had passed. He had died of a heart aneurysm moments after he had walked to work.

In that flash, God wiped all sorrow and tears from my heart. Ever since I have never had sorrow again over losing my father. Just the expectation that I will one day rejoice in heaven again with my dad.

God takes care of soul winners.

His life was ordered by his objective. Not for one moment did Jesus lose sight of his goal. The Master disclosed God's strategy of world conquest.[1]

—**Robert E Coleman**

But a life lived loving God bears lasting fruit, for the one who is truly wise wins souls.

—**Proverbs 11:30 TPT**

CHAPTER 6

Witnessing Jesus-Style

*J*esus was and is the **Master Evangelist**. After conversing with a woman at a well (John 4), a two-day revival ensued, saving most of the city. When we observe the Master Evangelist, we become highly effective witnesses. Jesus' conversation with this Samaritan woman is fantastic. Let us inspect *Jesus' Style of Witnessing*.

But first, let me tell you about an extraordinary conversion. This salvation spearheaded the Lagos, Nigeria revival. This **key conversion** contributed to 2,000 coming to Christ.

Keystone Species

In biology, there are *keystone species*. This species plays a crucial role in shaping the entire ecosystem. Without its keystone species, the ecosystem would change significantly or vanish entirely.

An example was the loss of the Otter population all around the Pacific Rim worldwide.[2] Between the 1700s and the early 1900s, hundreds of otters were extensively harvested for their beautiful pelts. They were almost wiped out. The kelp beds, home to many species of fish and other sea life, were dying off: the health of the waters diminished because of a significant decrease in CO_2 consumption. Sea urchins fed on the kelp,

Faith For Souls

and the otter was no longer abundant to feed on the urchins. The kelp beds were disappearing.

Then, in the 1950s, the US Fish & Wildlife Agency and others began conservation methods. Otters were transported from Alaska and repopulated along the western coast. The kelp beds revived. Sea life repopulated the kelp beds, and the waters were again healthy.

Key Salvations

In society, there are **key salvations**. Not that one soul is more important or more precious to God. But that person coming to Christ can affect many others coming to Christ. Anyone in a family can be that person. A dear friend, Pastor Stephen Fraser,[3] came to Christ, the youngest of six, and led his entire family to Jesus. Movie stars, professional athletes, business tycoons, the rich, and the famous could all be a keystone conversion. An essential salvation could be a minister of very humble beginnings whose ministry rose to prominence to reach thousands. Some examples would be D.L. Moody, Billy Graham, or John Osteen.

Nigerian Prostitute Brought to Christ

This Nigerian prostitute I had the privilege to bring to Christ was a **key salvation**, affecting the outreach that resulted in 2,000 receiving Jesus as Lord.

I stopped at the door of the *Coffee Bar* before climbing the three flights of stairs to my room at the *Stop Over Motel* in Lagos—a small room on the ground floor with a TV, tables, and chairs.

The black-and-white TV playing caught my attention. I leaned in the doorway and watched the television. The programming didn't impress me much as an American, yet I was momentarily captivated to watch it.

Witnessing Jesus-Style

As I did, someone spoke from within the dark room. A woman's voice. She said, *'Come in here.'* Weary of this invitation, but being a soul winner, I went in. We introduced ourselves. She told me her name was *Linda*.

The woman invited me to sit with her at the table. *'I'll be right back.'*

A Prostitute Is Downstairs; She Is Going to Get Saved!

I hustled up three flights of stairs and burst into my room. My roommate for this trip was Pastor Archangel (this wonderful man of God's actual name). *'There's a prostitute in the hotel, and she will get saved. Linda is going to get saved!'* We prayed together. I went back downstairs with expectations. (The right spiritual kind!)

Upon returning to the Coffee Bar, I took the chair across the table from Linda. Linda smiled and batted her eyelashes at me. (Now, when telling this story in a church service, I always do a role play. I select a man from the congregation to play Linda. I make him bat his eyes at me and talk icky-sweet. *It's hilarious!*)

I Have a Friend Who Wants to Meet You

To begin, I asked, *'Linda, I have a friend who wants to meet you. He thinks you are beautiful. Do you want to know his name?'* Linda, of course, said she did. But for emphasis, I asked her again, *'Linda, I have a friend who wants to meet you. He thinks you are beautiful. Do you want to know his name?'* (An angler knows he must 'sink the hook.') Linda nodded and faintly said, *'Yes.'*

Then, looking into Linda's eyes, *'His name is Jesus!'* Upon hearing my response, Linda rolled her eyes.

I shared the Gospel. I told her of the price Jesus had paid for her. She was so precious to Him; He died to give her life. As I continued,

Linda opened up a little. She told me she had made high marks in her religious class in school. Though unusual, she had her *final marks* (grades) in her purse.

Right around this time, Pastor Archangel popped his head into the room and greeted us. He intended to make sure I was winning, not Linda! Then he went on his way.

I invited Linda to receive Christ. We prayed together. I then asked, *'Linda, did you mean that prayer?'* She held up pinched fingers. *'Well, a little bit.'*

A Word of Knowledge- Do You Have a Five-year-old Daughter?

The Lord then gave me a Word of Knowledge. He told me she had a daughter who was about five years old.

'Linda, do you have a child?' 'Yes.'

'Is your child a girl?' She affirmed again, 'Yes.'

'Is she about five?' She said, *'Well, she just turned six.'*

I then got very bold: *'How much do you make every night doing this (turning tricks)?'* She told me, *'I do not do this every night.'* I asked, *'When you do, how much?'* She responded, *'100 Naira* (then about USD 20).' Then Linda hung her head and said, *'Sometimes only 50 Naira* (about ten US dollars).'

I leaned forward and made a challenge. *'Linda, I want to give you a challenge. I invite you to attend the church service in the morning. If you will, I will pay you 100 Naira.'*

Linda agreed she would meet me in the morning (for the money).

Early, Waiting for Linda

The minister's fifteen-passenger van was scheduled to leave at 8:30 a.m.; I arrived about ten past eight. I waited.

Looking again at my watch, *'No, Linda.'*

Closer to time, no Linda.

Then, at about 8:25, she arrived. A moment later, we climbed into the van, with about 7 or 8 other ministers already boarded. There was complete silence as we drove away from the motel.

I gave Linda a couple of Christian children's books I brought to Nigeria to give her daughter. She asked, *'What about the money?'* I then handed her an envelope. *'Linda, there is a note* (inside) *with the money that reads, "The devil has been paying you to destroy your life. Jesus will set you free and give you His life."'* She took the envelope and then seemed to relax.

Are You Ready to Get Serious?

'Are you ready to get serious? Do you want to make Jesus your Lord and Savior?' Linda nodded. We prayed together. The van with a dozen ministers was so silent you could hear the reverberation of the tires.

As we arrived at the church, I got out of the van with a Nigerian woman; I am sure eyes were upon me. I chose not to notice.

Linda was seated with me in the minister's section at the front. Someone had motioned to escort her elsewhere. I shook my head. The Helps Ministry staff served me a glass of water as the service began. I asked for one for Linda.

Linda, This Message is For You

This morning, the preacher arrived unannounced. He was a well-known Nigerian preacher, Bishop Benson Idahosa.[5] He preached two messages back-to-back. In his first sermon, he shared that until he was 18 years of age, he had never worn a pair of shoes. He spoke of the goodness of God, extending his foot toward the audience. *'But now, do you see my beautiful shoes?'* I leaned over to Linda and said, *'This message is for you.'* Linda gave a timid smile.

At the close of the second service, Bishop Idahosa gave an altar call to receive Christ and to be filled with the Holy Spirit. Linda arose and went up to the front.

After the service, sisters from the church reached out to Linda, taking her with them.

The following day, in front of the 200 believers who had come for the outreach, I began with, *'Did anyone see me come into the church service yesterday morning with a Nigerian woman?'* Several hands went up. I told the story. These believers were **ignited to win the lost**.

Jesus and the Samaritan Woman

Now let's turn to our text: John chapter 4, verses 1 to 26. I will organize this in a simple five-point outline and list the corresponding verses that go with each.

1. CONTACT   John 4:6-9
2. DESIRE   John 4:10-12
3. THE GOSPEL   John 4:13-15
4. CONVICTION   John 4:16-20
5. THE CHOICE   John 4:21-26

CONTACT

Now Jacob's well was there. Jesus therefore, being wearied from His journey, sat thus by the well. It was about the sixth hour. (v.7) A woman of Samaria came to draw water. Jesus said to her, 'Give Me a drink.' (v.8) For His disciples had gone away into the city to buy food. (v.9) Then the woman of Samaria said to Him, 'How is it that You, being a Jew, ask a drink from me, a Samaritan woman?' For the Jews have no dealings with the Samaritans.

John 4:6-9

We must rub shoulders with the world if we are going to win people to Christ. Yes, the Bible teaches to *'come out from among them and be separate'* (2 Corinthians 6:17). That speaks to your heart and lifestyle. It speaks to where you receive *your fellowship.* By all means, fellowship with brothers and sisters of like kindred faith! But do not snub the lost. **Look at Jesus.** Emulate His example.

What was Jesus often accused of? *'John came fasting and they called him crazy. I came feasting and they called me a boozer, a friend of the misfits. Opinion polls don't count for much, do they?'* Matthew 11:18-19 MSG. **Jesus loved people!**

That's why Jesus came. He came for the sick and the lost.

'On hearing this, Jesus said to them, "Those who are healthy don't need a doctor, but the sick. I have not come to call the righteous but sinners."'

Mark 2:17 NIV

Besides showing love for the unsaved, we must converse with them.

Look at what Jesus did here. He began the conversation. And what was His 'great spiritual' introduction? *'Give Me a drink.'* That is like us saying, *'How was your day today?'* Simple. Make conversation. But listen to your heart. So often, a thought comes, and I comment to someone. It could be, *'Your daughter's eyes are the prettiest green,'* or *'You must have the Serranos* (peppers)*!'* (I am a hot chili eater!) Just anything to begin.

Here is an uncommon idea in society today: *be friendly and kind.* Add genuine care and eye contact; we would be surprised at what might happen!

Lee and the Fisherman

For one of my *GCS (Great Commission Seminar)* meetings I conducted at a church, I took a friend named Lee Robbins with me. Lee is an avid soul winner. We drove my van and took our ten speeds with us. Before the services, Lee and I went for a bike ride. Going along a trail that followed the contour of a lake, we spied a lone fisherman. I looked at Lee. *'You want to stop, don't you?'* Lee said, *'Yes.'*

In our conversation, we learned the man had a back injury and was off work. We also discovered he had been watching a preacher on TV who prayed for the sick. We prayed for his back. And before we were done, Lee led him to Christ.

And what do you think was Lee's opening line? To a guy out at a lake fishing . . . *'Have you caught anything?'*

Do not be so hard on yourself. Stop feeling like you must have angels singing to you and God speaking in an audible voice to reach the lost effectively. I am exaggerating, but you get it. Just be touchable. And be yourself.

I guarantee that if you have read this far, several things are true:

1. You love the Lord.
2. You want His love to flow through you.
3. You want to bring more people to heaven with you.

Witnessing Jesus-Style

Let me tell you a little secret. God will use you mightily, just as you are, wherever you are on this journey. The first couple of guys I led to the Lord were water polo players. I played water polo in high school and one year in college. Hmmm ... do you think the Lord was gently guiding me where I was at the time? Remember, He loves *you*! Soul win from that vantage point. But start (or re-start if you have been inactive during the harvest).

> *Any little casual circumstance can be a crack in the door, an opportunity we do not want to miss. We may not know where such a conversation will lead, but God does—and he uses our availability.*[4]

DESIRE

> *Jesus answered and said to her, 'If you knew the gift of God, and who it is who says to you, "Give Me a drink" you would have asked Him, and He would have given you living water. (v.11) The woman said to Him, 'Sir, You have nothing to draw with, and the well is deep. Where then do You get that living water?' (v.12) Are You greater than our father Jacob, who gave us the well, and drank from it himself, as well as his sons and his livestock?'*
>
> John 4:10-12

News bulletin: You cannot get people saved talking about the weather. Some of us are comfortable around people. We can have a conversation. We engage well in conversing about many topics. But if eternity (spiritual matters) is never broached, you leave the encounter empty-handed. That has happened to me. It likely has happened to you, though your heart and mine were tugging for us to do more.

Let's go back to *the mentor*—**Jesus**. What did Jesus do here?

Jesus took the conversation and brought it into something eternal:

If you knew the gift of God, and who it is who says to you, 'Give Me a drink,' you would have asked Him, and He would have given you living water. (verse 10)

This got the Samaritan woman's attention.

The woman said to Him, 'Sir, You have nothing to draw with, and the well is deep. Where then do You get that living water?' (verse 11)

Jesus got her asking Him questions, 'What are you talking about?'

Peculiar Things Jesus Said

Jesus did this frequently. He said some of the most peculiar things. We find notable examples throughout the Gospel of John, beginning with His most famous declaration:

You must be born again.	John 3:7
(In you) *will be a well of living water.*	John 4:14
I am the Bread of Life.	John 6:48
Rivers of Living Water.	John 7:38
I am the Light of the World.	John 8:12
Before Abraham, I AM (God).	John 8:58
I am the Door.	John 10:7
I am the Good Shepherd.	John 10:11
I am the Resurrection.	John 11:25
Lord and Master.	John 13:14
Seen Me, Seen the Father (God).	John 14:9
I am the True Vine.	John 15:1

Why did Jesus make these statements? First, of course, because they were true. They describe who *the Son of Man* is in nature and dominion. But He also talked this way to prick people's attention. The soldiers who had failed to arrest Jesus reported, *'No man ever spoke like this man'* (John 7:46). Keep in mind His purpose. As Robert E Colman reveals throughout his book, *The Master Plan of Evangelism*, Jesus's goal was definite: world conquest.

God does not want anyone to be lost.

This means that contrary to man's perspective, the Lord is not late with his promise to return, as some measure lateness. But rather, his 'delay' simply reveals his loving patience toward you, because he does not want any to perish but all to come to repentance.

2 Peter 3:9 TPT

Jesus spoke in this manner to influence us. His intent is to wake us up! So, *hear what the Spirit is saying.*

Are you Born Again?

I have often used the expression and asked, *'Are you Born Again?'* This is effective for two things: to jump into eternal matters and learn if they are children of God. If a person is Born Again (even if not walking with Christ), they know it. If they are not, they rarely know what you are discussing—a perfect opportunity to expound the Gospel.

Remember the story of the two Mexican aviation students sitting by the pool?

Great Commission Seminars

Traveling throughout the United States, holding what I called *GCS—Great Commission Seminars*, I learned as I taught. Great Commission Seminars would take between 2 and 4 days. I preached the revelation of *Faith for Souls* and other messages, but my primary aim was to help the pastor by taking the church members out on outreach—so many beautiful meetings and outreaches. Believers who had never attempted to go out and share their faith led others to Christ. This happened every time in places like El Paso, TX, Toms River, NJ, San Jose, CA, and Lapeer, MI. I also conducted these meetings across the globe.

As in the Nigerian revival, we always returned from our outreaches and had time to share testimonies and encourage one another. In the coming chapters, I will share many of those testimonies.

Jesus Will Use Us to Help Teach One Another

While working with the believers, I also learned. Remember, we are enrolled in *Jesus' School of Evangelism*. You know well that God loves His people and loves to manifest Himself through them. He will use us to help coach one another in *Jesus' School of Evangelism*.

I remember a young believer from a church in San Diego, CA. He politely inquired if he could share how the Lord instructed him to explain becoming Born Again to street people. Of course, I said *'Yes.'*

Being Born Again Is Like a Lamp

The young man shared that he had to keep it simple when talking to a street person. So, he would explain becoming Born Again *like a lamp*.

Suppose your late grandmother gave you a beautiful lamp. You love it. Placing it on the table, you turn it on, but it does not work. You change the light bulb, but it still does not work. Then your friend says, 'Hey, you need to plug it in.'

You plug it in, and it works! It's wonderful. It's beautiful.

Like that lamp, we were made to have God's light. We were made to have God's love. He designed us to be beautiful. To be loved.

But sin tripped the cord. We are unplugged.

We must get plugged back into God. That is what it is to be Born Again.

Then, the brother would expound the Gospel of Christ, His death, burial, and resurrection.

THE GOSPEL

Jesus answered and said to her, 'Whoever drinks of this water will thirst again, (v.14) but whoever drinks of the water that I shall give him will never thirst. But the water that I shall give him will become in him a fountain of water springing up into everlasting life.' (v.15) The woman said to Him, 'Sir, give me this water, that I may not thirst, nor come here to draw.'

John 4:13-15

What is the Gospel? Let's get it from the Bible itself. Turn to 1 Corinthians, chapter 15.

*Moreover, brethren, **I declare to you the gospel** which I preached to you, which also you received and in which you stand,*

by which also you are saved, if you hold fast that word which I preached to you—unless you believed in vain.

*For I delivered to you first of all that which I also received: that **Christ died for our sins** according to the Scriptures,*

> and that **He was buried**, and that **He rose again the third day** according to the Scriptures,
>
> **and that He was seen** by Cephas, then by the Twelve,
>
> After that He was seen by over five hundred brethren at once, of whom the greater part remain to the present, but some have fallen asleep.
>
> After that He was seen by James, then by all the apostles.
>
> Then last of all He was seen by me also, as by one born out of due time.
>
> For I am the least of the apostles, who am not worthy to be called an apostle, because I persecuted the church of God.
>
> 1 Corinthians 15:1-9 (emphasis mine)

The *death, burial, and resurrection* of Jesus Christ. That is the Gospel. The power is in the Gospel. Paul declares in the Book of Romans:

> For I am not ashamed of **the gospel of Christ**, for **it is the power of God** to salvation for everyone who believes, for the Jew first and also for the Greek.
>
> For in it the righteousness of God is revealed from faith to faith; as it is written, 'The just shall live by faith.'
>
> Romans 1:16-17 (emphasis mine)

T. L. Osborn, *Preach the Gospel*

The great crusade evangelist T. L. Osborn was preaching the Gospel in Thailand.[6] The Thai people laughed at him as he shared how Jesus was crucified, buried, and rose again. They said, *'You Westerners are so violent. You even have blood in your religion.'*

Osborn fell on his face in the room that night and cried, *'God, I did not come halfway around the world to make a mockery of the Gospel.'* The Spirit of God answered, *'Preach the Gospel.'* Osborn argued, *'But Lord, I did.'* The Lord replied, *'No, you explained the Gospel. Preach the Gospel.'*

Osborn shared, *'The next night, I just got up and preached the Gospel. I just shared the Word and preached the Gospel. I (then) gave my call, and the Thai people responded.'*

Osborn looked up, and his interpreter was missing. He went behind the stage and found him crying. Osborn said, *'Come on, man!'* The interpreter said, *'No, you cannot cry in public in Thailand.'* T. L. grabbed him by the arm and said, *'You're going to learn how!'*

They went out and finished the meeting. Thousands were saved.

Osborn declared, *'There is a POWER of the GOSPEL I cannot explain.'*[7]

His words still ring in my heart today.

The Gospel Is Simple

I had the privilege of leading my oldest daughter, BreAnne, to Christ when she was 18 months old. To prepare for preaching at a rescue mission in North Little Rock, AR, I took a moment to pray on the side porch of our home. My precious little daughter came and sat beside me. She put her tiny hand in mine. I was impressed to ask, *'BreAnne, do you want to accept Jesus as your Savior?'* She answered, *'Yes.'*

As I prayed, she repeated. *'Heavenly Father,'* Bre said, *'Fatter.'* I continued, *'I ask Jesus.'* BreAnne said, *'Jezuz.'* I finished, *'Come into my heart.'* Bre just said, *'Heart.'*

Fatter, Jezuz, Heart. That was her prayer. She loves Jesus to this day. She is a mother of her own who runs her grandfather's ministry.

Simple. The Gospel is simple.

Daddy, I Saved Heather

Bre was talking to a friend on the family phone at six years old. I heard her tell her friend Amy, *'I don't think Heather is saved. I am going to share Jesus with Heather.'*

Bre had just been put down to bed a couple of nights later. As I walked down the hallway, little BreAnne exited her bed and approached me. You know when your child wants to tell you something. My eyes said, what is it, Bre? Beaming, she told me, *'The other day, I saved Heather!'*

Precious. Simple. The Gospel is so simple. *The power is in the announcement!*

[Yet the Gospel is often misrepresented. So, I have devoted a subsequent chapter to addressing the true and the false Gospel. See Chapter 11 *What Gospel Do You Have?*]

CONVICTION

> *Jesus said to her, 'Go call your husband, and come here.' (v.17) The woman answered and said, 'I have no husband.' Jesus said to her, 'You have well said, 'I have no husband.' (v.18) for you have had five husbands, and the one whom you now have is not your husband; in that you spoke truly.' (v.19) The woman said to Him, 'Sir, I perceive that You are a prophet. (v.20) Our fathers worshiped on this mountain, and you Jews say that in Jerusalem is the place where one ought to worship.'*
>
> John 4:16-20

First, let me tell you what the Lord told me. Back when I first attempted to share my faith (albeit without success) on my college campus during that final year. I felt pretty low, *'Well, again, I had failed'* when that person had not given their life to Christ.

Witnessing Jesus-Style

You Are NOT the Holy Ghost!

The Holy Ghost boomed within. He said, *'You are **not** the Holy Ghost!'*

Sharing and preaching the Gospel is our part. **Conviction** is His part. Look at John 16 as it reads in the *Amplified Bible*, Classic Translation:

> *However, I am telling you nothing but the truth when I say it is profitable (good, expedient, advantageous) for you that I go away. Because if I do not go away, the Comforter (Counselor, Helper, Advocate, Intercessor, Strengthener, Standby) will not come to you [into close fellowship with you]; but if I go away, I will send Him to you [to be in close fellowship with you]*
>
> *And when He comes,* **He will convict** *and* **convince the world** *and* **bring demonstration to it** *about sin and about righteousness (uprightness of heart and right standing with God) and about judgment:*
>
> *About sin, because they do not believe in Me [trust in, rely on, and adhere to Me];*
>
> *About righteousness (uprightness of heart and right standing with God), because I go to My Father, and you will see Me no longer,*
>
> *About judgment, because the ruler (evil genius, prince) of this world [Satan] is judged and condemned and sentence already is passed upon him.*
>
> John 16:7-11 AMPC (emphasis mine)

It is so important that we understand that the Holy Spirit is the one who **convicts, convinces,** and **brings demonstration** to the unbelievers. But we must rely upon and expect the Holy Spirit to do so. This empowers the Holy Spirit. How? By praying and expecting Him to work. Before every altar call, our pastor (at the beautiful church we attend) prays first. He prays that the Holy Spirit would move upon everyone in the service and those watching online who are unsaved to receive Jesus. We need to do the same before and after any soul winning endeavor.

The More You Believe the Gospel, The More Power Is Available

Paul makes a striking statement in Romans chapter 1 just before the verses about the Gospel (Romans 1:16-17).

> *So, **as much as is in me**, I am ready to preach the gospel to you who are in Rome also.*
>
> Romans 1:15 (emphasis mine)

I have found a direct correlation between how much we believe the Gospel and the power by which we preach it. I have had atheists tell me, *'You're real convicting,'* which is an anomaly. [Future chapters will explore these subjects in more depth: *Romans 1:15* (Chapter 9), *atheists* (Chapter 12), *the Gospel* (Chapter 11), and *Closing the Witness* (Chapter 8).]

For now, notice how the ministries of Jesus, the Apostles, and Steven are described:

> *And it was so, when Jesus had ended these sayings, that the people were astonished at His teaching,*
>
> *for **He taught** them **as one having authority**, and not as the scribes.*
>
> Matthew 7:28-29 (emphasis mine)

> *Now when **they saw the boldness of Peter and John**, and perceived that they were uneducated and untrained men, they marveled. And they realized that **they had been with Jesus**.*
>
> Acts 4:13 (emphasis mine)

> Witnessing Jesus-Style

And they were not able to resist the wisdom and **the Spirit by which he** *(Steven)* **spoke.**

And all who sat in the council, looking steadfastly at him, **saw his face as the face of an angel.**

Acts 6:10, 15 (emphasis and parentheses mine)

The power of the Gospel is directly linked to *our revelation of it.*

THE CHOICE

Jesus said to her, 'Woman, believe Me, the hour is coming when you will neither on this mountain, nor in Jerusalem, worship the Father. (v.22) You worship what you do not know; we know what we worship, for salvation is of the Jews. (v.23) But the hour is coming, and now is, when the true worshipers will worship the Father in spirit and truth; for the Father is seeking such to worship Him. (v.24) God is Spirit, and those who worship Him must worship in spirit and truth.' (v.25) The woman said to Him, 'I know that Messiah is coming' (who is called Christ). 'When He comes, He will tell us all things.' (v.26) Jesus said to her, 'I who speak to you am He.'

John 4:21-26

Ask them, *'Will you receive Jesus?'* No good salesperson would fail to ask. The difference between the top 20% of salespersons, who make 80% of the sales, is that they are the ones who *never* fail to ask for the sale.

They Prayed in between Phone Calls

Before I preached the Sunday morning service at a church in Colorado, one lady sitting near the front was beaming. I was compelled to ask, *'What has happened?'* The sister then explained that she had been in my Friday evening service and had received *Faith For Souls*! However, having to work on Saturday, she missed the outreach. However, this believer did not miss the *outreach*! She shared, *'I work as a telephone operator. During my shift between taking calls, I shared Jesus with the coworker beside me. Then I was impressed to ask her, "Will you receive Jesus?"* The coworker said, *"You mean now?"* The believer answered, *"Yes, now."* Then, bursting with joy, this sister exclaimed, *'We prayed together between phone calls. She was Born Again!'*

How to Get Them to Pray

I have frequently *asked* and *told* simultaneously. What I mean is that while I am asking, I am walking them through what we are going to do (already having shown them Romans 10:9-10).

> I will say, *'All we have to do is tell God what you told me, and He will forgive you and give you Eternal Life. You will be Born Again.'*
>
> *'I will pray, and you can pray with me....'*
>
> *'We will thank God that Jesus is Lord, and He is Your Lord.'*

Once we finish praying, I usually inquire, using their name(s), *'Did you really mean that prayer?'* (remembering my conversation with the Nigerian woman). This question exposed the doubtful sincerity in her prayer. Yet, most of the time, they are genuine. This question serves as a starting point to offer *the assurance of salvation*.

Then I will say, *'Let me show you what God's Word says about what you have just done.'* I show them the verse while reading it aloud (John 1:12).

But as many as received Him, to them He gave the right to become children of God, to those who believe in His name.

John 1:12

I address the person by their name and tell them, *'You have received Him* (Jesus as your Lord and Savior). *You now are a child of God. It is your right! Congratulations!'*

I pray for that sensitivity and to keep alert for openings to speak about the Lord, so witnessing is as natural for me as eating and drinking. The Holy Spirit gives me a nudge. I follow the opening in the conversation and speak for the Lord.[1]

—**Nellie Pickard**

I sent you to reap that for which you have not labored; others have labored, and you have entered into their labors.

—**John 4:38**

CHAPTER 7

Divine Appointments

The Greek word *logos* is used over three hundred times in the New Testament. Logos is often translated as **Word** (meaning God's word) but also denotes special revelation from God. *Jesus is the logos made flesh* (John 1:14). The *ACCU WORD* translation (a hyper-literal translation, written and translated by a friend of mine) translates logos as *'the logic of God.'*

What is the Logic of God Toward the Lost?

Let me take a little liberty here. Let's imagine what the *logic of God* is concerning believers witnessing of the Gospel to the lost.

First, let's suppose God has an available person. Maybe a young mom with two children, a senior couple, a small business owner, or a young college art student (my story). This person or persons are available. They yearn to see lost souls come to Christ. Willing to spend an hour or two in their day (or week), their heart cries for the lost to come to Christ.

Second, in any scenario, hundreds, if not thousands, of people are within a 2-to-5-mile radius of this believer(s).

Would You Orchestrate Events?

Third, as God (or an angel looking over His shoulder), you can orchestrate events enabling one person's path to cross another's. As God, you know the number of hairs (Luke 12:7) on every person's head (*you know everything about everyone*).

And fourth, as God, you sacrificed your most precious and only Son to die a criminal's death, to pay for the sins of all humanity. You want them saved!

> *He (Jesus) existed in the form of God, yet he gave no thought to seizing equality with God as his supreme prize.*
>
> *Instead he emptied himself of his outward glory by reducing himself to the form of a lowly servant. He became human!*
>
> *He humbled himself and became vulnerable, choosing to be revealed as a man and was obedient. He was a perfect example, even in his death—a criminal's death by crucifixion!*
>
> Philippians 2:6-8 TPT (parenthesis mine)

The second member of the Godhead made Himself to be but flesh, and He submitted to eternal separation on that hideous cross to appease the righteous judgment of sin for all humanity. He emptied Himself on the cross.

Now, do you suppose that if you were God, you would use your *logic*, your mind, *'to cause the right person* (the available soul winner) *to be at the right place, at the right time* (hearts prepared to receive) *and give that believer just the right words to say* (Matthew 10:19-20) *that would touch that heart to be saved?'*

The Right Person, the Right Place, the Right Time

This is what the Lord has impressed upon my heart to pray over every group of ready laborers, ready to go into the harvest, every time:

Lord, we ask that the right teams be at the right place, at the right time, to speak the right thing to the right people whose hearts have been prepared to receive right now.

He has always answered my prayer.

Would the Lord do that? Of course, He would. Would He do that every time? Absolutely yes! God is more vested and loves people more than any of us. What He needs is laborers (Matthew 9:37-38). Available laborers. If you are *shaking in your boots* but aspire to be used by the Lord, do you think the Lord will help you? You can bet your life on it. He bet His (His Son Jesus).

Amazing Divine Appointments

Let me share some of the most amazing stories where God did just this.

Englishman at the Munich, Germany, Train Station

I was doing back-to-back *GCS* (Great Commission Seminars) at *Wort des Glaubens* (Word of Faith) church in Munich, Germany, working with their Bible school. They had two sessions (schools), one in the morning and one in the evening. [After each day and evening outreach session, we would share testimonies about what the Lord had done.]

We gathered in the large church auditorium when the evening Bible school outreach students returned. Only the front portion of the sanctuary was lit. One student, a young man in his twenties from a team of three, came to the mic.

Our group was impressed to go to the train station. We were led to go up to a man who turned out to be English. We shared with him about Jesus dying for him, but he interrupted us, 'I am not interested.' So we talked to other groups of people.

Faith For Souls

After a while, the Englishman returned to us. And he 'wanted to hear what we had to share with him.'

As we talked, we learned that the man was suicidal, and in fact, he was there (at the train station) *to throw himself before an oncoming train.*

Praise God: that man received Christ!

On top of that, there was more to it. Sitting in the dimly lit sanctuary, the Englishman was identified by the young Bible student who declared, 'And this is him!' He was among his *new friends*—brothers and sisters in Christ! I had the opportunity to meet him face-to-face and shake his hand.

Nine Saved in One House in Plainview, Texas

I was doing a *GCS* at a church in Plainview, North Texas. These were country people, the very salt of the earth. We did six services: preaching Sunday morning and night, then preaching and outreach Monday morning and night, and then again on Tuesday.

Several of the teams were out witnessing in a mobile home park. During the first outreach, my partner and I called on a family at a mobile home. Two Hispanic women with three little children answered the door. We were invited in. Once inside, we met another young woman (only 14 years of age) with a newborn baby. After sharing the Gospel, everyone stood together, holding hands as the entire group (kids and all) received Christ.

The Pastor's Wife Led the Ex-Husband to Christ

Unknown to us, the pastor's wife and her partner had stopped to talk to the man parked under the carport. He was with a young woman. It turned out that the man was the ex-husband of one woman inside. He did not speak English, but the young girlfriend did. The pastor's wife led her to Christ. Then, the young girlfriend interpreted for her boyfriend (the ex-husband). He, too, became a child of God.

The next day, my team did a follow-up. I brought Christian children's books to share with the kids. The young 14-year-old mother answered the door. I greeted her, having met and prayed with her the day before. But she acted as if she had never seen me before. Then, one of the two ladies approached the door and introduced this daughter. Both women had 14-year-old daughters who both had newborn babies. This was the *other* daughter.

We were again invited into the home. I gave the kids the children's books. Then we shared the Gospel with this other new mom, and she was born again!

Nine people from one household accepted Christ as their Lord and Savior!

Suzie and the Punk Rockers

When I arrived at Pastor Larry Key's Church in Arnold, Missouri, a fifteen-year-old teen from his church greeted me with ecstatic joy. Her name was Suzie.

> *I am so excited that my church is going out* (to evangelize)*! My friends at the Baptist church go out. Finally, we are too!*

Pastor Larry gave me the back story about Suzie. At only fifteen, she was the spiritual pillar at her house. Her mom had different men in and out of the home. When offered a different living situation, Suzie refused because she had vowed to stay and protect her little sister. Someone in the church had offered to pay Suzie's tuition to attend the Christian school. Again, she refused. She had seen other friends go to a Christian school, and they had become lazy, starting partying and no longer living for the Lord. Suzie had her eyes set on Jesus.

[There will be another story (in a coming chapter) about this wonderful pastor. He is now *kicking it up* on the streets of heaven. I am sure he and my dad must be friends.]

Faith For Souls

When it came time for the outreach, Suzie was part of a team of four: two other teenage girls, a single mom in her thirties, and herself. The group traveled down a street, knocking on doors. They received multiple rejections. Some said, *'They have a church'* and refused to talk. Others just shut the door in their faces.

The Woman Said, Let's Tell Our Pastor This Does Not Work

The mom told the group, *'Let's go back and tell our pastor this does not work.'* But Suzie refused. She said, *'Brother Beelly* (my nickname to all who attend an outreach with me) *said there are divine appointments, and we are going to find ours!'*

The lady and the girls then approached a parked car with three punk-rocker-type guys (with the typical neon-colored spiked hair). They sat in the convertible with the top down. These guys were hanging out and drinking beer. Suzie and the group talked with them and shared Jesus for an hour and a half. Then one guy said, *'It's time for a beer run,'* and started the engine and took off.

Suzie Prayed. The Punk-Rockers Came Back and Got Saved!

Suzie and the group stayed put and prayed. They prayed those guys would come back. They prayed they would accept Christ as their Lord.

After about 15 to 20 minutes, the convertible pulled back up to the curb. After another 15 minutes of witnessing, the young men became somber. Soberness came upon them. All three punk rockers gave their hearts to Jesus!

Jesus Said You Would Reap

And he who reaps receives wages, and gathers fruit for eternal life, that both he who sows, and he who reaps may rejoice together.

For in this the saying is true: 'One sows and another reaps.'

I sent you to reap *that for which you have not labored; others have labored, and **you have entered into their labors**.*

John 4:36-38 (emphasis mine)

I like the Amplified for verse 38:

I sent you to reap a crop for which you have not toiled. Other men have labored, and you have stepped in to reap the results of their work.

It's like an actor who steps into the scene right after the stuntman has done the hard part. Or like receiving a paycheck on payday without ever having had to go to work. Talk about *divine appointments*. Believe for this!

Sowing seed is acceptable. This is a part of the process. But we often accept a lesser prize. I mean that if you can expect more, Jesus will give you more. More effectiveness. More impact. More souls won to Christ. You are reaping the rewards of your hard work and that of those who came before you.

Look at what Jesus is telling us! ***I sent you to reap*** *that for which you have not labored; others have labored, and **you have entered into their labors**.*

What Jesus Did and Did Not Say

Jesus didn't suggest, 'Let's try our luck at fishing, boys,' but made repeated promises.

*And (Jesus) said to them, 'Come **follow me** and **I will transform you into fishers of men** instead of fish!'*

Mark 1:17 TPT (parenthesis and emphasis mine)

And Jesus said to Simon, **Stop fearing.** *From this moment* **as characterized by what has just taken place, you shall be catching men alive.** *And having brought the boats to the shore, having abandoned all, they followed Him as His disciples.*

Luke 5:11 Wuest

Too many of us listen to what our church denominations, experiences, and understanding tell us. Things like, *'Not everyone has that gift,'* or *'At least I planted a seed,'* or *'If you do not reach them as children, few will come to Christ.'* Now, I am not knocking planting seeds. I do a lot of seed planting. But I also reap. I expect it. Why? Because Jesus—the Master Evangelist, my Lord and yours, told us, **'I sent you to reap.'**

Better Followers, Better Results

Let us switch gears here and talk about reaping. *Reaping* (and all effective ministry) occurs because of *our following*. If we follow His leading, we will be ambassadors of the Gospel and most effective.

Romans 8:14 tells us: *For as many as are led by the Spirit of God, these are sons of God.* You could say it this way: *the sons (and daughters) are led by the Spirit of God.*

Remember when the Lord instructed His disciples to *'Go and prepare the Passover for us'* (Luke 22:8)? The disciples asked where, and Jesus told them. They followed His instructions, and everything was carried out as it should. Now notice verse 13: *'So they went and found it just as He had said to them, and they prepared the Passover.'*

If we are willing, He will lead us, and *we will also find it, just as He has said.*

The Hidden Man of the Heart

Every person has a switch to their heart. What do I mean? Like the power button on your computer or the on/off control for a vacuum. You must find the switch to turn it on.

I love the phrase in 1 Peter 3 (referring to the person and character of a godly woman) that applies to us all:

> But let it be the inward adorning and beauty of **the hidden person of the heart**, with the incorruptible and unfading charm of a gentle and peaceful spirit, which [is not anxious or wrought up, but] is very precious in the sight of God.
>
> 1 Peter 3:4 APCE (emphasis mine)

This verse describes my precious wife. Because of her and the Holy Spirit, I am finally obeying God and completing the writing of this much-needed book on the freedom and ease of soul winning.

But let's notice the broader application here. Every one of us is a spirit man (or woman). The real you and the real me are not the ones we see. We are 'the hidden person of the heart.' And we (the hidden person deep inside) 'are very precious in the sight of God.'

That is the person Jesus spoke to all the time. But remember, I stated earlier:

*The Gospel is not a Gospel to the head. It is the Gospel **to** the heart.*

*And the Gospel is not a Gospel from the head. It is the Gospel **from** the heart.*

Jesus can help you reach that person. He will lead you to do so if you listen. Ask. In many witnessing situations, when I am tuned in to the Holy Spirit, I perceive my heart is praying, *'Lord, show me the door* (to their heart). *Help me find the switch.'* And He does.

Recognizing Divine Appointments

If we seek the Lord, He will lead us to divine appointments daily.

Some say that *the more sensitive and attuned we are to Him, the more softly He speaks.* Why shout at a child who listens? I find this to be true. Rarely has God had to raise His voice with me, but I must endeavor to be tuned in.

I remember another outreach in a different city in Texas. Most of the teams were again working in a mobile home park. Although summer was approaching, darkness had already set in. As I stood at a cross street and turned my head to the right, that street looked good. I motioned to my partner and said, *'Let's go down this street.'* Moments later, we were standing at a door with a dimly lit single porch light. A young woman answered. My partner (another guy) and I led her to Christ.

Musing upon this later, I thought how incredible it was that a young single woman would open her door and her heart to two guys sharing the Gospel with her on her poorly lit, isolated porch. God did that.

He will do the same for you.

The Holy Spirit Knows How to Lead

But even if our gospel is veiled, it is veiled to those who are perishing,

whose minds the god of this age had blinded, who do not believe, lest the light of the gospel of the glory of Christ, who is the image of God, should shine on them.

For we do not preach ourselves, but Christ Jesus the Lord, and ourselves your bondservants for Jesus' sake.

2 Corinthians 4:3-6

Those who are blind cannot perceive light. The god of this age has blinded souls so they cannot see. He uses darkness—spiritual darkness.

What does Jesus call us? *'You are the light of the world.'* He continued, *'Let your light so shine before men, that they may see . . .'* Matthew 5:14,16.

Listen.

Learn to listen to the Lord, even after the divine appointment. He will critique your witness. That is what a Master does in any field—especially in our commission to win the lost.

The Horsewoman

One such time in Omaha, NE, I and the pastor of a church had talked to a rancher. We conversed with this lady over the barbed wire fence. She was of a slight frame, but I could tell she was tough, a natural horsewoman.

We shared the Gospel with her. She said she had been a Catholic but was now an atheist. I knew better. We sowed the Word and dialogued back and forth for about 25 minutes. We left on a positive note.

As I lay in my bed that night, the Spirit of God talked with me about this woman. He impressed upon my mind,

'Do you remember how the woman said she had been a Catholic but now asserts to be an atheist?'

'Yes.'

'Do you also remember the witness you had at the time that this woman went through an abortion? That was correct—she had. The two facts are connected.' (No *good* Catholic woman could have an abortion.)

As you noticed, she was shattered inside, and her way to cope was to push me away and reject God.

The Lord then told me, *'Had you pursued that direction* (with my leading), *her heart would have been struck, and she would have surrendered to My Love.'*

'God is so patient. He never condemns.'[2] The voice of T. L. Osborn still plays in my heart. So Jesus the Master was instructing me.

Divine Appointments for You

Divine appointments are out there. They are everywhere. Meetings with eternity for men, women, teens, children, older adults, the rich, the poor, the fashionable, and the hobo. They abound. We must do three things:

1. Expect them.
2. Avail ourselves to them.
3. Declare our course now—*I will see. I will follow.*

Take a private moment now and make this declaration aloud:

My Declaration

God, I am shedding my skin. My old way of thinking is that I am insufficient or cannot be effective.

*I believe **Your** Word. Jesus, you said, 'that **I will reap** where I had not sown.' (John 4:38) You meant that people's hearts are prepared to receive all around me. Some other person has sown seed into their lives.*

They may be at a crossroads or have suffered a loss, but now they are open. Maybe not before, but now they are wide open to receive you as Lord and Savior—right now!

*I do not know who they are, where they are, or how to find them, but you do. But I am asking now that you give me **Divine Appointments**—divine appointments from Heaven!*

Divine Appointments

I do not yet know what I will need to say, but you do. You told believers facing persecution:

Not to worry about how or what you should speak. For **it will be given to you** in that hour **what you should speak.**
For it is not you who speak, but **the Spirit of your Father who speaks in you**.

Matthew 10:19-20 (emphasis mine)

When the divine appointment comes, I will hear, and you will speak through me—just the right words to touch their heart, and they will get saved.

Your Word says,

For as many as are led by the Spirit of God, these are sons of God.

Romans 8:14

*I am your child. Therefore, I am led by **You**. Even if I do not see it at first, you guide me to the right place at the right time, saying the right words and talking to the right person whose heart (s) has been prepared to receive Jesus as Lord.*

Make me become a great fisher of men *(people). I declare Psalm 2:8 as my request to heaven:*

Ask of Me, and I shall give thee the heathen for thine inheritance, And the uttermost parts of the earth for thy possession.

Psalm 2:8 KJV

Jesus, I am asking now! Give me Souls!

In Jesus' Name, Amen!

There is a place in every person's heart that God has placed there, and only He can fulfill and satisfy that place.[1]

—**Tommy Barnett**

That if you confess with your mouth the Lord Jesus and believe in your heart that God has raised Him from the dead, you will be saved.

—**Romans 10:9**

CHAPTER 8

Closing the Witness

I came across the audio recording of the meeting just before this first testimony I will share. I have included this word from the Lord to make a correlation.

A tongue and interpretation the Lord gave to me during a *GCS (Great Commission Seminar)*[2]:

Hallelujah. Hallelujah.

Thank you, Jesus.

By My Spirit says the Lord, by My Spirit, that I have poured out upon all flesh, I will bring in the masses of humanity. By this (By My Spirit), I have anointed My people to be My witnesses, My preachers, and My Victors of Truth upon the land.

It is by My Spirit, not apart from My Spirit, or without My Spirit, but by My Spirit,

says the Spirit of God, that they may effectively bring in the harvest.

I have poured out My Spirit upon young and old, male and female, of all races.

Faith For Souls

I have poured out My spirit, that those who look up to Me shall draw and drink in of My Spirit, to pour forth out of their belly. Rivers of Life will flow. Rivers of Life will flow.

But it is by My Spirit, says the Lord.

Oh, oh, oh, oh ... Yes, there has been an outpouring of the Spirit in days of old, and in truth, My Spirit has never left since that time 2,000 years ago.

On that Day of Pentecost, I poured out My Spirit upon all flesh.

My Spirit has been here. My Spirit of Revival. And those that will listen to Me, expect Me, and allow Me to manifest Myself are the ones who will benefit and see the results, says the Spirit of God.

This was the prayer that followed. Afterwards, the pastors, church members, and I went out for another time of outreach:

Father, we thank you in the Name of Jesus. Lord, it is not by power; it is not by might,

but by your Spirit. Father, we look to you.

Father God, thank you for divine appointments by the Spirit of God.

Appointments that no man could orchestrate, but your Holy Spirit has prepared

people's hearts to receive the Word of God.

And you give us the very words to speak. We do not know what to say, but by Your Spirit, we will have divine utterance and express the word that will make the difference in due season. That will drive home to the hearts, and they will cry out and say,

'Oh yes, I want Jesus. Oh yes, I will receive.'

Father, we thank you for it and give you all the glory, for man is nothing without you,

without the Lord Jesus, without salvation. And we give you all the glory.

In the Name of Jesus. Amen.

The Fastest Salvation I Have Ever Seen

This evening, my partner was the Associate Pastor of the church. We were working in an apartment complex. The pastor knocked at a door; a lady who used to attend the church answered. He encouraged and admonished her that she was missed and that it would bring her strength to return to fellowship. I concurred with the associate pastor.

However, my heart was burning to preach the Gospel to the lost.

Just then, an African American lady walked behind us on the sidewalk. (I mention her race only because a white man is approaching her—a stranger. We had never met.) *'Excuse me. Do you have peace with God? The Bible says, "Therefore being justified by faith, we have peace with God through our Lord Jesus Christ."'* (Romans 5:1 KJV)

The woman said, 'No, I do not.'

'Would you like to?'

'Yes.'

I reached out my hand; she took it, prayed, and made Jesus the Lord of her life.

'The Lord will now fill you with the Holy Spirit. He will fill you, and you will speak in a new heavenly language (tongues)*'* (Acts 5:32).

We prayed again, and the Lord filled her with the Holy Ghost, and she spoke in other tongues.

The whole event may have occurred in less than 3 minutes.

Saved and Filled in 3 Minutes. How?

In a moment, she is saved and filled with the Holy Ghost. That's God. Remember the interpretation of the message in tongues above? The emphasis was, *'By My Spirit'* and *'not apart from My Spirit.'*

Faith For Souls

If we are to experience what Jesus promised Peter, *'I will make you a fisher of men'* (and I am persuaded His promise is to all believers), then we must rely upon the Spirit of God.

Yes, I believe in 'door-to-door' evangelism. We founded a church by going door-to-door. But canvassing per se is not the key. The key is being led to the right person at the right time with the right words given by the Holy Spirit.

The First Outreach That I Led

I saw this in practice when I first received a *Faith For Souls*. Young adults from the 'College and Careers' Sunday school class went to share the Gospel one Saturday night. I was asked to lead the group that evening. Our location was the Bells Amusement Park[3] in downtown Tulsa, Oklahoma.

In groups of twos or threes, we went into the park.

One young man from our group stood at a distance from the entrance.

Upon finishing that evening, we gathered and shared the results. I had led a person to Christ. Teams shared whom they had led to Christ.

Then, the young man who had waited near the entrance shared. He had led seven to Christ. I remember asking how he led so many to Christ. He answered, *'I waited, watched, and prayed. The Lord then directed me to talk to this person. I did, and they prayed to receive Christ. Then the Lord directed to a couple of others, I approached them, and they also received Christ.'* He repeated this approach with others. They also were Born Again.

The Holy Spirit directed. He obeyed. People responded. Wow! Simple.

Practical Tools for Closing the Witness

Let me share simple tools that will help you in your endeavor to bring people into the Kingdom of God.

#1 Preach the Living Jesus

First, emphasize the living Jesus. People know He was crucified. They do not realize He is Risen! I have used the analogy often: *a dead firefighter cannot pull you from the fire. It takes a live firefighter to save you from the flames!*

To the woman at the well, Jesus was bold. *'I am [he], who am speaking to thee.'* (John 4:26 YLT). Moses asked God, *'What is his name? What shall I say to them?'* (the children of Israel) God answered Moses, *'I AM THAT I AM'* (Exodus 3:13-14 KJV).

At the close of presenting the Gospel admonishing the person to accept Christ as Lord, I have often said: *'Don't get Jesus.* **Get Jesus!'**

Examples in the Book of Acts

To the Ethiopian eunuch, Philip *'preached unto him Jesus'* (Acts 8:35).

On the day of Pentecost, Peter stood up and declared, *'(Jesus) you have taken, and by wicked hands have crucified and slain:* **whom God hath raised up**,*'* Acts 2:23-24 KJV. Then he nails it again, *'This* **Jesus hath God raised up**, *where we all are witnesses'* (verse 32).

Paul to the Greeks in Athens on Mars Hill proclaimed:

For the appointed day has risen, in which he is going to judge the world in righteousness by the man he has designated. And the proof given to the world that God has chosen this man is this: **he resurrected him from among the dead!**

Acts 17:31 TPT (emphasis mine)

Present the Resurrected Christ! Present Him *in* you. In others. In the Word. Entice them, *'Will you receive Him?'*

I Love This Quote from Oral Roberts

Oral writes in his excellent book, *A Daily Guide to Miracles*:

Do you know who you are talking to when you deal with Christ? You are dealing with the Man who scooped out the bed for the ocean, flung the stars from His fingertips, hung the earth on nothing, and put the fish in the sea. And He can tell them when to strike the net! You are dealing with THE MAN. You are dealing with Jesus. Have you ever realized how great He is?[4]

#2 Be Persistent, But Not Pushy

If they say *'No,'* inquire, *'Why is that?'* answer them from the Word of God, what He gives you now. Then, ask, *'Would you like to receive the living Jesus who paid for all your sins? Would you like to receive the gift of Eternal Life?'*

Paul, under custody by the Roman procurator, Porcius Fetus, gave his defense (Acts 26). Also present was King Agrippa. Paul shares his conversion before these men and the royal court (his unique story of meeting Christ—we all have one.) Learn how to present yours. (See the PostScript below) Paul spoke of being a persecutor of Christians: *'and when they were put to death, I gave my voice against them.'* He told of his confrontation with the living Jesus. He spoke of his transformation.

Paul preached the Living Christ. He declared Jesus' impact on his own life. Do the same.

Why should it be thought a thing incredible with you, that God should raise the dead?

As he spoke, Fetus decried Paul, a madman.

Closing the Witness

At this stage of Paul's defense, Festus said in a loud voice, 'You are insane, Paul! Your great learning is giving you to madness!'

Acts 26:8,24 BSB

But Paul stood resolute. He addressed Festus and the King: *'I am not mad, most noble Festus, but speak the words of truth and reason.'*

Paul persists with King Agrippa, *'For the king, before whom I also speak freely, knows these things . . . for I am convinced that none of these things escaped his attention, since this thing was not done in a corner.'* (v.25-26)

King Agrippa, I Know You Believe

Then Paul squares off with Agrippa: *'King Agrippa, do you believe the prophets? I know you do believe.'* Agrippa responds to Paul, *'You almost persuade me to become a Christian.'* (v. 27-28)

I love Paul's famous response to King Agrippa:

'I would to God that not only you, but also all who hear me today, might become both almost and altogether such as I am, except for these chains.' (v.29)

To Illustrate, Let Me Share a Fun Example

The Omaha pastor I mentioned earlier wanted his people to know how to win the lost to Christ. In two years, he had me come to hold a *GCS (Great Commission Seminars)* three times. I explained that I would preach the same series of messages. He had no problem with that.

Faith For Souls

On one of these occasions, his mother, a devoted believer and member of his church, was having an annual reunion with the ladies with whom she had worked. This reunion would be held at the church (which was also a summer camp) on Saturday morning. The pastor's mom invited me to the luncheon. She hoped these women would turn to Christ.

Little White-Haired Ladies and Tennies

I attended the luncheon and visited with a handful of these retired women. After lunch, they went for a hike. I smiled as I watched these white-haired women and their tennies hit the trail.

I headed back to my room. But the Holy Ghost was talking to me. He told me to address the group of women.

Evangelist David Allbritton

I did not want to. The idea of preaching to the little old ladies scared me! Then I remembered how an evangelist I admired had done something bolder. Back when Hal Lindsey's movie, *The Late Great Planet Earth*,[5] came out, this man preached. In the theatre version, the Gospel was not presented. No solution for the end of the world. This evangelist, David Allbritton, as a young man, obeyed God.[6]

While the movie was closing, he jumped to his feet and screamed, *'Sit Down! Sit Down! Sit Down!'* Everyone stayed in their seats—even the big tough guy with the knife scars on his face who sat before David.

Gospel Presented at the Movie Theater

David presented Jesus and gave an altar call. Across the theatre, people wept and got saved—even the guy with the scars. Afterward, the man thanked David.

Remembering this testimony, though still shaking, I returned to the church. A moment later, these elderly hikers came and sat, spread out across the sanctuary.

The Reason I Called You Here Today

Walking to the front, I raised my voice, *'The reason I have called you here today...'* I presented the Gospel, sharing God's great love and the gift of His Son.

Ladies standing in the back glared. Their stares were trying to bore a hole right through me. I could feel the hostility.

But I stayed the course. Then I gave my call. *'Now we are going to pray and invite Jesus, the Son of God, into our hearts. If you mean this prayer, you will be a new person. You will become a child of God. You will be Born Again.'*

After the prayer, I looked across the church and saw beautiful peace upon radiant faces.

The little old ladies did *not kill me*. Thank God!

#3 Listen to Them While Listening to The Holy Ghost

As you converse with a person about the Gospel, listen. Listen to them, but more, listen to God. Listen with a prayer in your heart: *'Lord, what do I need to do and say?'*

Don't get caught up in a debate. Jesus did not debate. The religious haters came to trip Him up; He did not play into their hands. *'By what authority do you do these things?'* (Mark 11:28 BSB). He responded, *'I will ask you a question. If you answer me, I will tell you by what authority I do these things.'* (v.29) The men refused to answer His question about the origin of John the Baptist's ministry. He did not answer them.

Learn to listen as Jesus did to His Heavenly Father.

#4 Proclaim Good News

You are not called to 'Go into the world, fight, contest, and argue the Gospel.' No, you are called to *'Preach the Gospel.' 'Proclaim the Good News!'*

Tell them God is not mad. Share that they could make heaven. Tell them whatever poisons their conscience has been appeased. The blood of Jesus has been shed to wash every heart. God accepts them. But they need to know it. They need to receive it.

> *But as many as received Him, to them He gave the right to become the children of God, to those who believe in His name.*
>
> John 1:12

Wonderful verse. Wonderful Gospel.

I Am Happy with My Religion

I was doing a *GCS* in a small town in the panhandle of Oklahoma. It didn't even have a hotel. (I was put up at a hotel in the city 20 minutes north).

Making one more call, I knocked on the door. My partner and I received a harsh response. A man in his mid-sixties retorted, *'I am Methodist. I have been a Methodist since I was 16 years old. I am happy with my religion, thank you!'*

What I instruct others, I had to do. *'If you do not know what to do,* **love** *them. If you do not know what to say, talk about* **Jesus***.'*

Loving this man and listening, the Lord gave me this response. *'Oh, my friend's grandmother is a practicing Methodist. She is in her 80s. She loves the Lord.'*

This response softened the man. It disarmed his hostility.

Wonderful When That Load Lifts Off

I continued: *'It is wonderful to house the orphans and feed the needy.* (Things I knew the Methodists were doing.) *But it is so wonderful when that load lifts off.'*

I paused as I spoke.

'It is so wonderful when that load lifts off. Understand that we are not doing things to be accepted by God, but we accept that God's Son died for us. Then, we become accepted by God. When we receive Him, everything changes.'

'Our efforts are no longer to be accepted. Our charitable deeds express our "Thank you to God for giving us Jesus."'

This precious Methodist man prayed to accept Jesus as His Lord and Savior. Glory!

#5 Other Keys to Winning the Lost

The more attuned you are to a person, the better you can communicate the Gospel to them. Two powerful things can locate a person: *their words* and *their eyes*.

Jesus said, *'For out of the abundance of the heart, his mouth speaks.'* (Luke 6:45) The Lord also told us, *'The lamp of the body is the eye.'* (Matthew 6:22). The exact phrase 'Eyes are Windows to the Soul' comes from Shakespeare, who often found inspiration from the Bible and biblical themes for his plays.[7]

These two things can help us determine where the person is. But we still have to listen to the Holy Spirit and discern. Let me give you an example.

Faith For Souls

Saved At the Dixy Dog

During the same *GCS* in Oklahoma I mentioned earlier, my friend Lee and I had another encounter. He and I led a waitress to Christ. We went to a burger place called the *Dixy Dog*. We were only in the business for 15 minutes.

Lee and I shared Jesus with this young 17-year-old waitress named Jody. At first, she did not respond. But her eyes told us she was hurt. As she left our table to place our order, Lee said he could see she also had low self-esteem. In our hearts, we perceived she aspired to be saved. She hungered for the love of God.

Jody came one more time to the table, asking if we needed ketchup. 'Yes,' We wanted her to return. We told her how much she was worth, the price of God's Son. Jody opened up. She prayed with us right there at the table.

However, words undiscerned can throw you off. Let me illustrate.

Debating or Sharing the Gospel

At the close of the Nigerian revival, where 1,800 came to Christ in the streets, the church's Senior Pastor sent one of his Associate Pastors to observe what I was doing. That day, we ended up in a small schoolhouse near the government housing. This was a one-room, dirt-floor building with wooden shutters (no windows). The teacher was an old guy in a 'wife beater' t-shirt. Several of his friends were also there, sitting around and smoking cigarettes.

Rather than observing me, the associate pastor engaged one man. I could hear them having a typical Muslim-Christian debate. After 15 minutes, he broke off, going to another. As I finished leading the schoolteacher to Christ, I went over to the man. That man prayed with me after a minute and a half to receive Christ.

Am I trying to brag? No, I am making a point. People can speak from their intellect, which does not reflect their hearts. Discern which: mind or spirit.

#6 The Dynamo of Sharing the Gospel

The more you share the Gospel, the more blessed you become. Why? Because the Gospel is God's testament of His love for us. We are reminded of how greatly Jesus loves us as we share Christ with others.

- The more we preach Christ, the more we know we are loved.
- The more you hear the Gospel, the more you appreciate your salvation.
- The more you appreciate salvation, the more you fall in love with Jesus.
- The more you fall in love with Jesus, the more life and power come through you.
- The more of Jesus's presence you experience, the greater your joy.
- The more life, power, and joy your preaching is compelling.
- The more compelling your preaching, the more people will come to Christ.
- The more you lead to Christ, the greater the soul winners' joy you will have.
- The more soul winners' joy you have, the more you will bring yet others to Jesus.

A dynamo is built, pouring life through your countenance, words, and presence. This is the vibrant life of God. You become, as Paul said of himself in Romans 1:15, 'So, **as much as is in me**, *I am ready to preach the gospel to you who are in Rome also.*'

We will examine this dynamo in the following chapter.

PostScript

This past year, I began an artist mentoring program called *Created to Thrive*[8] by Matt Tommy. This beautiful, all-encompassing Christian mentorship addresses all the artist's needs, from developing a style to marketing to the artist's mindset.

In one exercise, Matt challenges the artist to create a '3-second, a 30-second, and a 3-minute testimonial' of who you are as an artist, what makes you unique, and why clients should select your work. I had heard of this concept being used by top-selling sales trainers.[9] Doing the exercise was enlightening and encouraging.

This is an effective exercise for you to think about:

1) How to communicate why you are a Christ-follower.
2) Why others should want to hear the Gospel message of Jesus Christ.

It takes effort to reflect, write, evaluate, and critique, but is well worth it. Try it. Then, share your results with a supportive fellow believer and improve further. This tool is precious.

Reflective Questions

To illustrate, I will share my *homework assignment*. To begin, I had to answer the following reflective questions in my journal (you could adapt these into questions about how and why you became a Christian).

1. Who are you as a person and as an artist? (Or *Who are you as a person? And why are you a believer in Christ?*)
2. Why did you choose the materials you use in your artwork? (Or *Why did you become a Christ-follower?*)
3. How did you choose the techniques and mediums you use in your art? (Or *What is your story? How did you become a believer?*)

4. What inspires and motivates you to create art? (Or *Why are you so enthusiastic about Jesus?*)

5. What personalized message are you trying to communicate through your art? (Or *Why are you so passionate about others coming to Christ?*)

As I reflected and wrote my answers to these questions about my art, this became the basis for my three testimonials (3 seconds, 30 seconds, and 3 minutes) about why someone would want to select an art piece I have made.

3 Second, 30 Second, and 3 Minute

Here is my response to a person on an elevator if they were to ask, *'So, what do you do?'* Listed are my 3-second response, my 30-second response, and just a touch of the extended 3-minute response. Enough to help you share who you are, what you are about, and why someone should have this Jesus you love. Write down your thoughts on how you might respond in a *chance* meeting with a stranger. It will help you prepare how *to give an answer for your faith.*

3-Second Artist Statement:

'I create art that inspires your heart!'

30-Second Artist Statement:

'I create art full of light and beauty that makes your heart smile. My paintings capture moments that make you pause and exclaim, "Whoa!"'

Faith For Souls

3-Minute Artist Statement:

'I have known that I was gifted as an artist since childhood. During music appreciation in the 3rd grade, I would sketch portraits of those bearded composers. My teacher noticed my talent and said something to my mother. My mom then enrolled me in a Montessori summer class with high school students.' (here I am describing my past)

(Describe a concise version of your life before you knew Jesus.)

One of the masters' artworks I have been enthralled with all my life was Peter Paul Rubens's Elevation of the Cross[10] *[my Cover Art for the book]. He was a Baroque artist. This painting is the center of three large images in a triptych (3 pictures). Ten figures are in a swirling composition with strong darks and lights. The vibrant color is dramatic. But what captures me most is the face of Christ. As the rough burley soldiers lift the cross, Jesus looks up (into the heavens) as if He knows why he is there. I am struck to the core every time I see this artwork.*

(Explain why you were compelled to come to Christ [your testimony].)

[Note: As a California public high school art teacher, I used this painting on the first day of school, for each class period every year, to begin my course. This art allowed me to express to 175 students yearly that *'I was enthralled with the face of Christ on the cross—as if He knew why He was there.'* I was preaching the Gospel in a California public high school from day one. Do not be intimidated to be a Christian.]

Closing the Witness

I want to incorporate complex perspectives, dramatic light and color, and scenes that tell a story. I want to inspire and lift your heart.

(Here, you could share the Gospel)

I love my work and appreciate the opportunity to create with the brush. My aim is for the viewer to experience that same joy.

(Compel them, 'Would you receive the gift of eternal life?')

Spend some time reflecting and writing your answers to the above questions. It will help you see how much you love Jesus. It will help you develop a clear, powerful personal testimony that you can use to share your faith. Very effective exercise.

In me is working a power stronger than every other power. The life that is in me is a thousand times bigger than I am outside.[1]

—Smith Wigglesworth

So, as much as in me is, I am ready to preach the gospel to you that are at Rome also.

—Romans 1:15 KJV

CHAPTER 9

As Much As in Me Is

I Have a Lion on the Inside

The men in *The Finishing Strong* Life Group at church love to tease. One guy with a drug and alcohol background is greeted every time like he is in an Alcoholics Anonymous[2] meeting: *'Hello Hank'* is the chorus. The leader is our Associate Pastor, worship leader, and bodybuilder. He is told our reading group is a *Ladies'* Book Club. (I have been tempted to bring lace bookmarks for all the guys). I get teased for telling too many stories and talking too long. Life-changing encounters need to be told, especially when God shows off. But they can be challenging to do in a short amount of time.

Driving to the meeting, I prayed, *'Lord, help me watch I do not speak too much, but do not hold back what you give me.'* The evening went well. I shared what He led me to tell. Upon arriving home, my wife asked about the meeting, and I told her how it went. But then it burst out of my mouth, *'I cannot act like a mouse when I have a lion on the inside of me!'*

Ego. Boldness, especially in a Christian, can often be mistaken for ego. But was that the case with Jesus? Look at the proclamations Christ made of Himself.

He who has seen Me has seen the Father.

John 14:9

Even if I bear witness of Myself, My witness is true, for I know where I came from and where I am going.

John 8:14

Most assuredly, I say to you, the Son can do nothing of Himself, but what He sees the Father do; for whatever He does, the Son also does in like manner.

John 5:19

Most assuredly, I say to you, before Abraham was, I AM.

John 8:58

But you say, 'But that was Jesus.' Precisely.

That *was* Jesus. But why did He come?

Jesus' Purpose was to Sanctify Us

Look closely at Jesus' High Priestly prayer from the Gospel of John chapter 17.

Sanctify them *by Your truth. Your Word is truth.*

As You sent Me into the world, I also have sent them into the world.

> *And for their sakes I sanctify Myself, that they also may be sanctified by the truth.*
>
> *I do not pray for these alone,* **but also for those who will believe in Me through their word;**
>
> **that they all may be one**, *as You, Father, are in Me, and I in You; that they also may be one in Us, that the world may believe that You sent Me.*
>
> *And the glory which You gave Me I have given them,* **that they may be one just as We are** *one:*
>
> *I in them, and You in Me;* **that they may be made perfect in one**, *and that the world may know that You have sent Me, and have loved them as You have loved Me.*
>
> John 17:17-23 (emphasis mine)

Jesus sanctified us by His perfect sacrifice. The Greek word for *sanctify* is the same word for *holy*.³ His shed blood washed us and made our hearts completely new. *Nothing but the blood of Jesus*, says Robert Lowery's hymn (1876).⁴

Jesus' Purpose Was to Perfect Us

He made our hearts, our spirit man, brand new, *a new creature altogether!*

> *Therefore if any person is [ingrafted] in Christ (the Messiah) he is a new creation (a new creature altogether); the old [previous moral and spiritual condition] has passed away. Behold, the fresh and new has come!*
>
> 2 Corinthians 5:17 AMPC

The Born Again man has had God's nature restored in his heart. He is forgiven, but more. The nature of the child of God is *reborn*—made once again in the perfect image of God. The Holy Spirit has changed our spirit. He has made us *perfected into one.*

> *I in them, and Thou in me, that they may be perfected into one, and that the world may know that Thou didst send me, and didst love them as Thou didst love me.*
>
> John 17:23 YLT98

When a person comes into Christ, Christ comes into them—a divine change in the very nature of the person within. The Greek for *perfected* is *teteleiomenoi*.[5] The *Strong's Concordance* definition is *to bring to an end, to complete, perfect.*[6] What has been brought to an end? The *old fallen man*, the man of sin. Through the miracle of the new birth, we now assume the very nature of Christ in our hearts.

True, Jeremiah says *the heart is deceitful ... and desperately wicked* (Jeremiah 17:9).

The Deceitful Heart is Replaced

But this is before the new birth. Jeremiah later prophesied (Jeremiah 31:31-34, as quoted in the New Testament in the Book of Hebrews):

> *For this is the covenant that I will make with the house of Israel after those days, says the Lord: I will put My laws in their mind and write them on their hearts: I will be their God, and they shall be My people.*
>
> *None of them shall teach his neighbor, and none his brother, saying, 'Know the Lord,' for all shall know Me, from the least of them to the greatest of them.*
>
> Hebrews 8:10-11

Ezekiel also spoke of the new birth that God would do in the hearts of believers.

And I will give you a new heart, and I will put a new spirit in you. I will take out your stony, stubborn heart and give you a tender, responsive heart.

And I will put my Spirit in you so that you will follow my decrees and be careful to obey my regulations.

Ezekiel 36:26-27 NLT

We are talking about identification, or even more precisely, *identity*. The real question here is: *who are you?* Who am I? Who and what is a Christ-follower?

You're a Tomato

We all remember the creation account in Genesis 1:12, Which says *the seed is of itself.*

And the earth brought forth grass, the herb that yields seed according to its kind, and the tree that yields fruit, whose seed is in itself according to its kind. And God saw that it was good.

Genesis 1:12

So, *whose seed* are you? Ponder that. Yes, let's say it together:

Then God said, 'Let us make man in Our image, according to Our likeness: and let them have dominion over the fish of the sea, over the birds of the air, and over the cattle, over all the earth and over every creeping thing that creeps on the earth.'

> *So God created man in His own image; in the image of God He created him, male and female He created them.*
>
> Genesis 1:26-27

A Chip off the Old Block

We are a 'chip off the old block,' 'two peas of a pod.' We would be a tomato if our seed were from a tomato plant. Yet far too many believers in Christ sell themself short. And we preachers are partially to blame. Many watered-down versions of the Scriptures or outright untruths are prolifically proclaimed from our pulpits. To name a few, here are some of these *sacred cows*.

Sacred Cow # 1: 'I'm Not Perfect, But Forgiven.'

Yet we just read that Jesus prayed we would be *sanctified*. That word is *hagios* in Greek, the identical word (or a derivative of) the New Testament word for *holiness*. Jesus came to make a bunch of tomatoes—not cucumbers, avocados, or squash—you understand my poor analogy. *He came to duplicate Himself in us!*

The text in Hebrews concurs:

Jesus' Blood did it All!

> *Then He said, 'Behold, I (Jesus) have come to do Your will, O God,' He takes away the first that He may establish the second.*
>
> *By that will **we have been sanctified** through the **offering of the body of Jesus Christ** once for all.*
>
> *And every priest stands ministering daily and offering repeatedly the same sacrifices, which can never take away sins.*

> *But this Man*, *after He had offered* **one sacrifice for sins forever**, *sat down at the right hand of God,*
>
> *from that time waiting till His enemies are made His footstool.*
>
> Hebrews 10:9-13 (parenthesis and emphasis mine)

Jesus, by one sacrifice, forever has sanctified us. By His shed blood, and our faith in His blood, has washed our sins and replaced our sin-nature with His own.

Jesus Has Made Our Spirit or Heart Clean!

> *And by his one perfect sacrifice he made us* **perfectly holy and complete** *for all time!*
>
> Hebrews 10:14 TPT (emphasis mine)

The *Young's Literal Translation*, very accurate for the correct verb tense (though awkward to read), reveals how strong the Bible is here. Let's look at verses 10 and 14 again.

> *In the which will* **we are having been sanctified** *through the offering of the body of Jesus Christ once,*
>
> *For by one offering* **he hath perfected to the end those sanctified.**
>
> Hebrews 10:10,14 YLT (emphasis mine)

We having been sanctified; He has perfected to the end. Awkward—but awesome!

Sacred Cow # 2: 'When God Looks at Us, He Sees Jesus and Not Our Sin.'

What is the problem with this? The problem is that it drastically sells short what Christ came to do for all humanity! Jesus came to die for our sins. But unlike the Old Testament, sacrifices for sins by which sins were only covered before the eyes of God, as we already read in Hebrews above, Jesus's blood *takes away sin*, not just covers it! Our sin is not hidden from God; it has been eradicated. (This includes both our sin and our sinful nature.) Look at this profound passage of Scripture:

We are Nw Creations!

Therefore, if anyone is in Christ, he is a new creation; old things have passed away; behold, all things have become new.

Now all things are of God, who has reconciled us to Himself through Jesus Christ, and has given us the ministry of reconciliation,

that is, that God was in Christ reconciling the world to Himself, not imputing their trespasses to them, and has committed to us the word of reconciliation.

Now then, we are ambassadors for Christ, as though God were pleading through us: we implore you on Christ's behalf, be reconciled to God.

2 Corinthians 5:17-20

Remember, *a new creature altogether.* Something new, *Behold, the fresh and new has come!*

The One Who Knew No Sin Became Our Sin

For He made Him who knew no sin to be sin for us, that we might become the righteousness of God in Him.

2 Corinthians 5:21

God the Father made Jesus the Son *to be sin*. Sin that was not His own but our sin. He became our sin. So that something might happen—but what? That we would receive a new nature, and *we might become the righteousness of God in Him*.

The *Passion Translation* for this same passage is fantastic:

> Now, **if anyone is enfolded into Christ, he has become an entirely new person**. All that is related to **the old order has vanished**. Behold, **everything is fresh and new**.
>
> And God has made all things new, and reconciled us to himself, and given us the ministry of reconciling others to God.
>
> In other words, it was through the Anointed One that God was shepherding the world, not even keeping records of their transgressions, and he has entrusted to us the ministry of opening the door of reconciliation to God.
>
> We are ambassadors of the Anointed One who carry the message of Christ to the world, as though God were tenderly pleading with them directly through our lips. So we tenderly plead with you on Christ's behalf, 'Turn back to God and be reconciled to him.'
>
> For God made the only one who did not know sin **to become sin for us**, so that we might become **the righteousness of God through our union with him**.
>
> 2 Corinthians 5:17-21 TPT (emphasis mine)

We have been *enfolded into Christ*. The result is that we have *become an entirely new person*. Now *everything is fresh and new*. Because Jesus *became* our sin, we are no longer sinners. We are now *the righteousness of God through our union with him*.

Sacred Cow # 3: 'We All Know That Christians Sin Daily.'

Really? Jesus told more than one person to go and sin no more. He even warned, *'lest a worse thing comes on you.'* (John 5:14; 8:11) Was that a joke? Was that just an ideal or something to strive for?

Let the scripture address this lie—*'that we sin every day.'* What the Bible says is dramatically cross-cultural to what some Christians swallow as the norm today.

Christ Dealt with the Sin Problem

> *This is why he had to be a man and take hold of our humanity in every way. He made us his brothers and sisters and became our merciful and faithful King-Priest before God; as* **the One who removed our sins to make us one with him.**
>
> *He suffered and endured every test and temptation,* **so that he can help us every time we pass through the ordeals of life**.
>
> Hebrews 2:17-18 TPT (emphasis mine)

By holding to the doctrines of men (such as 'we are just sinners saved by grace'), we nullify the power of the written Word of God. When we were lost, sin was our nature, and it was our pattern. Now we are saved, righteousness is our nature, and holiness is the inherent pattern our heart directs.

Cling to the Truth by Faith

> *So then,* **we must cling in faith to all we know to be true**. *For we have a magnificent King-Priest, Jesus Christ, the Son of God, who rose into the heavenly realm for us, and sympathizes with us in our frailty.*

*He understands humanity, for **as a man, our magnificent King-Priest was tempted in every way as we are, and conquered sin**.*

Hebrews 4:14-15 TPT (emphasis mine)

Tell me, where does the Spirit of Christ dwell? Even a child who is a believer can answer correctly, *'In my heart.'* The One who beat sin, death, and the devil lives on the inside (1 John 4:4). Why do we want to proclaim defeat? Claim your new nature. *You have a **new** Lord.*

Focus on Jesus

*And **all who focus their hope on him** will **always be purifying themselves**, just **as Jesus is pure**.*

1 John 3:3 TPT (emphasis mine)

*God always makes his grace visible **in Christ, who includes us as partners of his endless triumph**. Through our yielded lives he spreads the fragrance of the knowledge of God everywhere we go.*

2 Corinthians 2:14 [TPT] (emphasis mine)

Christ in You!

The key is to *look*. We must perceive what Christ has finished for us, what He has done *in us*. Paul's burning revelation, *the mystery*, that was given to him to preach everywhere, was this:

The mystery *which has been hidden from ages and from generations, but now has been revealed to His saints.*

> *To them God willed to make known what the riches of the glory of **this mystery** among the Gentiles: **which is Christ in you**, the **hope of glory**.*
>
> Colossians 1:26-27

So, What Is *in You*?

In our initial text, Paul predicates his famous statement that *the Gospel is the power of God*, stating that he is ready to preach the Gospel. What makes him ready? Because of what was *in* him. *'As much as in me is.'* Paul knew *Who was in him*, and because of this, *he knew who he was*. That made him *ready to preach*!

You have to know *Who* is in you. Then you can see who you are.

Paul Had a Revelation

> *So, **as much as in me is, I am ready to preach the gospel** to you that are at Rome also.*
>
> ***For I am not ashamed** of **the gospel of Christ**: for it is **the power of God** unto salvation **to everyone** that believeth; to the Jew first, and also to the Greek.*
>
> *For therein is the righteousness of God revealed from faith to faith: as it is written, 'The just shall live by faith.'*
>
> Romans 1:15-17 KJV (emphasis mine)

Paul was not ashamed of the Gospel. But he was not ashamed of himself—whom Christ had made him to become. A brand-new creature that never existed before. Jesus saves us from ourselves![7]

Peter Had This Revelation, Too!

Peter had the same revelation. Remember the lame man carried out to the temple entrance at the gate called Beautiful? The man begged for coins as Peter and John approached. Peter looked the man in the eye, *'Look at us!'* The man expected to receive something. Then Peter proclaimed:

> *Then Peter said, 'Silver and gold have I none;* ***but such as I have give I thee****: In the name of Jesus Christ of Nazareth rise up and walk.'*
>
> *And he took him by the right hand, and lifted him up: and* ***immediately his feet and ankle bones received strength****.*
>
> ***And he leaping up stood****, and walked, and entered with them into the temple,* ***walking, and leaping, and praising God****.*
>
> Acts 3:6-8 KJV (emphasis mine)

What did Peter have? He had a revelation burning inside him: 'I cannot act as a mouse when I have a lion on the inside of me!' Peter had a *revelation* that *Christ was in him*! Do you?

This German Sister Has This Revelation.

Let me share this marvelous example about a German sister in Christ. This gal was a Bible school student at *Wort des Glaubens* (Word of Faith) church in Munich, Germany. I was there conducting a *GCS (Great Commission Seminar)* with the students. She was in her mid-fifties; I was in my thirties. Because I cannot remember her name, let us call her Joy.

For that outreach, Joy asked if I would witness to her employer. She worked at a beautiful hostel in Munich—a three-story marble, small, but luxurious hotel. Joy was not afraid. Just the opposite. Her *joy* and faith

Faith For Souls

in Jesus resulted in her being barred from working inside the hostel. She was assigned to work in the gardens. The owner could *'not take any more of her.'*

The plan was that another student and I would call upon the owner while Joy sat in her car nearby and prayed. I agreed.

Knocking on the heavy oak door, a little hatch or mini door opened. The small gray-headed owner peered through. I began.

I told her who I was and that I was there on behalf of Joy. The Holy Ghost gave me these words:

> *'I have just come to apologize. I apologize for Joy and myself because we are so full of joy and happiness at being saved and right with God. She (Joy) is sorry, but she cannot contain herself. And she wants you also to experience this same joy and wonderful peace.'*

The little hatch door shut. I thought it was over. That was all we were going to do. Then I heard a rustling, and the big, heavy oak door opened wide. The little gray-headed lady invited us in. She motioned for us to sit at one of the booths. This entire room was made of handcrafted oak—floor to ceiling. Gorgeous. We visited with her. I explained the teachings from the book of Romans, from Abraham's faith (chapter 4) up through receiving salvation (Romans 10).

Partway through, the owner left the table and then returned with two pieces of wonderful Bavarian chocolate cake and a couple of cokes. She stood next to the high wooden back of the booth as I ate cake and continued.

When I got to the part about *'if we confess with our mouth Jesus as Lord and believe in our heart God has risen from the dead, we shall be saved,'* she slapped the oak top of the booth and declared, *'That is what I believe!'* This was her declaration of faith.

Sister Joy wrote to me later that she was working inside the hostel again and that she and the owner shared the Word of God constantly.

What did Sister Joy have? She had what Paul and Peter possessed: *'as much as in me is,' I am ready to preach the Gospel* kind of faith. You can get it, too.

Declarative, Transformative, Causative

Some say that righteousness is only *declarative*—meaning that God has legally called and considers us righteous. He calls us and considers us righteous by the substitutionary work of Christ on the cross. Wonderful. But beyond declarative righteousness, Jesus Christ has *transformed* us from the inside out! He has made us become the righteousness of God in Christ. He has *caused* us to become a brand-new creature that never existed before—made into the righteousness of God. God has done this in our spirit man. *Our souls* (minds) *must still be renewed.*

> Therefore, **if anyone is in Christ, the new creation has come: The old has gone, the new is here!**
>
> *God made him who had no sin to be sin for us, so that in him we might become* **the righteousness of God**.
>
> 2 Corinthians 5:17,21 NIV (emphasis mine)

Purpose and Intent

I will not corroborate by scholarly argument or allude to the Greek verb tenses—honestly, they are out of my reach, though I do some reading and analysis of them. However, emphatically, I declare that Jesus Christ has completely *'changed us down through'* (AWT—ACCUWORD translation[8]) to become God's righteousness. This was God's original plan and intent.

Look at Creation

What do I mean? First, consider the creation account in Genesis. What was God's original plan for creating humanity (before we sinned)? Look at what our Creator stated as His purpose and intent:

> And **God said, Let us make man in our image, after our likeness**: and let them have dominion over the fish of the sea, and over the fowl of the air, and over the cattle, and over all the earth, and over every creeping thing that creepeth upon the earth.
>
> Genesis 1:26 KJV (emphasis mine)

Likeness and Image

Likeness. His image. Profound. God Almighty brought us into being, produced, conceived, designed, forged, generated, and brought us into existence . . . synonyms for the word *create*. He brought us into His life to be like Him as His offspring. God made us in His image—to be a family member.

Why Do We Want a Child of Our Own?

Why do couples want their own child? To become a member of their family. To become their child—of their making, an actual part of the mother and the father—of *their DNA*.

Why?

To love them, cherish them, and give them everything of themselves they can so their child can have the best life and be the best person they can be. All loving parents intend to do that. Jesus said:

If you, imperfect as you are, know how to lovingly take care of your children and give them what's best, how much more ready is your heavenly Father to give wonderful gifts to those who ask him?

Matthew 7:11 TPT

The Original Plan

Why is this significant? It is imperative to understand *why* God made us! His intent in making you and me (the human race) before we stepped out from a right relationship with our Creator was to make us like Him, like His very self. That means we were created to be holy, pure, beautiful, lovely, intelligent, creative, fabulous beings, *like God Himself*. Again, why is this significant? Because redemption in Christ was about restoration to God's Original Plan.

The Intent of God

This shows us why God the Father was pleased to bruise Him (Jesus). The *New International Version* is ghastly here:

> **Yet it was the Lord's will to crush him and cause him to suffer, and though the Lord makes his life an offering for sin,** he will see his offspring and prolong his days, and the will of the Lord will prosper in his hand.

Isaiah 53:10 NIV (emphasis mine)

The Father God's intent in crushing His Son was so that we could be fully restored to our holy, pure state before the fall of humanity. This occurs in our hearts (our spirit) when Born Again.

God Completely Restored Us

Why? So, God could fully and completely restore us to Himself, as holy, beautiful, and righteous as Himself, as we were (Adam and Eve) in the Garden with God before we all screwed it up! *Jesus came to fix us, not just patch us up!* I know I keep asking, 'Why?' We must seriously consider it! Salvation is about restoring every one of us to the beautiful state of being we were *conceived, designed, and forged, to be* in the first place, when man used to hang out with His Maker in the Garden in the cool of the day. (Genesis 3:8)

Explosive Revelation

Understanding who we are *only* comes from God. Who He says we are is **the** true and accurate view. His perception of us supersedes all others. God's acumen only comes through revelation disclosed by the Holy Spirit. He is the Teacher. Seek Him for this revelation.

> *But the Helper, the Holy Spirit, whom the Father will send in My name, He will teach you all things, and bring to your remembrance all things that I said to you.*
>
> John 14:26

The Holy Spirit Opens to Us the Mind of God

The Holy Spirit has come so He might open God's mind and intent to us. Regarding all things, but mainly:

- How we know and view God.
- How we view others.
- How we assess the situations of life.
- How we see ourselves.

Our view of ourselves is crucial because this becomes the lens by which we judge and discern everything else and everyone around us. We must see ourselves through God's eyes.

We Treat Others How We See Ourselves

I will never forget my pastor from thirty years ago, Pastor Billy Joe Daugherty, proclaiming in a sermon: *'People treat others ugly because they see themselves as ugly.'*[9] What we need most in life is to fix ourselves, not to fix the people and circumstances around us.

We need God's help to do this.

So how does that work? He does it by *explosive revelation*! What do I mean? Recall how Jesus made the following unique claim:

> *Then Jesus answered and said to them, 'Most assuredly, I say to you, the Son can do nothing of Himself, but what He sees the Father do; for whatever He does, the Son also does in like manner.'*
>
> John 5:19

As a man walking this earth, Jesus depended on His Father God. He assessed life, got direction, and decided on what he thought, said, and did based upon *one* thing—*what God showed Him!* Notice how Jesus said, *'The Son* (speaking of Himself) *can do nothing of Himself, but what He sees* the Father do.' We have no problem saying that Jesus *would do* nothing but what the Father had shown Him. But He stated He *could do* nothing.

We Must Do What He Shows Us

Our takeaway is that if we are going to do it right (all our thoughts, words, and deeds), there is only *one* way. *To be entirely dependent upon*

Faith For Souls

and obedient to God, and what He shows us. This occurs by *revelation*—the revealed plan and purpose for our lives in every detail. Oh, the mistakes I could have avoided had I had this perspective earlier.

> *Trust in the Lord completely, and do not rely on your own opinions. With all your heart rely on him to guide you, and he will lead you in every decision you make.*
>
> *Become intimate with him in whatever you do, and he will lead you wherever you go.*
>
> *Don't think for a moment that you know it all, for wisdom comes when you adore him with undivided devotion and avoid everything that's wrong.*
>
> *Then you will find the healing refreshment your body and spirit long for.*
>
> Proverbs 3:5-8 TPT

In Keeping, We See

> *Jesus answered and said to him: 'If anyone loves Me, he will* **keep My Word** *and My Father will love him and We will come to him and make an abode with Him. The one not loving Me does not keep My Words and the Word which you hear is not mine but of Him having sent Me (by) the Father.'*
>
> John 14:21 AWT (emphasis mine)

Keep to Obey

Some translations substitute *'obey'* for the word *'keep,'* but most texts translate this as *'keep.'* In Greek, the word is *teron*:

keep *(teron)* *from the word* <u>teros</u>, *meaning 'a watch' like a guard on duty.*

1. *to guard by keeping the eye upon.*
2. *to hold fast.*
3. *to keep.*
4. *to preserve.*
5. *to watch over.*

It carries the connotation of *'keeping a valued treasure.'*

That is what we are supposed to do with the Word of God: to treasure it. How is that different from *obeying*? After all, we are to obey the Word. The difference is stark and profound.

Guard the Word in Your Heart

Using the term *'obey'* points to our own effort. However, to *keep* the Word (guarded in our hearts as a treasure) positions us for a miracle. We hold God's Word as dear and precious—as a jewel. As we behold our most precious gem, God reveals its splendor.

This is a miracle of sudden understanding—revelation given to us by the Holy Spirit. Suddenly, we have the ability to do it. We see ourselves doing the Word. This originates from God. It is not our willpower (like Peter, 'Though all deny you, I will die with you, Lord'—and we know how that came out!). But this is 'such as I have' (revealed plan, will, and worth revealed from God). *Stark difference!*

Suddenly We Can See

God set up a natural progression: *the seed is in itself.* Everything produces after its kind. That includes the Word of God made flesh: Jesus.

Suddenly, we see what was once unseen as His Word comes alive in us. Something we lacked before, we now possess *the ability to do*. To do what God says we are supposed to do, not through our willpower, but because of the breath of the Holy Spirit upon the Word of God, treasured and allowed to germinate *in our hearts*.

Outward Evidence

Then, it becomes outwardly evident in our lives by our actions. This is miraculous, and it is God's method of producing after His kind: *the righteousness of God through Jesus Christ in and through our lives.*

This is *the secret* to a transformed life. A loving Father has given a heavenly gift to us.

So how do you get this? How do you get this revelation to burn within you? Let's look at simple yet essential, practical steps.

Practical Application

Step 1: *Find scriptures that show where your identity comes from according to God.* You are in Christ, and He is in you. Find several (if you like, you may choose from any listed in this chapter to begin).

Step 2: *Meditate upon the scriptures you have chosen.*

Meditate – *to murmur, ponder, imagine, meditate, mourn, mutter, roar, speak, study, talk, utter.*

As you do this, look up other verses that come to mind, investigate the meaning of an unclear word, contemplate the scripture verse by saying it aloud, and then repeat the process. So often, the Lord gives me guidance, solutions, and creative ideas when I first wake. My mind is still, but my heart has been communing with God through the night (Psalm 4:4; 1 Corinthians 2:11-12).

Why is this important? Because your heart is a furnace to produce the things that God has revealed to you, *you must cook the Word in your heart* for the savory juices of understanding (and ensuing practical application) to be produced in your life. As we meditate on the Word, the Holy Spirit reveals.

> **But God has revealed them** *(the things which God has prepared for His people) to* **us through His Spirit**. *For the Spirit searches all things, yes, the deep things of God.*
>
> *For what man knows the things of a man except for the spirit of the man which is in him? Even so no one knows the things of God except the Spirit of God.*
>
> **Now we have received**, *not the spirit of the world, but* **the Spirit who is from God, that we might know the things that have been freely given to us by God**.
>
>   1 Corinthians 2:10-12 (emphasis and parentheses mine)

Step 3: *Stop listening.* Block the voices of those jackals telling you that you cannot live powerfully in Christ. Stop listening to the sacred cows constantly mooing about your defeat, saying you are less than. No! **You are an overcomer** in Christ!

Step 4: *As you see, do.* What do I mean by this? The Lord told Joshua that as he held the Word of God dear and meditated upon it, *he would see differently.* He would see himself as able to do what God told him he could do.

> *This Book of the Law shall not depart from your mouth* (keep it on your tongue), *but you shall* **meditate in it day and night, that you may observe to do according to all** *that is written in*

it. ***For then you will make your way prosperous, and then you will have good success.***

Joshua 1:8 (emphasis and parentheses mine)

Know that we cannot do the Christian life in our own strength. Notice I said *we*. *We can only be and do the God-in-Sandals life by the Holy Spirit, as He opens God's Word and transforms us from the inside out.* It is of God. And it is supernatural. *Expect miraculous help* to be like Christ; that is *His* plan.

[**NOTE:** Those *enfolded into Christ* have become an entirely new person and are unique in their spirit. But the soul (the mind, will, and emotions) has yet to be and must be renewed by the Word of God. In the next chapter, Chapter 10 *Spirit & Soul: the Renewing of the Mind*, I will discuss the difference between 'soul and spirit' (Hebrews 4:12) and the renewing of the mind. God has done His part. It is time for us to do ours.]

Conclusion

I address *identity* in a soul winning book because *we are to be witnesses* rather than just going out to witness. To win souls to Christ, we must know who we are, *Whose* we are, and *Who* is in us. Also, this is central to living a successful life as a follower of Christ.

A Precious Example

I experienced this precious event on one of my trips to India. May it inspire you!

We had a 3:30 a.m. departure by a van leaving our hotel in the village. We had to catch our domestic flight in the city to get to our international connection home. Our Indian contact pushed the young driver hard to the point of recklessness, passing trucks in the dark on blind curves to make our flight time. Being late for the domestic flight check-in meant missing the flight to the US. We arrived on time but discovered the ticket agent had already re-sold our seats. Because we were Americans, they agreed to put us on the evening flight to the coast without charging us again, which still allowed us to make our international flight. The airport was in the South-Central Indian city of Madurai. Having been there the previous year and knowing of a hotel, we booked a room to relax for the day.

You, the Godman!

At lunchtime, we went down to the hotel's restaurant. As our server approached, I recognized him. My associate pastor and I led this man to Christ the previous year. We had led two waiters to Christ: one named Philip, who had a Lutheran upbringing, and this young man named Jayaraj, who had been a Hindu. I greeted Jayaraj and asked, *'Do you remember me?'*

His reply stunned me. With exuberance, he said, *'Oh yes! You, the Godman that met me Jesus!'*

My heart was struck. Then I reasoned, *'Well, I am a man, and I am of God, so yes, I'm a Godman!'*

After all these years, that greeting still warms my heart! Jayaraj had already begun attending Bible college and was starting a Christian school for children! Amazing! His introduction to Christ the year before was the catalyst.

You are a Godman or a Godwoman!

Know this: you are a *'Godman'* or a *'Godwoman.'* Know *who* you are and *Whose* you are!

The man who says he can, and the man who says he can't, are both right.[1]

—Charles Capps

So, get rid of all uncleanness and the rampant outgrowth of wickedness, and in a humble (gentle, modest) spirit receive and welcome the Word which implanted and rooted [in your hearts] contains the power to save your souls.

—James 1:21 [AMPC]

CHAPTER 10

Spirit & Soul: Renewing the Mind

You Are a Spirit

*Y*ou have been wonderfully Born Again. A new creation—you are a new creature, made by God Almighty. But this new birth is in *your spirit man*—your heart, not your head or mind. Human beings are 3-part beings. Each of us has a body. We have a mind (though today, using that mind may be rare!) But we are more; we have a spirit. Or *we are a spirit*. An accurate description of a person: *you are a spirit, you have a soul (mind, will, emotions), and you live in a body.*

> Now may the God of peace Himself sanctify you completely; and may your whole **spirit, soul,** and **body** be preserved blameless at the coming of our Lord Jesus Christ.
>
> 1 Thessalonians 5:23 (emphasis mine)

Change Your Stinkin' Thinkin'

What becomes complicated and often confusing for many Christ-followers is this: if I am indeed a Christian, why do I still think ungodly things? The answer is simple, but the application takes real diligence. We must renew our minds. My father, teaching the Junior High School kids at church, used to say: *'You have to re-program your bio-computer. You must change your stinkin' thinkin."*

> *And do not be conformed to this world, but be **transformed by the renewing of your mind**, that you may prove what is the good and acceptable and perfect will of God.*
>
> Romans 12:2 (emphasis mine)

Acting Like Fools

We have all undoubtedly seen Christians act like fools. I won't ask you if you have (so I do not have to tell on myself!). We have witnessed these people say they love God, say Jesus is their Savior and Lord, and yet *act ugly*. This should not be so.

But why? Why do Christ-followers not act like Christ?

The answer is simple: *we must change the way we think.*

A famous poet accurately nailed this idea.

> Sow a thought, reap a choice.
> Sow a choice, reap an action.
> Sow an action, reap a habit.
> Sow a habit, reap a character.
> Sow a character, reap a destiny.[2]
>
> *Ralph Waldo Emerson*

It Begins with Your Thought-Life

It all begins with thoughts or *your thought life*. Your thought life is *a pattern of thoughts* we constantly give place to or dwell upon. Successful athletes see themselves running a play, making a shot, or outmaneuvering an opponent. They practice, yes, but even more than practice, they *dwell on* the move or action.

They see themselves doing it right!

What We Image, We Do

I played water polo in high school. In my senior year, we were national champions. Most of the team comprised average guys who worked hard and were coached well.

Except for two guys, Mike and David.

They were the top players on the West Coast. Mike probably was the top high school water player in the nation. These guys were muscular, powerful, and effective. But far more, they did something the rest of us did not do. They obsessed over the game. David even had a regulation water polo goal in his backyard pool. They ate, breathed, and thought about the game constantly. Their *imagination of themselves* playing the game was just as important as the game itself. Together, they were an art form.

Marble-Playing Devil

I vividly remember a men's breakfast where the senior pastor of the large church where I served as his associate was ministering. The topic was Christian growth and maturity. The pastor asked the entire group of 300 men,

'How many of you played marbles as a boy?' he asked.

Almost every hand went up.

Then he posed a follow-up question: *'How many of you play marbles now?'*

No hands went up (except for a few guys who had younger sons).

The pastor continued: *'Why? Did you have a marble-playing devil cast out of you? No, something happened to you: you grew up!'*

He then quoted this verse:

When I was a child, I spoke as a child, I understood as a child, I thought as a child; but when I became a man, I put away childish things.

1 Corinthians 13:11 (emphasis mine)

How Do We Grow Up Spiritually?

How do we grow up spiritually? We let the Word of God change how we see the world. In cooperation with God, we transform the way we think. We receive the instruction of the Bible.

Every Scripture is God-breathed (given by His inspiration) and profitable for instruction, for reproof and conviction of sin, for correction of error and discipline in obedience, [and] for training in righteousness (in holy living, in conformity to God's will in thought, purpose, and action),

So that the man of God may be complete and proficient, well fitted and thoroughly equipped for every good work.

2 Timothy 3:16-17 AMPC

The New Birth is instantaneous. The nature of our hearts has changed, but our mental actions dictate whether we embody a spiritual or worldly Christian lifestyle. The interjection of the Word of God will meticulously divide, like a surgeon's knife, between God-led and self-fed.

> *For we have the living Word of God, which is full of energy, like a two-mouthed sword. It will even penetrate to the very core of our being where soul and spirit, bone and marrow meet! It interprets and reveals the true thoughts and secret motives of the heart.*
>
> Hebrews 4:12 TPT

Thirst for the Word to Grow

When my second son was six months old, I often helped with early morning feedings. Caleb would bawl. He would be so hungry. I would pick him up from his crib, change him, then carry him downstairs. With him in one arm, I would get a bottle out of the fridge, put it in the microwave for a few moments, test it on my arm, and then carry both baby and bottle to a chair in the living room. As soon as I got positioned, I would give Caleb his bottle. Boy, did he take the bottle! It was like he inhaled it! Sometimes, I would have to get him a second one.

While feeding him, I would put my Bible in my lap and have *quiet time*. One day, I happened to be reading from 1 Peter:

> *Therefore, laying aside all malice, all deceit, hypocrisy, envy, and all evil speaking,*
>
> **as newborn babes**, *desire* **the pure milk of the word, that you may grow thereby**,

Faith For Souls

if indeed you have tasted that the Lord is gracious.

1 Peter 2:1-3 (emphasis mine)

As I read, I looked at Caleb. I looked at the text again. I looked at my son. Then back again at the verses.

Suddenly, *I got it!*

To grow up, or you could say *to grow out of childishness, immaturity, and foolish acting,* **we need to feed upon the Word of God** to alter our thoughts. The Bible will change our *thought-life.* Caleb is now a man, 6'4" tall, wrestles Jiu Jitsu, and has shoulders like volleyballs.

He has grown!

Don't Be a Meathead!

The key to growing out of carnality (a Bible term meaning we are acting like *meatheads*—immature, selfish, and *'acting the fool'*) is that we must *make a diet of the Word of God!* We must renew our minds.

I have heard and used this preacher's story more than once to help folks understand how to grow up, become mature, and stop *acting the fool*:

> Two of the best boxers would engage in a heavyweight championship bout. They were the same weight and size. Both were champions with many victories, beating many tough fighters.
>
> One guy was taken to a premium training camp. He was given the best high-protein meals, plenty of rest, muscle massage, physical therapy, and training.
>
> His opponent was locked up in a cold cell with just bread and water.

They were brought to the ring for the Championship Fight a month later.

Who do you think won the match?

Without hesitation, everyone asked that question always chose the first fighter.

Why?

The guy who was starved did not stand a chance.

Feed Your Faith; Starve Your Doubts

A great man of God once put it this way:

Feed your faith and starve your doubts to death.[4] Lester Sumrall

I was highly privileged to sit under an extraordinary man of God at Bible College, Kenneth E. Hagin. I often heard him say: *'I have made it a practice to feed on the subjects of faith and healing.'*[5] Hagin was raised off his deathbed by faith in God's promises as a teenager. He was not supposed to see adulthood. He passed away at the ripe old age of 86.

What do you want in life? The answer lies in what you are feeding upon.

I Make a Diet of Faith, Compassion, and Soul Winning

I make a diet of *faith, compassion,* and *soul winning*. I listen, read, study, and meditate upon the Word of God. I also read books, listen to messages, watch preaching, and attend meetings of other preachers reaching the lost. *'Evangelism is more caught than taught.'* Robert E Coleman, in The Master Plan of Evangelism,[6] writes:

Faith For Souls

They (the disciples) needed an experience of Christ so real that their lives would be filled with His presence. Evangelism had to become a burning compulsion within them purifying their desires and guiding their thoughts. Nothing less than a personal baptism of the Holy Spirit would suffice. The superhuman work to which they were called demanded supernatural help- an enduement of power from on high.

Before I boarded a plane to preach a *GCS (Great Commission Seminar)*, I would listen again to my own tapes and the messages of other evangelists and soul winners. In addition, I vigorously pursued opportunities to minister the Gospel in my daily life. I still do every day. (I asked three individuals today if they knew Jesus as their Lord and Savior and gave my own *The BULLET*[7] tract to several more.) To be an influential soul winner, we must get our minds renewed and keep them renewed.

On a funny note, I once asked Charles Capps who he was listening to (noticing the earpiece in his ear and the tape player in his pocket.). With a straight face, Charles answered me, *'My favorite preacher.'* And then, without skipping a beat, he added, *'Myself.'* He quipped with a cajole, *'You better be your own favorite preacher. You will hear yourself more than anyone else.'*

Important Application

I am addressing the subject of *Spirit & Soul: Renewing the Mind* here because:

1. We need it. To live victorious, we need to exchange our thoughts for His.

2. We must be Spirit-led if we hope to be effective witnesses for Jesus Christ, affecting those around us with the wonderful Gospel (God's great love & forgiveness).
3. Being Spirit-led begins with having our minds renewed to the Word of God.

The Spirit of God will bring the Word of God to our remembrance. Therefore, we need to sow God's Word into our minds so that He can bring it to our memory!

But the Helper, the Holy Spirit, whom the Father will send in My name, He will teach you all things, and bring to your remembrance all things that I said to you.

John 14:26

We need *to see* God's viewpoint on life. Our thinking needs to reflect His. This includes, foremost, how we see ourselves. It's hard to convince others to follow Christ if we think poorly of ourselves. If we see ourselves as *schmucks*, it's difficult to believe we can influence another.

Your Nature Became New

Unfortunately, many mis-teach or misrepresent the subject of *mind renewal*. What do I mean? Preachers teach about how bad your natural man is without Christ. True, we were sinners without Christ. I was a quiet teenager. Outwardly, I was a pretty nice guy. But inside was envy, jealousy, hatred, and the evil imaginations that come with them. I needed to be saved! When I received Jesus as my Lord, I became a new man. Now, I am no longer a sinner. My nature became different. I became a lover of God because He had first loved me (1 John 4:19).

Faith For Souls

The characteristic nature of my heart was now different. I became a new creature in Christ.

Recognize Your Identity in Christ.

Mind renewal awakens you to your identity in Christ. **The old self is not the target of mind renewal.** My old man died. This is also true for you if you're Born Again.

> *Or do you not know that as many of us as were baptized into Christ Jesus were baptized into His death?*
>
> *Therefore we were buried with Him through baptism into death, that just as Christ was raised from the dead by the glory of the Father, even so we also should **walk in newness of life**.*
>
> *For if we have been united together in the likeness of His death, certainly we also shall be in the likeness of His resurrection,*
>
> *knowing this, that **our old man was crucified with Him**, that the body of sin might be done away with, that we should no longer be slaves of sin.*
>
> *For **he who has died has been freed from sin**.*
>
> *Now if we died with Christ, we believe that we shall also live with Him,*
>
> *knowing that Christ, having been raised from the dead, dies no more. **Death no longer has dominion over Him.***
>
> *For the death that He died, He died to sin once for all; but the life that He lives, He lives to God.*
>
> ***Likewise you also, reckon yourselves to be dead indeed to sin, but alive to God** in Christ Jesus our Lord.*
>
> Romans 6:3-11 (emphasis mine)

Spirit & Soul: Renewing the Mind

The scripture commands us to walk in *the newness of life.* Our *old man was crucified with Christ.* He is dead, just as Christ died on the cross. Dead men do not sin: *he who has died has been freed from sin.* Death and sin no longer have dominion over us. So what is the key? How do we enjoy this freedom to live as we should?

Notice verse 11 states, *Likewise, you also, reckon yourselves to be dead indeed to sin, but alive to God in Christ Jesus our Lord.* The English Standard Version says it this way:

So you also must consider yourselves dead to sin and alive to God in Christ Jesus. ESV

Who must consider yourself dead to sin and alive to God? You. We must agree with God.

Once, in a college-age Sunday School class, the instructor, while teaching about hearing God's Voice, made a statement that has always struck me.

If God says, 'We hear His voice' (John 10:3-4;27), and we say we do not. Somebody is mistaken. Who is lying because it is not God?'

We must realize that anything and everything we think and believe *contrary* to what God says in His Holy Word about us *is a lie.*

Let me illustrate this truth another way.

To quote Charles Capps, *'I'm going to say this so many ways you get it!'*[8]

You're Dead

My oldest son, Zac, was quite a character to raise. Kids go through funny phases. At about 11 years of age, Zac had this saying he liked to repeat, and he would sometimes say it to me. He'd say: *'You're dead!'* (Most likely quoting from some bully in a movie he had seen). I did not particularly like him saying this. Around that time, in my Bible reading, I came across Colossians 3:3, which states:

> *For you are dead, and your life is hidden with Christ in God.*
>
> Colossians 3:3 KJV

I decided that the next time Zac made that tough-guy face and said to me, *'You're dead,'* I would reply: *'You're right! I am dead, and my life is hidden with Christ in God!'*

The plan worked like a charm! Once I answered him this way, his face dropped, and he got quiet. I do not believe he ever used that line on me again (maybe stopped it altogether).

Dead Men Commit No Crimes

Have you ever thought about it? Dead men commit no crimes! What are you? What am I? We are walking dead men. My union with Jesus' death on the Cross is complete, 100 percent. So is yours. His work on the cross is finished. In Him, I died. Believer, so did you. On the cross, He took it all.

This *'realm of death'* describes our former state, for we were held in sin's grasp. We are forever alive and forgiven of all our sins, having been resurrected from the realm of death!

> *He canceled out every legal violation we had on our record and the old arrest warrant that stood to indict us.* ***He erased it all—our sins, our stained soul—he deleted it all and they cannot be retrieved!*** *Everything we once were in Adam has been placed onto his cross and nailed permanently there as a public display of cancellation.*
>
> Colossians 2:14 TPT (emphasis mine)

Spirit & Soul: Renewing the Mind

What God Thinks Is Everything

To renew the mind is to align our thinking with God's perspective of us. This is a transformation of how we see the world. Now, we view everything through God's lens of what He says and thinks about us. We are His kids. The precious blood of His Son, Jesus Christ, has redeemed us from our sins. We're washed inside out. Learn it! Get ahold of it! Perceive this—*then ponder*. Think about yourself and your life. You are not a shmuck! Neither am I. We are brothers and sisters of the Lord Jesus. And He likes us! (As a public school teacher, I found that persuading students that 'my teacher likes me' is an excellent tool to impact classroom behavior.) You are the Creator's beautiful masterpiece.

> *This is why he had to be a man and take hold of our humanity in every way. He made us his brothers and sisters and became our merciful and faithful King-Priest before God; as the One who removed our sins to make us one with him.*
>
> Hebrews 2:17 TPT

Alla Prima Bootcamp

I am developing my particular oil painting style by participating in an intensive art mentoring program called *Alla Prima Bootcamp*.[9] Part of this process is observing artworks I admire and then executing practice paintings of those Master Studies. I love the work of Joaquin Sorolla, John Singer Sargent, Michelangelo, Peter Paul Rubens, and more. So, I am doing small, one-to-two-hour studies of a part of one of their paintings. I then do an original (with a similar subject, lighting, and composition), attempting to do it in the same style as the master's painting. Working in this manner, you see things you did not know existed. The way these artists approached their paintings makes sense to me. My thinking is beginning to align with theirs (at least partially).

Let me tell you about a unique experience I had in art school long ago.

When I Sketched My Mom, I Saw My Mom

I was sitting on the couch next to my mom, doing a sketch. She had her glasses on the tip of her nose and looked down at the sewing handwork she was doing. My drawing was of her. I captured her in a non-complementary pose, double chin and all. The sketch was not well-received by my mom. But at that moment, I remembered forever what my mother looked like. How many times have we seen our own mom? The careful observation allowed me to see my mother's features and likeness in a new light.

Only God's View Is Accurate

Renewing our minds to the Word of God is similar to this. We know our Father God, and we know ourselves. *Yet, many times, we do not perceive God's intent.* Nor do we see ourselves accurately, not seeing ourselves as God does. **Only God's view of us is accurate.** Every other idea is short-sighted or untrue at worst. To be redundant—we are not an idiot (a synonym for shmuck!) We are the righteousness of God through Christ Jesus. We are *God's MASTERPIECES*!

The Correct God-View

A correct God-view is necessary to make a meaningful impact on the world. Those who see themselves as ugly treat others as ugly. When we can dare to *see ourselves as loved and cherished* by our loving Heavenly

Spirit & Soul: Renewing the Mind

Father, then and only then do we emanate *a beautiful aroma* that draws others to our Jesus.

> *Exhort servants to be obedient unto their own masters, and to please them well in all things; not answering again;*
>
> *not purloining* (stealing), *but shewing all good fidelity* (being honest); *that they* **adorn the doctrine of God** *our Savior in all things.*
>
> Titus 2:9-10 KJV (emphasis & parenthesis mine)

Our lives are to *adorn the doctrine of God*, like a garnish on the plate of a beautiful meal. Other translations convey this concept of how our lives affect the appeal of the Gospel:

> **advertise** *through all they do the beautiful teachings* [The Passion Translation]
>
> *their good character will* **shine through** *their actions* [The Message]
>
> *in everything they may be* **an ornament** *and do credit* [Amplified Bible]
>
> *they will make the teaching about God ...* **attractive** [New International Version]
>
> *the teaching of God ... they may* **embellish** *with honor* [Wuest]

Renew your mind to who God says you are. See whom God reveals Himself to be. Align your thoughts to how God views those around you. Learn to perceive others as God sees them—*with deep, compassionate love*. Then you will win them because others will *want what you have*.

Perceive How God Sees You

I want to close the chapter with the passage I began, laying it out in context. Usually, I would start a message with the surrounding text. Here, I recommend leaving you with that context. *Think about it. Meditate upon it.* Let it sink in; let *it help* **renew your mind.**

> So my friends, **don't be fooled** by your own desires!
>
> **Every gift God freely gives us is good** and perfect, streaming down from the Father of lights, who shines from the heavens with no hidden shadow or darkness and is never subject to change.
>
> **God was delighted to give us birth by the truth of his infallible Word** so that we would fulfill his chosen destiny for us and become the favorite ones out of all his creation!
>
> My dearest brothers and sisters, take this to heart: Be quick to listen, but slow to speak. And be slow to become angry,
>
> for human anger is never a legitimate tool to promote God's righteous purpose,
>
> So this is why we abandon everything morally impure and all forms of wicked conduct. **Instead, with a sensitive spirit we absorb God's Word, which has been implanted within our nature,** for the **Word of Life has power** to continually deliver us.
>
> Don't just listen to the Word of Truth and not respond to it, for that is the essence of self-deception. So always **let his Word become like poetry** written and **fulfilled by your life**!
>
> If you **listen to the Word** and don't live out the message you hear, you become like the person who looks in the mirror of the Word to discover the reflection of his face in the beginning.
>
> You **perceive how God sees you in the mirror of the Word**, but then you go out and forget your divine origin.

*But **those who set their gaze deeply** into the **perfecting law of liberty** are fascinated by **and respond to the truth** they hear **and are strengthened by it—they experience God's blessing in all that they do!***

James 1:16-25 [TPT] (Emphasis mine)

If you ever see Jesus, you will never be the same again. He will show Himself to you in a way that you will know that He is alive and that He loves you.[1]

—**T.L. Osborn**

For by grace, you have been saved through faith, and that not of yourselves; it is the gift of God.

—**Ephesians 2:8**

CHAPTER 11

What Gospel Do You Have?

*W*hy would we even need to ask such a question? After all, the Gospel is so simple:

> Moreover, brethren, I declare to you **the gospel** which I preached to you, which also you received and **in which you stand,**
>
> **by which also you are saved**, if you hold fast that word which I preached to you—unless you believed in vain.
>
> For I delivered to you first of all that which I also received: **that Christ died for our sins according to the Scriptures**,
>
> and **that He was buried**, and **that He rose again the third day** according to the Scriptures.
>
> 1 Corinthians 15:1-4 (emphasis mine)

Christ's death, burial, and resurrection is the Gospel. We agree. But notice Paul said, 'Which also you received and in which you stand.' So, my question could be, yes, you were saved by trusting in Christ, but what are you trusting in today? Christ, and Christ alone? Or in ourselves, 'trying to follow Christ?' Can you do that? Is it even possible?

You Cannot Save Yourself, Nor Can You Live the Life

As a pastor, I have declared to my congregations often:

Saving ourselves is impossible. Only our faith in Christ can save us. Neither can we live the Christian life. Only by faith in Christ alone can we live for Christ.

Is this a big deal? The Apostle Paul considered it a huge deal!

Cursed for Preaching the Wrong Gospel

*I marvel that ye are so soon removed from him that called you into the grace of Christ unto **another gospel**:*

*which is not another; but there be some that trouble you, and would **pervert the gospel** of Christ.*

*But though we, or an angel from heaven, **preach any other gospel** unto you than that which we have preached unto you, **let him be accursed**.*

*As we said before, so say I now again, If any man **preach any other gospel** unto you than that ye have received, **let him be accursed**.*

Galatians 1:6-9 KJV (emphasis mine)

Cursed. Yeah, that is a pretty big deal.

What is Paul talking about?

He is talking about switching from grace to be saved and then to works to keep you saved. You cannot do it.

Let me expound upon the Gospel and lay it out. But first, let me share this testimony to give a visual image of *the grace of the Gospel* of Jesus Christ.

Washed Away

Years ago, a man in my church who had been an international banker shared this testimony. An English pastor he knew told him this story: A man in the English pastor's congregation had come to Christ after living a dark life. This brother wished to be baptized in water. But he was ashamed to be water baptized because his body was covered in tattoos, notably, the large letters across his chest that spelled S A T A N. He could not do it.

The pastor encouraged him as this man grew in his walk with Christ. The man came to believe that he was a new creature in Christ. He was no longer worried about his past life or his tattoos.

The Man Came to be Baptized

Eventually, the man came to be baptized. The believers gathered to rejoice that their brother openly declared his faith in Jesus, the risen Son of God. The pastor declared,

> *'I baptize you in the Name of the Father, the Son, and the Holy Ghost. You are a New Creature in Christ.'*

He dipped him under the water. Up he came, glorifying God.

But something was missing. All the tattoos were just as they were, but for one. The name of the devil was *miraculously washed away* from his flesh.

So, too, are you miraculously *washed by the blood of Jesus Christ*. By the blood alone.

That alone is the Gospel.

The Gospel of the Lord Jesus Christ

For God so loved the world that He gave His only begotten Son, that whoever believes in Him should not perish but have everlasting life.

For God did not send His Son into the world to condemn the world, but that the world through Him might be saved.

John 3:16-17

Precisely: God, in His love, slew His Son, Jesus, that we might spend eternity with Him.

To expound: God had a Master Plan.

God Had a Master Plan

God created His man and woman to know Him. We see this in Genesis, where God joined his man (humanity) in the garden *in the cool of the day* (Genesis 3: 8).

The Creator had given the reign of the entire planet into His man's hands.

Then God said, 'Let Us make man in Our image, according to Our likeness; let them have dominion over the fish of the sea, over the birds of the air, and over the cattle, over all the earth and over every creeping thing that creeps on the earth.'

Genesis 1: 26

He even gave us authority over creeps!

Now, this delegation is very significant. Why? People complain, 'How could a loving God . . .' as they name a terrible atrocity. God put humanity in charge of this entire world system. He is not screwing it up—we are. To sovereignly take away the reins, God would be a thief and a liar. That's the devil, not God.

The Earth Is Leased to Mankind

God made a contract with His creation. The earth is the Lord's, but He entrusted humanity to manage it. Planet Earth has been *leased* to humanity.

The earth is the Lord's, and everything in it. The world and all its people belong to him.

Psalm 24:1 NLT

God is the 'land owner;' we are the 'tenant.' In so doing, humankind has certain rights and responsibilities over the earth. Therefore, God has no right to enter as a property owner by force.

> *Tenants are entitled to exclusive possession of the premises they rent, even to the exclusion of the landlord. Owners, landlords, property managers, or the landlord's agents cannot simply enter a tenant's unit anytime they please and for any reason.*[2]

God needs our permission to operate on the earth. This concept is difficult for many people to comprehend, and it seems radical to most.

Shared Jurisdiction

Consequently, prayer takes on a vital role of shared jurisdiction rather than begging petition, which is often misunderstood. Correctly comprehending the believer's position in prayer empowers the Christian to take proper dominion over his affairs and to influence the lives of others. Biblical prayer is a partnership with the Almighty.

It is interesting to note that the account of Abraham being asked to sacrifice his son Isaac in Genesis 22 is not some bizarre anomaly of scripture.

God has carried out His covenant (contract). In Genesis 15:1-6, we see God entering an agreement, *a covenant*, with a man, Abram (later to be called Abraham). Why?

A Man Had to Give God Legal Access to Work on the Earth

This covenant with a man with *complete* legal dominion on the earth gave God legal access to work on the planet. God had given humanity power all over the world. For God to intervene and violate man's jurisdiction, no matter how much He wanted to help humanity, would make God a liar and a thief. God is not the thief—Satan is.

In the Genesis 22 account, God requires His covenant partner, Abraham, to work his end of the life-death contract (covenant) so that later, God could have a legal right to sacrifice His Son, Jesus Christ, on the earth. Some Christian scholars miss the significance and absolute necessity of Abraham's offering of Isaac.

The Gospel Removes Sin-Consciousness

Most know that scripture teaches 'that man has sinned and fallen short of the glory of God' (Romans 3: 23). The church has propounded this truth. Unfortunately, it often leaves men in a sin consciousness without sharing the Gospel's Good News—that we are new creatures in Christ and forever forgiven by the shed blood of Christ.

Sin means *to miss the mark*. A Holy God created humankind to fellowship with Him. To do so, we must be holy. It takes only simple observation to see that we are not. Therefore, humanity has a problem.

Only One Solution

To fellowship (walk intimately) with a Holy God is impossible— except for *One Solution*. God Himself solved this problem. He solved this problem, *our problem*, in the person of His Son, Jesus Christ. The scripture tells us:

> *For He* (God the Father) *made Him* (the Son Jesus) *who knew no sin* (did not sin His own) *to be sin for us, that we might be made the righteousness of God in Him.*
>
> 2 Corinthians 5:21 (parentheses mine)

Reconciliation by Judication

God wholly restored *all men* to Himself by judication.

> *For God was in Christ, reconciling the world to himself, no longer counting people's sins against them. And he gave us this wonderful message of reconciliation.*
>
> 2 Corinthians 5:19 NLT

People often believe He did it *by* mercy. He did not. He *judicated* His mercy.

Reconciliation is *the act of coming to an understanding and ending hostility, as when former enemies agree to an amicable truce: acceptance.*[3] In Greek, the word is *katallasso*.[4] This is a compound word, *kata*, 'down to the exact point,' and *allasso*, 'to change.' The definition from the Greek is 'Properly, decisively change, as when two parties reconcile, when coming together (changing) to the same position.'

How can we come into 'the same position' with God? God does not change.

> *For I am the LORD, I change not; therefore ye sons of Jacob are not consumed.*
>
> Malachi 3:6 KJV

The only way we can resume holy communion with God is by judication. Judication is *the power, right, or authority to interpret and apply the law; the authority of a sovereign power to govern or legislate; the power or the right to exercise authority: control.*[5]

God poured His full wrath on Jesus on the cross to pay for all our sins. He then exercised His judication (full authority) to pronounce us reconciled.

Incredible!

The Son of God Became Flesh to Receive the Wrath of God

On the cross, Jesus, the Son of God, relinquished His Deity, becoming fully human.

> *You must have the same attitude that Christ Jesus had.*
>
> *Though he was God, he did not think of equality with God as something to cling to.*

> *Instead, he gave up his divine privileges; he took the humble position of a slave and was born as a human being. When he appeared in human form,*
>
> *He humbled himself in obedience to God and died a criminal's death on a cross.*
>
> Philippians 2:5-8 NLT

Jesus took and endured God's wrath (Isaiah 53:10; Hebrews 12:2). If all of God's wrath had not been poured upon Christ, we would still owe a debt. Christ finished it!

God Has Reconciled All of Humanity

You and I, and all humanity, are *reconciled* to God, whether or not we believe. However, to benefit from this reconciliation and all the incredible benefits of walking in harmony with God can only occur by *faith*.

Faith—the Currency of Heaven

Faith is the currency of heaven. Money, we all understand. Using the Mexican peso down at the corner gas station will not work.

What most people think is prayer also does not work with God. Why? Because it is not of faith or done in faith. Many petition, complain, argue, justify, and plead, but do not trust.

> *For indeed the gospel was preached to us as well as to them; but the word which they heard did not profit them, not being **mixed with faith** (trust) in those who heard it.*
>
> Hebrews 4:2 (emphasis & parenthesis mine)

To Come to God, We Must Trust

Some would say this is unfair—God is unkind and too hard. However, to come to God, we must trust Him.

> *But without faith (trust), it is impossible to please Him, for he who comes to God **must believe that He is**, and that **He is a rewarder** of those who diligently seek Him.*
>
> Hebrews 11:6 (emphasis & parenthesis mine).

Judication Satisfied the Court of Heaven

I must reemphasize that God was in Christ reconciling the world unto Himself, not by mercy. He did this by judication. The holy court of heaven has given a verdict. The **shed blood of Jesus** has already paid for the sins of every man, woman, and child of all races and for all time, making them righteous before God. His justice (Jesus taking all our sins) *allows* God to pour out His great mercy.

Only one thing remains—a decision.

Rejection of the Gospel Is Death

We can *reject* God. We can do this to the extreme—as an atheist, *I reject God's right to exist* (as I once did). Or, like many, we can do this more passively and claim *that is not how we believe* (one's own choice of religious system or practice) or say, *not now, maybe later*. It makes no difference.

All have sinned. All have fallen short. The wage of sin is death—not the cessation of physical life, but eternal separation from a loving God.

None can resolve his debt.

One Thing Required by God

All the goodness, kindness, and even self-sacrifice in the world cannot accomplish the one essential thing God requires for us to know Him now and throughout eternity. That *one thing* is that we must *be holy as God is holy* (Matthew 5:48; 1 Peter 1:16).

Only the Blood of Jesus shed on the cross can wash us white as snow. Therefore, Peter preached:

> *Nor is there salvation in any other, for there is **no other name under heaven** given among men **by which we must be saved**.*
>
> Acts 4:12 (emphasis mine)

God is not intolerant; He is just. Jesus Christ paid your debt; He paid mine.

We Must Have a Choice to Believe or Not

That is why the third chapter of John concludes with:

> *He who believes in the Son has everlasting life; and **he who does not believe the Son** shall not see life, but **the wrath of God abides** on him.*
>
> John 3:36 (emphasis mine)

For a loving God to have a loving relationship with each of us, He must give us a choice. Belief by coercion does not exist. In today's environment, people are protesting around the globe over mandates. Regardless of your or my view, compliance because of compulsion is tyranny.

God is not, nor ever will be, a tyrant. He gives all of us the privilege to believe and receive eternal life. He also provides us with the right not to accept and receive eternal separation and damnation—not because He is unjust, but because we rejected His Love.

What Will We Do with This Knowledge?

What will we do with the knowledge of His Love poured out through the sacrifice of His Son ... His only Son? One cannot even imagine what it would be like to give the life of a beloved child for someone else. I cannot.

This Is the Gospel

Salvation is by the grace of God. This is the Gospel.

Walking in harmony with Christ is also by the grace of God. This is the Gospel. We must hold on to and preach it.

God did not say to *'go into all the world and tell them to clean up their act.'* He commands us to *'Go into all the world and preach the Good News to everyone,'* (Mark 16:15, NLT).

> *And he said to them, 'As you go into all the world, preach openly the wonderful news of the gospel to the entire human race!'*
>
> Mark 16:15 TPT

The Progression Is Essential

These three verses in Ephesians Chapter 2 eloquently lay out the doctrine of salvation and living the Christian life. We must not change this progression of truth. Follow it as God gave it:

> *For **by grace**, you have been **saved through faith**, and that **not of yourselves**; it is **the gift of God, not of works**, lest anyone should boast.*
>
> Ephesians 2:8-9 (emphasis mine)

Salvation is by grace and grace alone. I like what the Lord told Brother Charles Capps before he got up to minister. The Spirit of God told him, *'Grace is my willingness to use My power and My ability on your behalf, even though you don't deserve it.'*[6] That is so true.

Saved by Grace, Now What?

The next verse in this sequence lays the foundation for how we will walk in life following Christ. Verse 10 of Ephesians 2 reads:

> *For we are His workmanship, created in Christ Jesus for good works, which God prepared beforehand that we should walk in them.*
>
> Ephesians 2:10

How can we do these *good works*? By being created in Christ Jesus. How were we created in Christ Jesus? Or you could ask, who made us in Christ Jesus? Did I—did you? No.

Look at *Young's Literal Translation* for these verses. The YLT is a very literal translation. Difficult to read, yet strictly follows verb tense and word order.

> *For by grace ye are having been saved, through faith, and this not of you—of God the gift,*
>
> *not of works, that no one may boast;*

> for **of Him we are workmanship, created in Christ Jesus to good works**, *which God did before prepare, that in them we may walk.*
>
> Ephesians 2:8-10 YLT

Salvation doesn't originate from you. It is *of God the gift. Not of* (our) *works.*

Of Him We Are Workmanship

But also notice who is forging this artistry. *For of Him, we are workmanship.* I love it—it sounds like a Russian tough guy in a movie telling you straight, *'Of Him we are workmanship!'* In plain English—He did it, not us. Even the works we are to produce are not by our effort, ability, determination, or human will. They are by *grace*! By His grace, the Gospel is at work *in* us. This is how we are to live the Christian life—by the grace of the Gospel of Christ.

This is The Gospel in which you stand, by which also you are saved, if you hold fast that word which I preached to you, (1 Corinthians 15:1-2). Hold it fast.

The Whole Christian Experience in One Verse

Let me do you one better. One verse in the second chapter of the Book of Galatians reveals our entire life in and through Christ.

> *I am crucified with Christ: nevertheless I live;* **yet not I, but Christ liveth in me:** *and the life which I now live in the flesh* **I live by the faith of the Son of God**, *who loved me, and gave himself for me.*
>
> Galatians 2:20 KJV (emphasis mine)

From start to finish, the entire Christian life is all because of Jesus Christ. Emulating our blessed Savior and revealing heaven to others hinges entirely on our dependence on Him in all parts of our lives. The preposition **of**, in the stanza, *I live by the faith **of** the Son of God*, reveals it all. *Of* as a preposition denotes 'belonging to somebody; relating to somebody.'

We Live by the Faith *of* the Son of God

Who could it be referring to? To Christ. We live *by the faith **of** the Son of God*.

We live by His faith. Our faith comes from His faith. Our love comes from His love. A godly life comes from His life. Remember, *we love Him because **He first loved us***. (1 John 4:19)

Follow me as we look at the Greek, which is even more awkward than *Young's Literal Translation*. Greek word order differs from the English. So, I will have to lay it out in phrases so that we can see it. (And no, I am not a Greek scholar nor a theologian. I am just passionate about the true Gospel of the Lord Jesus Christ.)

First, let me give you a sample of the word order in the Greek from *The Englishman's Greek New Testament: An Interlinear Translation*.[7]

Hands They Shall Lay, Well They Shall Be

The word order for Mark 16:18 in Greek is marvelous:

*Upon (the) infirm **hands they shall lay, well they shall be**.* (emphasis mine)

I love it! *Hands we lay* (our part), *well they shall be* (His part). We trust our Lord and do what He instructs. And then He will confirm His Word. Beautiful.

Let's look now at Galatians 2:20 from the Greek text.

Galatians 2:20 from the Greek

Here is Galatians 2:20, the English transposed from the Greek text:

> Christ, I have been crucified with, yet I live, no longer I, but lives in me Christ; but that which now I live in the flesh, in faith I live, **that of the Son of God**, who loved me and gave up himself for me.
>
> Galatians 2:20 [Interlinear Greek] (emphasis mine)

For English speakers, the Greek New Testament sidebar adjusts the word order for clarity.

> I have been crucified with Christ: nevertheless, I live; yet not I, but Christ liveth in me: and the life which I now live in the flesh **I live by the faith of the Son of God**, who loved me, and gave himself for me.

You Cannot Live for God, Apart from God

Beautiful. It all comes from Him. That is the Gospel. Why would we want to burden new believers that 'now that you are saved, you need to clean up your act' and live for God? You cannot live for God, apart from God. That would not be the Gospel.

This is the Gospel of Grace, which we preach.

> But none of these things move me; nor do I count my life dear to myself, so that I may finish my race with joy, and the ministry which I received from the Lord Jesus, to testify to **the gospel of the grace of God**.
>
> Acts 20:24 (emphasis mine)

The Gospel We See Is the Gospel We Preach

How you see (perceive) the Gospel will predicate your preaching (sharing). Which gospel do you have—one based upon the grace of God or one that puts the burden upon the follower of Christ? Our burden is to rest in Him.

> *So there is a special rest still waiting for the people of God.*
>
> *For all who have entered into God's rest have rested from their labors, just as God did after creating the world.*
>
> Hebrews 4:9-10 NLT

My dear friend, Melchizedek from Andhra Pradesh, India, recently published a book about the grace of God titled **Grace Realities: Where Sin Has No Dominion**.[8] In this excerpt, Melchizedek reveals how the way we present the Gospel can affect the new believers for the rest of their Christian walk. Listen to this:

> Today, when we see people living in gross sin, some of us would like to warn them about their eternal destiny in hell to get them saved.
>
> We ask questions like, 'Do you know where you will go if you die tonight?' We put the fear of judgment in them and then offer salvation through faith in Jesus Christ. We have just won a soul who believed just to save his skin from hellfire. To him, Jesus Christ is just a fire escape.

You Stand a Chance to Make Heaven

> But how about asking them, 'Do you know that if you were to die tonight, you stand a chance to go to heaven?' And when they unbelievingly ask, 'How?' we could tell them that Jesus Christ paid the penalty for all their sins, and if they believe in this provision of God and in the name of the Lord Jesus Christ, they can gain entry to heaven.

The former approach is condemning, and an unhealthy fear of God is instilled. We should not blackmail people to believe in the Lord Jesus Christ.

In the latter approach, we are introducing a loving God who sent His only begotten Son, Jesus Christ, to die for the sins of the world. The person thus saved will begin to develop a healthy and loving relationship with God the Father and our Lord Jesus Christ.

The Gospel Is Good News!

My writing has led me to discover books I never knew I owned in my library. A great one is called *The Joy of Evangelism,* written by Jonathan Gainsbrugh. Listen to these quotes:

The Gospel is properly called (In Greek) the 'Euangelion': the Good News. It is not the 'pretty-good' News, not the 'mediocre' News, or the 'not-too-bad' News! It is 'the most wonderful news ever announced,' for it gives Life to people who are dead in their hearts, and light to those full of darkness! It gives forgiveness to the guilt-ridden and heals the sin-infected souls and spirits of all Mankind.[9]

We have a spiritual pardon from the Ruler of the Universe for every human being who currently, without Christ, is imprisoned in sin, living on Death Row! The world is spiritually starving to death, and we have Christ, the Bread of Life! The world is spiritually blind, living in darkness, and we have Him, the Light of Life! The world is dying of spiritual thirst while we splash liberally, daily, in Christ, the Well of Salvation![10]

There's no better news than the Gospel of Jesus Christ! Preach it that way.

Oh Ya, It's *Good* News!

Getting 200 workers out onto the streets in Nigeria was no small task, especially since I had never worked with a large church before. Another minister led half, five groups of twenty, out to evangelize. I took the other half.

I directed my last group of twenty toward a particular neighborhood. Almost simultaneously, they all stepped over a small concrete trench (gutter) as I looked down the row. I called out to the whole group, 'Have Fun!'

They all looked up and stared. Then, abruptly, they all smiled. They remembered, 'Oh ya, this is Good News!'

Preach Good News!

I will finish with another beautiful event. May it imprint upon your heart the urgency of preaching the *correct Gospel—a gospel of God's extraordinary grace*, not a gospel of works.

Woman with a Tough Question

One more door. Sharing the Gospel outdoors is always compelling and challenging to interrupt. We were out in the community in the small Oklahoma town of Cordell. I glanced at my watch: a quarter to nine. But I told my team (a man and woman from the church) *just one more door*.

I knocked. A man answered, but a lady behind him addressed us and invited us into the home. During the discussion, we had the privilege of leading the man, this lady, and her 10-year-old red-headed daughter (with a cast on her arm) to Christ.

But before we left, the woman asked me a question. She shared that she had three children, all from different fathers. I thought the man who opened the door was not her husband. (This story was like the Samaritan woman in John 4.)

God Had an Answer

I did not know what the woman would ask, yet I knew God already had an answer. My heart was eager to see Him work.

The lady continued. Two different churches, as well as the Jehovah's Witnesses, had visited her. She told them of her situation. She then inquired, *'They* (each of these groups) *said* (because the kids were of different fathers) *my kids were bastards. What do you say?'*

Immediately, the Lord reminded me of a scripture. I opened my New Testament, turned to the book of Romans, and read these verses to this woman as I answered her question.

> *For you did not receive the spirit of bondage again to fear, but ye have received the Spirit of adoption by whom we cry out, 'Abba, Father.'*
>
> *The Spirit Himself bears witness with our spirit that we are the children of God,*
>
> Romans 8:15-16

They Can Say What They Want

By then, the 10-year-old redhead had come over and sat between her mom and me. I told the woman:

> *Your daughter has received Jesus as her Lord and Savior. She is now a child of God. They* (the other churches and the Jehovah's Witness) *can say what they want.*

I then patted the girl on her knee, looked squarely into Mom's eyes, and said, *But I am telling you, now, she is the righteousness of God in Christ.*

The mother exclaimed, *I found me a church!*

That Is the Gospel. Preach the Gospel.

PostScript

For thirty years, I have known Brother Melchizedek. I have been to his home. He has been to mine. Melchizedek walks in peace, joy, love, and victory. He does so because of his understanding and dependence upon the Grace of God.

He and I have worked together conducting pastor conferences in India. We witnessed healings and a sovereign outpouring of the Holy Spirit without the laying on of our hands. God's grace was responsible. The Gospel of Jesus Christ in demonstration.

Together, we hosted a ten-day open-air campaign. Workers made more than 3,500 decision cards for Christ. We witnessed miracles. The city's top advocate (lawyer) had an enormous growth that vanished immediately during the mass prayer for the sick. I never laid hands. A mentally disabled young man regained his mind and could converse in everyday conversation. Deaf people heard. And other miracles. Why? Dependence and reliance upon God's majestic Grace. The Gospel of Christ.

Brother Melchizedek has authored a book about God's grace, *Grace Realities: Where Sin Has No Dominion*. Reading this work, I realized the depth of Brother Melchizedek's revelation and dependence upon God's wondrous grace. Today, every believer must live infused with God's Grace because this is the Gospel of the Lord Jesus Christ.

To be a good fisherman for Christ you must possess endurance. You must be willing to fight the storms of opposition, stem the floods of criticism, and labor in the face of seemingly fruitless endeavor. Tenacity and doggedness must be your constant equipment.[1]

—**Lester Sumrall**

Because what may be known of God is manifest in them, for God has shown it to them. For since the creation of the world His invisible attributes are clearly seen, being understood by the things that are made, even His eternal power and Godhead, so that they are without excuse.

—**Roman 1:19-20**

CHAPTER 12

I Don't Believe in Atheists

*A*theist. *'A person who disbelieves or lacks belief in the existence of God or gods.'* Without saying it, you cannot even define what an atheist is or what atheism is as a belief structure. God. *'One who believes there is no GOD.'* I bet many atheists choke on that.

Darkness is *'the partial or total absence of . . .* 'light. The rest of the definition is *'wickedness or evil.'* Boy, that pretty much says it all.

I Was Once an Atheist

I used to be an atheist. In the latter part of high school, my family took in an exchange student from Sweden. He was from a socialist country. And he was an atheist.

The following year, we took in another student. This young man was from the former Yugoslavia. A monarchy previously ruled Yugoslavia, but it was abolished after WWII. In 1945, a communist government was established, renaming it the Federal People's Republic of Yugoslavia.[2] This exchange student was also an atheist.

I treasured my foreign brothers and grew to love them.

Faith For Souls

My family rarely attended church. When we did, I found it stiff, liturgical, and dry. No god seen or felt there.

As a high schooler, you talk and reason with friends, other students, and teachers.

From all of this, I deduced that there is no God.

I Want to Challenge You to Ask If God is Real

In my junior year, for a brief season, I dated a young lady who was a Mormon. In keeping with her upbringing, she invited me to her church and asked if missionaries could visit my family. My dad enjoyed the visits—always up for a lively conversation. My mom hid in the kitchen. Those *'religious people scared'* her.

As a quiet art student, I wasn't sure what to think.

They visited twice. Twice, my dad answered and asked questions of these two friendly, polite young men.

Upon leaving on their last visit, standing under the hanging light at our front door, one of these guys asked me a question. Face to face, a few feet apart, he asked, *'Bill, I want to challenge you to ask if God is real.'*

Nervous but intrigued, I agreed.

I Remembered the Challenge

Maybe that night, or perhaps a week later, as I lay in my bed *'thinking about things I had done—that you don't tell your mother,'* I remembered their challenge.

I got out of bed and picked up the Book of Mormon they had left and found where the *Lord's Prayer* (Matthew 6:9-13 KJV) is recorded. Down on my knees on the wood floor, just the streetlight peering through the window, I read aloud:

Our Father which art in heaven, Hallowed be thy name. Thy kingdom come. Thy will be done in earth, as it is in heaven. Give us this day our daily bread. And forgive us our debts, as we forgive our debtors. And lead us not into temptation, but deliver us from evil: For thine is the kingdom, and the power, and the glory, forever. Amen.

The Presence of God Came into My Room

The Presence of Almighty God came into my bedroom! I did not see Him. I heard nothing. No music played, and no angels sang. There was not a bright light. No sound disturbed the stillness. But *HE CAME*.

Decades later, a holy awe falls upon me as I write. I knew *GOD WAS REAL*.

How? *Because I asked.*

[Now, I was not yet Born Again because I did not know enough to understand the Gospel. That happened at college when a water polo teammate was bold enough to share *The Four Spiritual Laws*[3] gospel tract with me after practice. But I knew God was real. When the Gospel was presented, I was ready! Because for 18 months, I knew God was Holy, and I was not.]

I Had Prayed This Prayer Before

I had prayed this prayer before in church services. The minister would instruct us to turn to the page number as we read in unison. But it was more like a dirge. *Life* was nonexistent, and there were no expectations for it.

But that day, that night—it *all* changed in my life.

God had walked into my bedroom. I knew **He was real!**

I am so grateful that God used those earnest Mormon young men. I cannot embrace their doctrine, but I cling to the scripture. My Bible tells me, 'For whosoever calls on the name of the Lord shall be saved' (Romans 10:13 KJV)—even an atheist challenged by a Mormon.

That is true for a Muslim, a New Ager, or the heathen.

This statement applies to religious people, even if their religion is atheism. Atheism is a religion, *a pursuit or interest to which someone ascribes supreme importance.*[4]

He Is as Close as Your Breath

'So, you're asking me to believe in this Jesus I've only just heard about?'

'Yes, but He is as close as your breath.'

I was talking with an East German man. The Berlin Wall had been down for about a year and a half.[5] We were on the streets in Salzburg, Austria. (This was where my mother had become pregnant with me 35 years earlier.) Working with the Bible school at a friend's church, our group talked and shared with many.

My divine appointment that day was this East German man. Steeped in atheism, my witness puzzled and intrigued him. He wanted to talk more. The fellow invited me to have lunch with him at the local McDonald's restaurant. Unfortunately, as this conversation was beginning, we had to leave. I prayed and trusted those words by the Holy Ghost would resonate.

Why a True Atheist Does Not Exist

I believe there's no such thing as an actual atheist, and I want to tell you why. Millions claim to be so. Yet, I believe God's Word. True atheism cannot exist.

I Don't Believe in Atheists

Let me explain.

Considering our text, let me lay it out again here in the *Passion Translation*:

> *In reality, the truth of God is known instinctively, for God has embedded this knowledge **inside every human heart**.*
>
> *Opposition to truth cannot be excused on the basis of ignorance, because from the creation of the world, the invisible qualities of God's nature have been made visible, such as his eternal power and transcendence. **He has made his wonderful attributes easily perceived, for seeing the visible makes us understand the invisible.** So then, this leaves everyone without excuse.*
>
> Roman 1:19-20 TPT

Two things are said to be inherent in every human being, as per our text:

1. *Consciousness* of our *conscience*.
2. *Consciousness* of the very world we live in, *the creation*.

First, let me deal with the *consciousness* of our *conscience*.

The New King James uses the phrase *'what may be known of God is manifest in them.' The Passion* says it even more plainly: *'The truth of God is known instinctively, for God has embedded this knowledge **inside every human heart**.'* This is talking about awareness of *the conscience*.

The Term *Conscious*

Let's start by discussing the term *conscious*. The Merriam-Webster dictionary defines *conscious*[6] as:

1: having mental faculties not dulled by sleep, faintness, or stupor: AWAKE

Faith For Souls

2: perceiving, apprehending, or noticing with a degree of controlled thought or observation

3: personally felt

4: **a:** likely to notice, consider, or appraise

b: being concerned or interested

c: marked by strong feelings or notions

5: done or acting with critical awareness

6: capable of or marked by thought, will, design, or perception

7: SELF-CONSCIOUS

8: *archaic*: sharing another's knowledge or awareness of an inward state or outward fact.

Beyond the standard definition of just being awake, notice some of these phrases:

- perceiving
- apprehending
- noticing with a degree of controlled thought or observation
- personally felt
- to notice, consider, or appraise
- being concerned or interested
- marked by strong feelings or notions
- acting with critical awareness
- capable of or marked by thought, will, design, or perception
- self-conscious
- awareness of an inward state

'Perceiving,' 'controlled thought,' 'personally felt,' 'consider,' 'being concerned,' 'marked by strong feelings,' 'acting with critical awareness' these all speak of a hidden guidance system placed **inside every human heart**. We are *'capable of or marked by thought, will, design, or perception.'*

We all are moral beings created by a righteous God, and we know it.

Our consciousness exists. I like the *archaic* definition: *'awareness of an inward state.'*

The Term *Conscience*

Now let us examine the term *conscience*[7]. (As also defined by Merriam-Webster.)

1: **a:** the sense or consciousness of the moral goodness or blameworthiness of one's own conduct, intentions, or character, together with a feeling of obligation to do right or be good

   b: a faculty, power, or principle enjoining good acts

   c: the part of the superego in psychoanalysis that transmits commands and admonitions to the ego

2: conformity to what one considers to be correct, right, or morally good: CONSCIENTIOUSNESS

3: sensitive regard for fairness or justice: SCRUPLE

4: *archaic*: CONSCIOUSNESS

For clarity, let us emphasize some of these key phrases:

- the sense or consciousness of the moral goodness
- blameworthiness of one's own conduct, intentions
- character together with a feeling of obligation
- obligation to do right or be good
- conformity to what one considers to be correct, right, or morally good
- sensitive regard for fairness or justice

- (having) scruples- *an ethical consideration or principle that inhibits action, mental reservation*

Wow! This is huge! *'sense of moral goodness,' 'intentions,' 'obligation to do right or be good,' 'what one considers to be correct, right, or morally good,' 'sensitive regard for fairness or justice,'* or having *scruples*!

Together, They Are Mammoth!

Putting these two terms together: *consciousness* of having a *conscience*—baby, you can run, but you cannot hide! You see now why a favorite term I use from Scripture when sharing the Gospel with the lost is *'the hidden man of the heart'* (1 Peter 3:4). Or, as I like to rephrase it, *'the real you deep down inside—nobody knows but you and God!'*

The atheist knows. (I have encountered many more male atheists—I will expound later.) They know they have a conscience. Over the past few years, I have had more conversations with atheists than in the previous three decades. Never has an argument been made for a solid explanation as to *'why or what to do about the conscience'* possessed by all human beings.

Atheism is impossible, just like darkness cannot exist. [Darkness is only the absence of light. The atheist lives in the *absence* of knowing God.] Yet they know in their conscience. Inside the spirit or heart of a person, just like the beating of the physical heart, is *the moral beating of the human conscience*—and he (the atheist) knows it. Is self-concealment possible? I've encountered an atheist who asserts that humans lack a spirit and are only a physical body with a biological brain (the mind). He has to *try* to do something to ignore his conscience.

Why and How Did They Leave?

Let's look back at the confrontation Jesus had with the Pharisees in John 8:1-11 over the woman *caught* in adultery. You remember he wrote in the sand, then stood and said that famous fifteen-word sentence:

'He who is without sin among you, let him throw a stone at her first.' (v. 7)

You remember what happened—they all left. But let's analyze again about who and how they left:

Then those who heard it, being **convicted by their conscience**, *went out* **one by one, beginning with the oldest even to the last**. *And Jesus was left alone, and the woman standing in the midst.* (v.9) (emphasis mine)

Notice these three facts:

1. Each was *convicted by his conscience*.
2. They left *one by one*.
3. The men left, *beginning with the oldest even to the last*.

Every man left—but they left because of *themselves*! And to be more accurate, they left because of their own individual *conscience*. Not for the other guy. Not by peer pressure. They left because of intense pressure within—*within their* **own** *conscience*.

The Heart Must Be Pierced, Especially with an Atheist

As I stated in Chapter 5 *Handling the Religious*, Jesus showed me He loved those Pharisees by saying, *'He that is without sin.'* How? If you are going to assist someone in becoming a child of God, the first thing that must be bent is man's pride.

For the self-righteous, which is a hallmark identifier of an atheist, the heart must be pierced. This is undeniably the work of the Holy Ghost, but He uses the believer. God works through the words you speak (the Bible) and your very person (shrouded with the presence of God).

Let me mention this truth: The older we are, the more our conscience will convict us of sin. The common myth taught in churches nationwide that *you must reach them when they are young or few will believe* is unequivocally false, according to the Word of God. Stop listening to tradition.

Listen to and get renewed by God's Word. Anything is possible.

The key to reaching the atheist or anyone full of themselves is cooperating with the Holy Ghost to bring conviction.

More Male Atheists Than Female

In my conversations and dealings with atheists, I've come across more men who declare themselves atheists than women. This is just my observation. It may be because, as a man, I am more likely to engage another man. However, there exists another reason.

To be an atheist (as opposed to an agnostic—*who does not know if there is a God*), you have to be very defiant. You adamantly assert that God does not exist. Bold. But more, they are outrageously arrogant. How dare you declare to the One who made you, *you cannot make me thus.*

> *Who in the world do you think you are to second-guess God? Do you for one moment suppose any of us knows enough to call God into question? Clay doesn't talk back to the fingers that mold it, saying, 'Why did you shape me like this?' Isn't it obvious that a*

potter has a perfect right to shape one lump into a vase for holding flowers and another into a pot for cooking beans?

Romans 9:20-21 MSG

In my experience, women are less likely to have this level of arrogance compared to men.

Classes or Levels of Atheists

I find classes or levels of atheists. Some are humble in person but defiant in belief. Others are arrogant in both. Still, others are intensely angry, and others are so enraged that they become vile. I have engaged all but the last group. (However, there is one former teacher I want to share with who is such a man—belligerent and profane. I am praying.) Men, as a gender, are much more likely to be full of pride. Yes, women, too, but we men have them beat. We can be so full of ourselves that we become blinded.

As an artist, I know that one can experience sight without perceiving. Once you begin to see as an artist sees, you will inherently improve your drawing skills.[8] Often, we see but don't notice. I also know this being a man: *'Honey, when did we get the new lamp?'* Her response was, *'Six months ago.'*

The Solution: Preach the Gospel

But the solution in all these cases, with anyone who is not born again, is to *preach the Gospel*. Pray for a door of utterance and preach the Gospel. *Declare* if preaching sounds too difficult.

And listen to the Holy Spirit. That very neighbor who is so rude or the scary guy next door, when the Holy Ghost says, *make a plate of your favorite cookies and take it to him*—do it! When we get those specific promptings, *trust*. God has something in the works you and I do not know about. Maybe that scary guy just had his best friend killed in a motorcycle accident. Or perhaps that mean rude neighbor just had been diagnosed (or his wife) with cancer. You do not know. But when the Holy Spirit is tugging on your heartstrings, respond. He is opening a door.

Lapeer Days, the Atheist, and the Tough Guy

A Michigan pastor had coordinated the dates for the *GCS (Great Commission Seminar)* I was to conduct to coincide with the annual *Lapeer Days* summer event. Chili contests and beer tents brought the crowds. The strategy proved astonishingly effective. His church was housed in one of the oldest brick church buildings in the downtown area- within walking distance of the event.

Once out on the street, I approached a guy in a hat, holding a beer in one hand and a pack of cigarettes in his shirt pocket. After only a few words, he told me he was an atheist. While still shaking his hand, I responded,

'Bob, (my memory default for a name always comes out "Bob." Maybe his name was Murray.) *Let me ask you one question. Jesus is the Son of God. He died but has risen from the dead, and He is coming back. If He could prove Himself to you that He was alive, would you accept Him as your Lord and Savior?'*

Bob answered, *'You're real convicting,'* as he withdrew his hand.

How does an atheist *get convicted*? Just like any of us—by the *conscience*.

Others Were Afraid

As the outreach there at the Lapeer Days ended for the day, we all walked back to the church. A couple of teams were ahead of me.

I watched as they veered to the side, avoiding a big, tough-looking bearded dude dressed in all-black—biker boots and chains hanging from his belt.

Purposely, I walked towards him. I greeted him. Then I asked him the same question I had asked Bob (Murray?) earlier. This man and I stood face to face. He spoke softly, *'Yes.'* So, I prayed with him, not yet to become born again, but I prayed God would make Himself real to him as He had done for me. With a tear in his eye, this man shook my hand and said, *'Thank you.'*

Believer, I implore you to renew your mind about who God says you are. *'You are the light of the world'* (Matthew 5:14-16).

The Second Witness

> *In reality, the truth of God is known instinctively, for God has embedded this knowledge inside every human heart.*
>
> *Opposition to truth cannot be excused on the basis of ignorance, because **from the creation of the world**, the **invisible qualities of God's nature** have been **made visible**, such as his eternal power and transcendence. **He has made his wonderful attributes easily perceived, for seeing the visible makes us understand the invisible.** So then, this leaves everyone without excuse.*
>
> Roman 1:19-20 TPT (emphasis mine)

So now, let's look at the second witness: consciousness of the very world we live in—*creation*. Every person can perceive it. We live in and on it, the earth.

*Opposition to truth cannot be excused on the basis of ignorance...
because from the creation of the world, the invisible qualities of God's nature
have been made visible, such as his eternal power and transcendence.*

Transcendence means *extending or lying beyond the limits of ordinary experience.*

We know or perceive things. Unlike the person who claims, *I can only accept what I can see or touch* as real. Have you seen or touched your brain—are you sure you have one?

Seriously though, how about love? A person can be profoundly affected by the presence or absence of love. Having been a foster parent for dozens of children, I can state that the damage that can occur to a baby not having a healthy bond with a parent—especially a mother—is undeniable. It is called RAD—Reactive Attachment Disorder.[9] Love eludes touch and sight (unlike touching a tree), yet it unequivocally exists. Perception does not define reality; many intangible things are real. However, God, in His providence, showed the *invisible* with the visible.

This fantastic world in which we live shows His existence.

He has made his wonderful attributes easily perceived, for seeing the visible makes us understand the invisible. *So then, this leaves everyone without excuse.*

Romans 1:20 TPT

When My Dad Stopped Being an Atheist

As an adult, I sat with my father and talked with him about his faith. I wanted to make sure he had a Born Again conversion. Although he inclined towards spiritual matters, not all were centered on Christ, which might lead the soul astray.

He told me of when and where he received Christ as his Savior. The conversation took us back further. Then my dad told me he used to be an atheist. I asked, 'What changed you?'

He said, 'When I held my first-born son (me) *in my hands, I believed. I knew there was a God.'* Hmmm . . .

Deflection by Criticism

I have been going back and forth with an atheist Englishman. We have PM—personally messaged—each other on Facebook off and on since last year. One consistent trait in every response is criticism, citing all the flaws in the creation (of the planet, the universe, and humanity). Why?

Because if he ever *allows himself to see* the wonder right before his eyes, he will behold the Maker. He is constantly deflecting.

I must address his core resistance, but I have yet to reach that point. He told me early on that he gets passionately angry when people (even others besides Christians) state that he hates God. But that is the core of his problem. He is hyper-critical (inferring he could have honed a better creation) because he has issues of hurt and anger toward God.

How can you be angry at someone that does not exist? [That was the confrontation line between the Christian student and the atheist professor in the movie *God is Not Dead*.[10]]

See the Beauty of Creation

While ministering and sharing my adventures around the globe, I have often been asked what is the most beautiful or amazing thing (around the world) that I have seen. I give them three. Here they are.

Fjords of Norway

First, the *Fjords of Norway*.[11] I was 18 years old, with a backpack, traveling by train across Europe with a few other Americans after high school. The exchange students who had formerly lived in our homes implored us, 'When you graduate, come to Europe!' On a student Euro-rail pass, we traveled to thirteen countries in Europe. (This was the summer before I became Born Again.) Traveling north up to Oslo, Norway, the rail ended. We struck out by foot, hitchhiking—our destination: Alesund, Norway. The inland route to this coastal port is frozen most of the winter, and there are no train routes (at least not when I was 18).

We hiked to the outskirts of Oslo. Nightfall approached. I suggested we make camp (not considering that we were in the Borrel Forrest[12] with timber wolves—we could have been eaten in the night). One other suggested we try hitchhiking. We did and got picked up by a trucker. He spoke no English, and we, of course, spoke no Norwegian. He pointed on the map to his destination for his load of apartment building doors, then to himself and Alesund, his home.

The three of us slept in the cab as he drove. We awoke at his delivery location, helped him unload, and continued traveling. Arriving about three in the morning, this man allowed us to set up our tent on the heavy tundra of his yard. He offered for us to sleep inside—but we were more than grateful for the tent in the yard.

In the morning, his wife came and woke us up and motioned to the three of us to come to the house. Smoked meats, cheeses, homemade breads, and jams were spread out in a magnificent display. Wonderful! These people were so kind. I have often wondered if they were Christians and had *helped pray me into the Kingdom*. I wholeheartedly expect to meet them in heaven one day.

I Don't Believe in Atheists

Midday, the trucker drove us into town and to the ferry station. He helped us buy tickets for that night's voyage through the fjords back down to Oslo.

Late into the night, awakened from another sleep nap, I looked and beheld. Amazing! Mountain peaks that thrust down into the mirrored dark waters of the sea inlets. Occasionally, there would be a small piece of earth where the land had eroded over the centuries, making a flat area with a cluster of 30 or 40 homes. These people are entirely isolated for months every winter. What an existence to live on the fjords! Surreal.

The Himalayas Mountains

I went to preach about *Faith For Souls* at my friend Deborah Strong's[13] intense three-week Bible School in Katmandu, Nepal. These mountain pastors, who had access to little training, came to sit under preaching and teaching morning, noon, and night.

For this trip, a couple from the church I pastored, Ron and Kelly, had felt God had led them to join me. They believed God, and He provided. However, to make it as easy as possible for them, I booked the cheapest airline reservations possible. Big mistake. We literally had to take *ten flights* to get from Tulsa, Oklahoma, to Katmandu, Nepal. It took us *almost three full days to travel one way*!

During our time with Missionary Strong,[14] Ron, Kelly, and I took a 24-hour excursion to the lower Himalayas. Ron wanted to get a glimpse of the world's most majestic and highest mountains. I tend to be an all-work-and-no-play kind of guy, so this was a welcome break—an excellent idea.

We had reserved a house-type hotel at about 9,000 feet elevation.

At approximately 5:00 a.m., Ron rapped on my door. *'Let's go!'* He and I hiked for 30 or 40 minutes up and down mountain paths while getting a little higher and closer to the *big guys*! Finally, we picked a place to wait and watch. The sun was breaking through cloud formations. We were high enough to be in the clouds. Abruptly, we got a clear view.

Majestic white glistening peaks. We could not see the tops, but they were huge! I do not think we saw Mt. Everest, but we saw the range of the *higher Himalayas*. Over 110 peaks tower at an altitude of over 24,000 feet.[15] Breath-taking!

The Sahara Desert

I flew from Paris, France, to Accra, Ghana, West Africa. This was the first of two trips working with Tommy O'Dell,[16] the grandson of T.L. and Daisy Osborn. He is a brilliant guy, ex-druggy, and prolific soul winner and missionary. He and his wife Elisabeth are still *tearing it up*, reaching the unreached around the world.

I would apprentice under a Ghanaian, Brother James, to learn how to set up an evangelistic campaign. (I include some of the ministry testimonies of this trip in Chapter 14 *Minding My Own Business*, while discussing the association of miracles with the Gospel.)

My flight to the capital city, Accra, was late afternoon. The over-six-hour flight allowed me to reflect on what I would encounter. Sitting next to the window, my eyes focused on what was below me.

Underneath were fantastic swirls and waves of golden brown, glistening in the aureate light of the afternoon. The Sarah Desert stretched as far as the eye could see. It covers 9 million square kilometers (3,500,000 square miles), representing 31% of Africa.[17] The patterns and brush strokes from the desert winds were to me like a *giant finger painting by the hand of God*. Awestruck!

Why the Atheist Cannot See?

To claim that this is all by chance and that the human body, which is far more complex than this entire planet,[18] is foolishness.

I Don't Believe in Atheists

The [empty-headed] fool has said in his heart, There is no God. They are corrupt, they have done abominable deeds; there is none that does good or right.

Psalm 14:1 AMPC

I selected the *Amplified* Translation here to make a point: *[empty-headed] fool*. Not only are they foolish and presumptuous. But they are genuinely empty-headed; they are not thinking right. This passage in 1 Corinthians tells it accurately:

For the message of the cross is foolishness to those who are perishing, but to us who are being saved it is the power of God.

For it is written: 'I will destroy the wisdom of the wise, And bring to nothing the understanding of the prudent.'

Where is the wise? Where is the scribe? Where is the disputer of this age? Has not God made foolish the wisdom of this world?

For since, in the wisdom of God, the world through wisdom did not know God, it pleased God through the foolishness of the message preached to save those who believe.

1 Corinthians 1:18-21

Don't doubt yourself because you think you are not smart enough, or wise enough, to speak to the atheist. You, my friend, are plenty bright—you chose God. Pull on Him to help you in the moment.

So, What Is It Going to Take?

What does it take to reach anyone? It takes love, faith, and persistence. I love Lester Sumrall's stance in his quote above. Now listen as he shares the following testimony.[19]

Faith For Souls

Dr. Chalmers and the Infidel

From all visible evidence, you might as well talk to an Alaskan totem pole as to ask some people to accept Christ. There seems to be absolutely no soul response toward God. However, the fisher of men does not work according to outward evidence, but by the principle of being faithful to God. In too many instances, the fisherman gives up too soon. It is a challenge to read the account of Dr. Chalmers of Glasgow, Scotland, who visited an infidel twenty-two times, seeking admission to witness for Christ. The infidel was known to the minster, who, when he heard that the infidel was seriously ill, resolved to speak to him about eternity. Twenty-one times, Dr. Chalmers knocked on the door and asked for an interview with the dying infidel—but twenty-one times, he was refused. The twenty-second time, the infidel found no power to resist. Upon permitting Dr. Chalmers to enter his sick room, he commented, 'I want to see the man who could be refused twenty-one times!'

Family Members Came to Christ

Some of my family members received Christ because I prayed for them (over the phone) about a crisis they were facing, just like I would with any brother in the Lord. Jesus gave me the grace, boldness, and gentleness to do this. God answered prayer; unbelief dispelled to faith.

Another time, my faith had to be uplifted to try yet again. (Again, over the phone) I chimed, *'For your birthday today, I am going to share again the wonderful message of God's gift of Salvation.'* To my delight, after decades, they said *'yes'* and *'prayed to make Jesus Lord.'*

Each one of them declared himself to be an atheist during a specific time in their life.

Believe the Word, Do Not Be Intimidated.

My heart and my intention in writing about atheists is not to belittle or conjure disdain. No, not at all. I want you, as a believer, to believe God's Word. Believe what God says to overcome the intimidation of trying to reach the atheist.

While serving full-time as a public high school teacher (in California), I completed a Master of Educational Leadership (Administration).[20] I achieved this entirely online with the University of Cincinnati. During this season, I raised my three younger children as a single parent. I also pastored the small local church we attended (for ten years). Each Sunday afternoon, my three teenagers knew to be quiet in the house as *'Dad is writing a paper.'* They knew their friends would have to go home if they got loud.

Online Master's Program

Another significant part of this online degree program was a weekly *asynchronous discussion*. Each student would have to weigh in on a particular topic while reading and responding to at least three other students' responses and weighing in regarding their threads. This was done asynchronously. Each would read and write whenever their schedules permitted, but this was rarely done in live time. Most of these students were in the Eastern portion of the United States. Living in California, my 'morning posts' were early as I would write in the late evening. But my deadline for the Sunday paper was only 9:00 p.m. instead of midnight as for the other students!

The program was rigorous and tough. But it expanded my knowledge of education. This helped my confidence in the classroom and standing firm in my dealings with my administration at my school site. Covering School Law was highly emboldening to me as a believer. We studied *'published research regarding the rights of students and personnel.'*

I realized I was one of *those personnel*. This helped me be a witness for Christ in the classroom and greatly aided my dealings with my cohorts (fellow master's degree students).

Asynchronous Debate

At one point, one particular very liberal atheist cohort and I went round and round in our responses to one another. No other student nor the instructor dared weigh into our debate, but they all had access and were likely reading every word.

This younger man poured out his doctrines[21] of atheism, but especially defending forced acceptance of gender identity and evolution. He became belittling, other times defensive, and then angry. He tried to diminish my riposte because *'I was just an art teacher,'* but grew muted when I told him I was also a certified high school science teacher. Eventually, he quit the discussion.

I do not tell you this to gloat. He became a regular subject of prayer for my wife and me. But further, I gained confidence through going toe-to-toe with an *educated atheist*.

They are just people.

They are like someone standing in profound darkness. It does not make them bad. They just cannot see because they do not have the light. *Give them the light.*

A Final Thought

In Billye Brim's book, *The Blood and the Glory*,[22] she shares a prophetic word given by Sister Wilkerson. I remember a few occasions when I attended services in Tulsa, Oklahoma, where Sister Wilkerson gave *a word*. She was known as a great woman of prayer. I had heard she had spent years praying for hours daily, seeking God.

On those occasions, she would stand (usually in the back) and deliver a word from the Lord. It came out with such force, such authority, it sounded like thunder. Among two or three thousand, the word pierced the air—without using a mic.

Billy Brim shares this word Sister Wilkerson gave in a meeting:

Tell the people not to be concerned over My soon appearing because of lost loved ones. Tell them to name them to Me in prayer. Those whose names they call to Me in faith, I will see that they make it if I have to wrestle them on their beds in the nighttime.[23]

Call the names. Call the names of the atheists you are trying to reach. My wife and I almost daily call out the English fellow, an atheist salmon fisherman, and certain relatives.

I told her today while we sat and prayed together, *'I can just see (the Englishman) and (the fisherman) kicking and fighting as they go up in the rapture! And then relaxing, being so glad to be saved.'* They are part of my inheritance.

Ask of me, and I shall give thee the heathen for thine inheritance,
And the uttermost parts of the earth for thy possession.

Psalm 2:8 KJV

When fear rears its ugly head, you have the right and authority in the name of Jesus to point the finger of God at fear and say, 'In the name of Jesus, I refuse to be afraid!' And until you start doing that, fear is going to dominate you.[1]

—**Frederick K.C. Price**

For God has not given us a spirit of fear, but of power and of love and of a sound mind.

—**2 Timothy 1:7**

CHAPTER 13

Bold, Not Brash

Bold is courageous and daring. *Brash* is impetuous or rash, insensitive or tactless, impudent or shameless.

As soul winners for Christ, we need to be bold and unintimidated. But we must not be brash and rude.

Unique Bold Healings

Sometimes, the distinction between the two becomes blurry. Let me begin by sharing an exceptionally unique healing in a village in India. It was undeniably bold, but not brash. The difference is how the Holy Spirit led to minister in His power and love.

We had a small mob of people thronging us. The new village church was being dedicated for the third night. For two nights, I preached the Gospel and then ministered healing by having the new believers lay their hands upon their bodies as I prayed en masse. My intent, to do as T.L. Osborn would minister, was for the people to use their own faith to receive.

My team members had pressured me to alter my method this last night in the village and lay hands on some. They insisted that some would not receive healing without the laying on of hands.

Faith For Souls

He Cast Out a Demon, the Blind Saw

When I invited the crowd to come forward to have hands laid upon them by the team of ministers to be healed, some three hundred surged the little platform. My interpreter, Brother Lazarus (his Christian name), was off to my left. I could not see him, but I could hear him praying forcefully. Later, I learned that as Lazarus touched a blind man, he instantly perceived a demon. He hollered as he prayed in tongues—or his tongue. I could not discern which.

The man fell to the ground. Lazarus firmly kept his hand on him and kept praying fearlessly.

When everything concluded, the man stood up, liberated, and his sight restored!

A Mute with a Demon

While this was happening, a mother brought her son to me. Her son was likely about 16 or 17. She said he could not talk. He stood before me in a stupor. The boy had a blank stare in his eyes. His mouth hung open. She explained he could not talk. *'All he does is furiously rip up his clothes, cuss her, and tear up their house.'* I perceived the boy had a demon spirit.

The Lord instructed me on what course of action to follow. It would be bold.

But First, the Back Story

But before I continue, let me tell you the back story of how I came to be in India on this trip. It will encourage your heart to know that God makes a way for us to minister and bring life to people.

Beautiful Provision of the Holy Spirit

God had done many beautiful things over the previous year.

Bold, Not Brash

Before this ministry trip to India, I had been waiting on the Lord at the end of the year prior, seeking *'what the Lord would have for the coming year.'* The Holy Spirit gave me a clear direction. He told me:

> *You are to build three churches in India and three (fresh) water wells. Go and hold the dedications of these churches. You are not to try to raise money by taking extra meetings outside pastoring your church.*

> [I was pastoring full time. We had weekly services every Sunday morning and Wednesday night. It would have been easy to book speaking engagements at other churches on Sunday evenings across the state and beyond. But God was emphatic that I was not to do so. He instructed that I *'wait on Him.'*]

> *You must wait in My Presence. You cannot accomplish this mission unless you wait in and upon My Presence.*

[An opportunity had been presented to support an American ministry, Mike Francen Ministries,[2] doing just this. The Lord was now giving me the *green light* to partner with them. However, I was to go to India and do the church dedications myself. We would provide the funds for the churches and freshwater wells to be built. I would preach the dedications.]

Happy That I Listened and Obeyed

You know how we often beat ourselves up for what we should have done and *should have listened to* God? Well, I am happy to tell you this was one time I just listened and obeyed.

I did as the Lord said and concentrated on my church. But I also did what He had instructed and spent many sessions in prayer, just *'waiting upon the Lord.'* (Acts 13:2)

Glorious things happened. We had many corporate times of prayer each week. I also had private times of waiting in the *Presence of God*

(Isaiah 6:1-8). Usually, I would go into the sanctuary, put the lights low, and play soft worship music. And then, I would lie on my back behind the podium on the platform. I would pray in the Spirit or get still (Psalm 46:10). His presence would descend upon me. Often, it felt like I was being pushed down through the floor or sinking into a warm, glorious pool of His Love and Presence (Revelation 1:17). Beyond words.

He Gave His Paycheck

As I did this one day, I joked with my secretary, *'Don't disturb me. But if the President* (naming the then sitting President of the United States) *needs me, get me.'*

After spending an hour or more in the church sanctuary, I emerged refreshed with the tantalizing presence of His glory all over me. On this day, Cathy, the secretary, shared with me that *'a man had come by and left this.'* She handed me the man's paycheck endorsed to the church. This fellow got paid weekly. But this was a *'five-week month, so this was an "extra" paycheck.'* The brother was driving by the church, felt impressed to stop, and left his check. He said, *'He was unsure, but the Lord may have him do this again.'* (He did.)

This man did not attend our church, and he and I never met.

Tumultuous Student Finds Peace

This season, I ran a minister's school at our church, *Practical Minister's School*. Functioning as a supplemental year to a Bible college, students received the practical experience necessary for successful ministry. We concentrated on personal soul winning, individual discipleship of new believers, helps ministry (each student served throughout the church on rotation), practice preaching, and missions (to graduate the 18-month program, each student would take part in a mission trip).

On one occasion, one of my students stopped by the church while I was waiting upon the Lord. She had some personal struggles and quit and returned to the program. That day, unknown to me, she had opened the back door of the sanctuary and looked up to the platform. She told me later that she saw me lying on the platform and a golden light over my entire body (Luke 9:29). She finally grasped the concept I had been sharing about waiting in the Lord's presence. With the help she received, she completed Practical Minister's School and graduated.

[Her mission trip was to Mexico. The Holy Ghost impressed me to allow her to bring her teenage daughter on this trip. The Lord used them both.]

'Pastor, You're Ripping Us Off'

A man's wife in the school confronted me one Sunday before service. Her name was Karen. She was a small-framed, redheaded woman. Both she and her husband, Mike, were devout believers. Little Karen looked up with piercing eyes and said, *'Pastor, you are ripping us off.'*

Humbled (and in shock), I asked her, *'What do you mean?'* Karen explained. *'Pastor, you tell us* (the church congregation) *about these wonderful trips, but you never allow us to sow* (our finances) *into them. You are ripping us off!'*

I had never seen it this way before. I believed fulfilling my calling as an evangelist was not the burden or responsibility of those I pastored. Too often, I had heard of situations where pastors and ministers had misused or even abused their power and authority as ministers to influence their people to give money. (I had heard of multi-level marketing schemes passing through churches where the pastor made a substantial profit, but others in the congregation did not.) I was bent on never being guilty of such abuse of my influence.

That day, I repented. I apologized to Karen. And I repented to the Lord.

As I ministered in those villages at year's end, standing on the shores of India, there was a remarkable boldness. Unlike any previous trip, what a covering of love and a beautiful prayer partnership. Stacy, a single mom with young kids who sang on the worship team, informed me before the trip that she and each child had all sown into it, including her youngest child, who gave a few pennies.

I cannot tell how this blessed me. I knew I was representing Jesus, but I also knew I was a representative of each family from my church.

Instead of Buying a New Car

In agreement with her husband, one dear sister, Lydia, sowed their insurance settlement. Instead of buying a new car, they settled for a used one and gave the largest single donation towards building the three churches and three water wells. Their gift paid for an entire church and water well. (I had their name put on the sign on that church along with the ministry that instituted this program. Despite never meeting the village believers, they will have the chance to do so in heaven one day!)

Wash One Another's Feet

During corporate prayer, the Lord impressed a lady from our church that *we were to wash one another's feet* (John 13:2-17). She told me that the Lord told her this and that she was to begin with the pastor (to wash *my* feet first).

As I sat on the chair on the platform and removed my shoes, I will never forget what I saw. When I lifted one foot over the pail of water before she washed my foot, I saw Jesus' nail-pierced foot. It happened in a blink, a mere micro-second, yet I can still recall it. Fear, humility, overwhelming gratitude, and holy awe swept through my being. *Oh, Jesus... how could you have done this all for me, for my sins? For each of us, for all our sins?*

Angelo Mitropoulos

Also, before fulfilling this assignment to build churches in India this year, I was blessed to meet Evangelist Angelo Mitropoulos.[3] Angelo had trained and had done street ministry under R.W. Schambach[4] in the Bronx, Coney Island, and other parts of New York. The Lord had given Angelo an exceptionally comprehensive teaching and revelation, precisely diagnosing the healing processes of the New Testament, mainly focusing on the ministry of Jesus.

Evangelist Mitropoulos taught these things at our Practical Minister's School and my church. God used these teachings to help me work healings and miracles on the mission field. His ministry aided me in connecting with the Holy Spirit and helping others in receiving.

[Both these dear men of God, R.W. and Angelo, have passed on to glory. I can picture my dad regularly hanging out with these guys, knowing him as well as I do.]

We Made It!

So many beautiful events happened that year before this trip to India. And we made it!

By year's end, we had the entire amount to have the three churches and freshwater wells built and my plane ticket to go preach. Glory to God! He is so faithful. But it happened His way—by waiting upon the Presence of God.

Consider this familiar verse:

*But those who **wait** on the Lord Shall **renew** their strength; They shall mount up with wings like eagles, They shall run and not be weary, They shall walk and not faint.*

Isaiah 40:31 (emphasis mine)

I want to call attention to two words here: *wait* and *renew*.

Wait, in Hebrew, here is *qavah* (kaw-vaw'). The verb is translated as:

> **Wait for** (probably originally *twist, stretch*, then of *tension* of enduring, waiting: *wait, cord; be strong, strength*, also *strand* of rope; *endure, remain, await, threads*, so spider's *threads, web*).

Renew in Hebrew is *chalaph* (khaw-laf′). The verb is translated as:

> (A prime root) *to pass on* or *away, pass through*.

Using the literal meanings, this verse is telling us:

> But those who **bind together by twisting with the Lord, like strands of a rope** (we) Shall **pass away (abolish) (our own)** strength; They shall mount up with wings like eagles, They shall run and not be weary, They shall walk and not faint.

We exchange our strength for His. When we wholeheartedly understand and practice what it truly means to wait upon the Lord, we come out clothed with God Himself.

You can understand why God's instructions to me at the onset were so critical:

> *And you must wait in My Presence.* **You cannot do this mission if you do not wait in and upon My Presence.**

Now, Back to the Boy with the Demon

Thank you for allowing me the diversion; now let's get back to the demonized 17-year-old tearing up his mom's hut and his clothes and cursing but not talking.

As the boy stood before me, the Lord abruptly brought to my memory a comparable situation Brother Kenneth E. Hagin[5] had encountered. Someone had brought such an individual to the prayer line in his service. This man had been brought from a mental facility. He had no expression and did not talk. Hagin had laid hands upon the man and then proceeded down the line, praying for others. As Kenneth looked back down the row toward this comatose-like, non-responsive man, this time, he saw a demon sitting on his shoulder. (This is a manifestation of the Discerning of Spirits spoken of in 1 Corinthians 12:10. Hopefully, in a later book devoted to Signs and Wonders, I will teach on this.) The small demon looked like an ugly monkey on his shoulder with its arms clenched around the man's head.

Hagin Told the Demon Go!

Hagin, now seeing this demon, spoke to it. *'Leave him. In Jesus' Name, go!'* The devil unlocked its arms and fell to the ground. Brother Hagin spoke again, *'Now go! Get out of here.'*

The monkey-like demon looked sorrowful, like a sad puppy. Hagin said, *'Get!'* and it ran out of the back of the church. The man was cured and *'as normal as you and me,'* said Hagin.

Recalling this testimony, I knew I was dealing with a similar situation with this young man. Not seeing the demon, I felt impressed to deal with the monster another way. (I laid hands on the boy, but then the Spirit directed me to use more force.)

Tell the Mom I Won't Hurt Her Son

I told my interpreter, Dr. David Livingston (his Christian name), to speak to the mother. Tell her, *'I will not hurt him.'* (Remember, I stand 6 feet 2 inches tall, and almost all the Indian people are much shorter and smaller than I am.) Immediately, I grabbed his head, locking my arms around his skull. I put a headlock on this devil! I squeezed him forcefully (he was not going anywhere!) I pressed hard, but not enough to hurt the boy, for maybe 30 to 40 seconds (though it seemed much longer).

Inside my heart, my faith concentrated on the anointing *burning that devil right off* his head!

I let go.

The teen wobbled a little.

I then asked his mother (via my interpreter) to take him aside and check him. She did. We ministered to others; Mom returned to the line with her son. With a soft smile, she said, *'he is talking to me.'* The next day, I got a picture of me and the young man standing together, him with a big radiant smile. [See below]

Bold. Not brash.

We must be bold in the Lord to help people. It may seem aggressive, but done in love, led by the Spirit, it gets the job done. Your heart's motive is the deciding factor. Are you sincerely trying to help or just trying to show out (as they say in the South)?

Let me further illustrate this for you with a couple more testimonies.

A Vet Named Bill

There lived a Vietnam veteran named Bill in my apartment complex during my time as a Bible school student. He was pretty much crazy. But I wanted to win him to Christ. Talking with him one day, he invited me over for dinner. I agreed.

Being there just for a few minutes, he lit up a joint, so I said, *'I am going to go.'* Bill said he *'would put it out'* and did. So, I stayed.

He got the food off the BBQ, and we sat at his coffee table, him on his couch, me sitting on the floor. Bill was muttering a lot of nonsensical things. He sang incoherent phrases from different country music songs. Inside, I grew angry, not at Bill, but at the devils messing with this man. I knew I needed to fight *fire with fire*. I locked my eyes with Bill and intently prayed aloud in other tongues (1 Corinthians 14:2). He stared back and got quiet. The crazy singing stopped. The room got still.

Then it arose in me, *'Bill, would you like Jesus to come into your heart and save you and give you peace?'* To my joy and my delight, Bill answered, *'Yes.'*

I prayed with Bill to receive Christ into his heart to be saved! Praise God.

A couple of months later, Bill got kicked out of the apartments. He and the guy across from him had shot through the walls at each other. No one got hurt—thank God. Bill was still a big work in progress.

Young Guys Hanging Out

We were in Rogers, Arkansas. I was doing another *GCS (Great Commission Seminar)*. One night, my team approached some young people hanging out by their cars. Several of the teens accepted Christ. But one guy was too cool to give us much interest. I knew that if I were going to get through and reach this guy, it would take something different.

I walked over to him and said,

> *Let me ask you a question. Let's suppose instead of carrying a Bible (I have a pocket Soul Winner's New Testament, well used), I had a 45-caliber pistol. And instead of talking to you about Jesus, I came right up to you and BLEW YOU AWAY. Lifeless as the cold steel of this pickup truck* (as I slapped the top side wall of his truck). *Where would you be right now?*

I paused just for a second to let that sink in. And then I continued,

> *Now let's suppose instead of me, you have the 45. And you just blew me away. Now I have angels protecting me. They are here right now, so you couldn't do it. But let's just suppose you did—you blew me away.*
>
> *Do you know where I would be right now? I would be in heaven for eternity with God. The Bible says, 'to be absent from the body is to be present with the Lord'* (2 Corinthians 5:8).

We led that young fellow to Christ.

Showmanship—brash? No. Bold. Sometimes, they will not come without it.

A Simple Test

A simple test to know if you (or another) are operating in the Boldness of the Lord or just being brash, arrogant, and rude is to check the motive of your heart. Understanding another person's heart motivation is not a straightforward task, but their words often disclose their intent (Luke 6:45). Ask yourself:

- Why am I doing this? (Or why do you intend to do this?)
- Are you pulling with all your heart, trying to get what you need from God to set a soul free?
- Is it a concern for you that Jesus gave up His life for the redemption of humanity?
- Is your heart filled with Him, His love and grace, zealous to reach the lost at all costs?
- Is this about helping others come to Christ?
- Or is it about making a name for myself?
- Or drawing attention to you?

[To be honest, I have pulled back and not witnessed because I was worried that other believers present would think I was showing off. Rid yourself of that fear, too. You are operating as a *spiritual first responder*—you must do your job.]

If you pose such questions to yourself and your sincere responses align with a desire and effort to assist souls in escaping the clutches of hell and embracing Christ, then you are in line. His Holy Boldness empowers you to reach souls.

Bold, Not Brash

A Roll Call of the Bold

We could spend hours and days reciting the mighty acts of saints in both Testaments that operated under such an anointing. But let's think about one incident of Peter and John after they healed the lame man at the temple gate called Beautiful.

> Now when they **saw the boldness** of Peter and John, and **perceived** that they were unlearned and ignorant men, they marveled; and they took knowledge of them, that **they had been with Jesus.**
>
> Acts 4:13 KJV (emphasis mine)

My best advice: seek God with all your heart for the souls of men, and He will manifest as He knows best when you are out in the fields, reaping His sons and daughters back to Him.

A wise man once said, *If you bow before God, you will stand before men.*

This was the young man from that Indian village. I laid hands. However, the Lord impressed me to use more force, and then I put him in a headlock! In my spirit, I knew *the devil was getting burned off his* life. Look at that smile. You should have seen his mom's smile! God is good! **Bold in Love**.

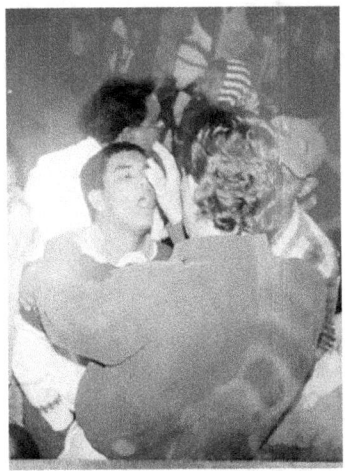

Jesus' message was with evidence. His Gospel was with proof! His preaching was with demonstration![1]

—T.L. Osborn

And having gone forth, they preached everywhere, and the Lord working with (them) and confirming the word by accompanying signs.[2]

—Mark 16:20 BLB

CHAPTER 14

Just Minding My Own Business

*J*ust minding my own business, leading a good Muslim to the Lord. And God brought a miracle my way. As recounted in Chapter 3, *1,800 Saved in Eight Days*, while leading the Muslim man to Christ, the mom of the deaf girl sought me out. The Holy Spirit directed, and I followed. She heard! Dad and daughter walked the aisle that night and gave their hearts to Christ.

Preach the Gospel. God will confirm His Word with miracles.

The bolder we preach, the pure Gospel of Christ, the more He comes.

This is HIS Gospel, and He will confirm it. Notice our text now in *The Passion*:

And the apostles went out announcing the good news everywhere, as the Lord himself consistently worked with them, **validating the message** *they preached with miracle-signs that accompanied them!*

Mark 16:20 TPT (emphasis mine)

The Lord himself consistently worked with them. But notice why He worked with them:

'validating the message they preached.'

What was the Lord doing? He was, and He is, validating **the message**. The message is everything.

How does He validate? **With miracle-signs** that accompanied them!

Look now to the *Young's Literal Translation*. A crucial distinction has been made:

And they, having gone forth, did preach everywhere, the Lord working with [them], and confirming the word, through the signs following. Amen

Mark 16:20 YLT

Please notice that the reference to *them*, the apostles, is in brackets. This indicates that God did not directly confirm the apostles or disciples. He is confirming *His Word*—every time. We preach Him, and He proves Himself.

[You will find the same thing in the *King James Version* and the *Berean Literal Translation*. The reference to the disciples or apostles is in italics. *Them* is not in the original Greek.]

Why is this significant? It holds importance for two reasons.

1. The pressure is on the Gospel—not on you.
2. God will confirm you—but only when you preach Him.

Everything revolves around the Gospel.

Beautiful Deaf Girl Hears

This was my fourth visit to India. Missionary Jerry O'Dell and his Indian counterpart, Pastor Sam, had devised an effective tool for bringing in the Indian harvest. They called it *The Indian Harvest Plan*.[3] It comprised three parts. They would set up an outdoor crusade in a larger village (with a population of 30,000 to 50,000), a hub for smaller villages. The students and staff would then evangelize the villages and advertise the Good News campaign. Then buses were hired to bring people to the meeting. After the weeklong campaign, a church started with the new converts, and then some Bible school student graduates would lead the church.

On their ministry website, Jerry writes of these students:

By the time they graduate from the two-year program, they have gained confidence that the power to produce salvation and miracles lies in the message of the Gospel, not the messenger.[4]

I had the privilege of observing this model in operation on multiple occasions. I witnessed demoniacs come before the platform while Jerry and Sam (interpreting) were preaching. In eye-opening wonder, I watched. They would contort, grimace, and yell. Then, they would collapse as if dead.

Witnessing the testimonies, I was astonished as these former demoniacs boldly proclaimed Jesus as their Lord.

So many healings. So many deliverances. So many salvations. Wonderful!

A Church Is Started

Often, two crusades were scheduled back-to-back in neighboring villages. In between, several days were devoted to the opening services for the new church plant.

Faith For Souls

I arrived just as the church was launched (and then attended the second village crusade). The man preaching the first night was Stephan Steindler. He was the director of the Bible school in Germany, where I had held *GCS (Great Commission Seminars)* for two consecutive years. He was a wonderful brother and an excellent minister.

While he preached, I sat on the little platform with other ministers. Over two hundred were packed into the building, sitting close to one another on the floor. Stephan had their attention. He preached a simple message about putting faith in God for healing. A beautiful little girl sat in her mother's lap right before me. I could feel their unwavering gaze on me. The pretty little girl smiled. But the mom looked with longing. She would touch her fingers into the ears of her daughter, then cup her hands in a pleading gesture towards me. She repeated this act over and over as Brother Steindler preached.

My Heart was Pulled

I knew what she wanted. My heart was pulled. Her longing was for her daughter to hear. And the mom wanted me to pray for her daughter.

Stephan finished. He gave his call. Stephan spoke of believers laying hands on the sick, and they would recover (Mark 16:18—I love the Greek, *'hands they shall lay, well shall they be'*). As people got up and came forward, he directed the ministers on the platform to go to them.

Without hesitation, I made my way to the mother and daughter. I put my fingers in the girl's ears and commanded, *'Come out, you deaf spirit! Be opened!'* I turned the girl around to face her mother. I snapped my fingers on one side of the girl's head by her ear, then the other. Each time, her head twitched in that direction. But momma's face said it all. She beamed, eyes wet with joy. God had opened the little girl's ears.

God confirmed His Word—He always does. I had not preached, yet He affirmed His Word with a beautiful healing of the little girl's ears. God is good.

Mangaluru (Mangalore) Crusade

This marked my sixth visit to India, this time for almost an entire month. I was the Campaign Manager setting up a crusade for Tommy O'Dell in Mangalore[5] along the west coast of India. He is Jerry's son and grandson of T.L. Osborn. There's much to say about this trip, but I'll concentrate on one short story.

Alongside the preparations for the crusade, which involved local and state officials, obtaining the grounds for the campaign, logistics, advertising, equipment, and promotion, we also dedicated time to street evangelism.

My interpreter this afternoon was a young 18-year-old brother. (I have not yet located my diary for this trip to give you his name.) While his understanding of English was good, he faced a problem. He stuttered. All his life, he struggled to speak. He tried to turn down my request to interpret. I told him not to worry. I believed God would help us. He would help him. We prayed and went out with the other teams.

People were brought to Christ. We gave personal invites to Tommy's crusade, but something else is what I remember most. This young man spoke plainly. He did a superb job interpreting the Gospel without stuttering.

This was on a Friday afternoon. On that Sunday, I spoke at a church. The young guy and his parents attended this church. The parents came to me ecstatic. With their son interpreting, they said, *'Since Friday afternoon when he went with you to preach the Gospel in the neighborhood, he has not stuttered once. He has never done that before!'*

God honored and confirmed His Word—He always does. This time, a believer, a soul winner, was the beneficiary. Praise God.

Cape Coast, Ghana

It was the year before the Mangalore, India, crusade. I went on this trip *to learn how* to set up a crusade. I was mentoring under a cheerful and experienced Ghanaian man, Brother James. This was my first trip traveling and working for Tommy O'Dell. (I spoke earlier of gazing from the plane window at the beautiful Sarah Desert flying from Paris to Ghana.)

Now, I was traveling by car up the coast from the capital, Accra, about 3 hours to Cape Coast, where Tommy would conduct a smaller crusade on the beach.

Again, so much to tell.

Sitting in the front passenger seat, my mind wandered. Just then, Brother James spoke. He reached his arm over the back seat, padded my chest, and enthusiastically said, *'Brother Bill! You are going to preach in the churches. People will be saved. They will be healed. Many will come to the crusade!'*

What If I Mess Things Up?!

I panicked! *'What if I mess everything up? If I pray for the sick and no one is healed, will no one come to Tommy's crusade because of me? What if . . . ?'* Have you ever been there? Ever worried that you might mess things up trying to do things for God?

Just then, I gazed up at the car right before us. The back of the vehicle had a scripture reference hand-painted on it. *Isaiah 41:10*. I hastily looked it up.

Fear thou not; for I am with thee be not dismayed; for I am thy God: I will strengthen thee: yea, I will help thee; yea, I will uphold thee with the right hand of my righteous.

Isaiah 41:10 KJV

God is so good and merciful! Hang in there—he will use us if we keep looking to Him and finally figure out how to get our eyes off ourselves!

Effective in the Churches

For the three and half weeks before Tommy's arrival, I spoke and exhorted the believers during church services, Bible studies, and leader's group. Believers were stirred up to come to the beach Crusade. One man paid for a taxi to carry a cripple to Tommy's meeting. He had to carry the man to put him down in the sand. During the prayer that night, the man stood and walked.

Praise God—the Lord honored this man's faith because he confidently proclaimed Christ. Similar to the paralytic carried by four and let down through the roof (Mark 2:1-12).

God confirms His Gospel, even for others, when we dare to trust Him.

I Preached a Bush Meeting

On one occasion, I was scheduled to preach at a *Bush Meeting*. Brother James explained that several churches were coming together to pray and seek God for the coming crusade. It would be held outdoors, out in the bush (amongst the forest trees in this coastal area). I was scheduled to speak for the morning meeting. The pick-up time was 8:00 a.m.

At 7:00 a.m., I was still pondering the topic for my sermon. I knew I needed to deliver what the Lord had given me. About then, the Spirit of the Lord came upon me. His Presence visited me gently yet unmistakably.

I laid back on the bed. Gentle waves of His Love and Presence ministered to my heart. I still had no notes for the meeting, but I knew He had it under control.

I glanced at my watch. *'Getting close. Still no word or direction* (for the meeting).' But I lay there, resting in His glory.

He Spoke Two Words

Then He spoke. Two words, but He avouched. The words *'I will'* resonated in my spirit. I understood.

The Lord expounded further as we drove, showing me how to begin.

Standing before hundreds of Ghanaian believers, I recounted the events that had taken place. I told them about the Holy Spirit coming upon me. I told them I had no word. Then He spoke, *'I will.'* My text was Mark 1:40-42 KJV (emphasis mine).

> *And there came a leper to him, beseeching him, and kneeling down to him, and saying unto him, 'If thou wilt, thou canst make me clean.'*
>
> *And Jesus, moved with compassion, put forth his hand, and touched him, and saith unto him, **'I will;'** be thou clean.'*
>
> *As soon as he had spoken, immediately the leprosy departed from him, and he was cleansed.*

I declared God desires you to undergo healing. *'I will heal you.'*

To the Africans, I Spoke About Slavery in America

I described to these African brothers the abolition of slavery in my nation. I spoke of two prominent leaders. President Abraham Lincoln announced the Emancipation Proclamation.

> *President Abraham Lincoln issued the Emancipation Proclamation on January 1, 1863, as the nation approached its third year of bloody civil war. The proclamation declared 'that all persons held as slaves' within the rebellious states 'are, and henceforward shall be free.*[6]

The Lord had directed me to compare receiving healing to slavery at the very seat of where the slave trade began. Just a few miles away lay the Cape Coast Castel,[7] the site where Africans brought enslaved people to sell to the white man. How could the Lord lead in this bold way? To teach. To free. Truth sets free.

We Must Stand in Our Healing

The Lord then directed me to speak of another man: Martin Luther King, Jr. King's words caused a seismic shift in our nation, leading to cultural change and equal rights for all races.

> *So powerful was the movement he inspired, that Congress enacted the Civil Rights Act in 1964, the same year King himself was honored with the Nobel Peace Prize.*[8]

I continued,

> *Both men lost their lives for the freeing of the black man in my country.*
> *But only when men seized their freedom did they start to exercise and embrace it.*

Jesus Christ gave His life for all men to be free from sin and to be healed in body. He says this morning, 'I will.' Just like to the leper, He says now to you, 'I will heal you—it is MY WILL. Now take it!'

Backs were healed. People with crippled conditions stood and jumped. God performed His Word.

God-Partnership

At the beginning of this chapter, I stated God confirms the Gospel. He confirms us when we preach the Gospel. This is crucial to understand for two reasons:

1. The pressure is on the Gospel—not on you.
2. God will confirm you—but only when you preach Him.

Everything revolves around the Gospel.

God confirmed the ministry of Jesus. *HE IS THE GOSPEL*. Salvation is in no other.

> *Neither is there salvation in any other: for* ***there is none other name*** *under heaven given among men, whereby we must be saved.*
>
> Acts 4:12 KJV (emphasis mine)

Jesus Relied upon the Father to Speak

Jesus relied on God the Father to confirm His message as He walked and ministered on earth as a man.

> *Let this mind be in you, which was also in Christ Jesus,*
>
> *who, being in the form of God, did not consider it robbery to be equal with God,*

> *but made Himself of no reputation, taking the form of a bondservant, and **coming in the likeness of men.***
>
> *And being **found in appearance as a man**, He humbled Himself and became obedient to the point of death, even the death of the cross.*
>
> *Therefore God also has highly exalted Him and **given Him the name which is above every name**,*
>
> *that at the name of Jesus every knee should bow, of those in heaven, and of those on earth, and of those under the earth,*
>
> *and that every tongue should confess that **Jesus Christ is Lord**, to the glory of God the Father.*
>
> Philippians 2:5-11 (emphasis mine)

> *For I have not spoken on My authority; but the Father who sent me gave me a command, what I should say and what I should speak.*
>
> *And I know that His command is everlasting life. **Therefore, what I speak, just as the Father has told Me, so I speak.***
>
> John 12:49-50 (emphasis mine)

Jesus, operating solely as a man, depended entirely on the Father. In what He spoke (His teaching) and in His actions (His ministry), Jesus based the validity of His whole life's work upon saying and doing as God the Father instructed him:

> *Do you not believe that I am in the Father, and the Father in Me? The words that I speak to you **I do not speak on My own authority; but the Father** who dwells in Me does the works.*
>
> *Believe Me that I am in the Father and the Father in Me, or else **believe Me for the sake of the works themselves**.*

> *Most assuredly, I say to you, he who believes in Me, **the works that I do he will do also**; and greater works than these he will do, because I go to My Father.*
>
> John 14:10-12 (emphasis mine)

Jesus Relied upon the Father to Heal

God *endorsed* the ministry of His Son through *miracles, wonders, and signs.*

> *Men of Israel, listen to this message: Jesus of Nazareth was **a man certified by God** to you by miracles, wonders, and signs, which God did among you through Him, as yourselves know.*
>
> Acts 2:22 BSB (emphasis mine)

I like that. *The Berean Study Bible* says that Jesus *was a man **certified by God**.*

The Young's Literal says *a man **approved** of God among you by might works.*

The Amplified Bible, Classic Edition, uses these phrases:

> *You men of Israel, listen to what I have to say: Jesus of Nazareth, a Man **accredited** and **pointed out** and **shown forth** and **commended** and **attested to** you **by God** by mighty works and [the power of performing] wonders and signs which God worked through Him [right] in your midst, as you yourselves know.*
>
> Acts 2:22 AMPC (emphasis mine)

- **accredited**
- **pointed out**
- **shown forth**

- ***commended***
- ***attested to***

God is in the business of *confirming the* ministry He endorses. And *He advocates the Gospel!* Preach the Gospel. As quoted from the Introduction of F.F. Bosworth's *Christ the Healer*:

> *Yet, deep within the hearts of sincere men there is a longing to rescue the Book of Acts from becoming nothing more than an historical record and to put it back in its proper place as a pattern for the modern church whereby God can continue to confirm His Word and give proof of the Resurrection of His Son in this day of universal unbelief.*[9]

The God-Partnership is with Christ

The Gospel and miracles have a divine partnership. Why? Because God always backs up His Word. Paul knew it. That is why he declared:

> *And I, brethren, when I came to you, did not come with excellence of speech or of wisdom declaring to you the testimony of God.*
>
> *For I determined not to know anything among you except **Jesus Christ and Him crucified** (the Gospel).*
>
> *I was with you in weakness, in fear, and in much trembling.*
>
> *And my speech and my preaching were not with persuasive words of human wisdom, but **in demonstration of the Spirit** and of **power that your faith should** not be in the wisdom of men **but in the power of God.***
>
> 1 Corinthians 2:1-5 (emphasis & parenthesis mine)

The scripture tells us:

> How **God anointed Jesus** of Nazareth **with the Holy Ghost and with power**: who went about **doing good**, and **healing all** that were oppressed of the devil; for God was with him.
>
> Acts 10:38 KJV (emphasis mine)

Jesus was the Word, and *the Word became flesh and dwelt among us* (John 1:1,14). The *Amplified* is so powerful here:

> IN THE beginning [before all-time] was the Word (Christ), and the Word was with God, and the Word was God Himself. [Isa. 9:6]
>
> And the Word (Christ) became flesh (human, incarnate) and tabernacled (fixed His tent in flesh, lived a while) among us; and we [actually] saw His glory (His honor, His majesty), such glory as an only begotten son receives from his father, full of grace (favor, loving-kindness) and truth. [Isa.40:5]
>
> John 1:1,14 AMPC

Let me tell you something: *Jesus is the same, yesterday, today, and forever.* (Hebrews 13:8) He has not grown weary, Jesus is not 'worn out,' and He is not about to retire! God still confirms *the GOSPEL* (Jesus *is* the Gospel) with *signs, wonders, and miracles*. Our job is simple: preach (share, declare) the Gospel. Preach Jesus. Expect God to *'show out'* (that is Southern vernacular for *show off!* God will show off, do mighty stuff!) Get this revelation:

> *If I present Jesus Christ and His saving grace to the lost and dying world around me, I will not be doing it alone. It pleases God. It's my calling. God, the Father, will endorse His Son if I declare Jesus Christ. He always has, and*

He still is today. That means I can expect God to perform signs, wonders, and miracles when I preach Christ.

God confirmed the ministry of Jesus. HE IS THE GOSPEL.

I want to propound these truths into your mind and heart. Remember:

1. The pressure is on the Gospel—not on you.
2. God will confirm you—but only when you preach Him.

Everything revolves around the Gospel. So, preach the Gospel. Expect God to show up. He will.

Miracles on the Beach!

When Tommy O'Dell arrived, the miracle rally began. I saw wonders! A woman came up to testify. She brought her nine-year-old daughter and X-rays in her hand. The daughter had been born without most of her ribcage, so she was left without the ability to support herself. She could not stand or walk. The girl stood as the mother patted her daughter's chest. The X-rays displayed the absence of most of her ribs in her boyish frame. Now, she had a complete, healthy set!

[Recently, I corresponded with Elizabeth, Tommy's wife. We spoke about this miracle. And Elizabeth told me, *'And we still have those ex-rays!'*]

I witnessed two completely blind people receive sight. One was an older man, and one was a young boy. Both had that typical white film over the iris of the eye. Before us, the cloudy film disappeared, and they each could grab Tommy's nose!

Many came to Christ—an incredible sight. God validated the message of the Gospel with wonders.

Faith For Souls

Do You Want to Play Scrabble?

As we drove back to our motel, sitting next to Tommy, I supposed he would want to go back and pray. Undoubtedly, that is what you must do after a night like this. But Tommy turned to me and asked, *'Do you want to play Scrabble?'* Incredible! Tommy is just a guy doing the Lord's work. He's remarkably natural, entertaining, and genuinely authentic.

Oh, and he clobbered everyone playing Scrabble!

The next night, we played Bible Trivia. I thought I could win—people from my church would call me *Bible man*. Nope—he wiped us all out again!

What is so amazing was that as a teen, Tommy had OD'd on drugs. His friends had pulled his limp body out of the car and dragged it behind an abandoned house on that snowy night in Tulsa. They just knew he was dead. Tommy tells the story of God saving him, healing him, and even restoring his drug-crazed mind. He says, *'He* (the Lord) *made me smarter than before!'*

Get This Revelation

We need to get it into our spirits how extremely serious God is about the lost coming to Christ that if we do our part, He will absolutely do His. That might be unusual conversions of those we thought would never come to Christ becoming saved. Healings could be involved. Deliverances. Signs. Wonders. Whatever He wants. But I can guarantee that we are not in this fight alone- this fight for the souls of men. We are doing this with Him. *Get this revelation.*

The Apostles Had This Revelation

Peter and John had this revelation at the Gate called Beautiful. What did Peter say to the cripple (of over forty years)? *'Silver and gold have I none; but **such as I have** give I thee: In the name of Jesus Christ of Nazareth rise up and walk.'* Acts 3:6 (emphasis mine). You know the story. He walked! He stood and entered the temple, *walking, leaping, and praising God.*

When the people wondered, Peter was quick to clarify:

*So when Peter saw it, he responded to the people: 'Men of Israel, why do you marvel at this? Or **why look so intently at us**, as though by our own power or godliness we had made this man walk?*

*The God of Abraham, Isaac, and Jacob, **the God of our fathers, glorified His Servant Jesus**, whom you delivered up and denied in the presence of Pilate, when he was determined to let Him go.'*

Acts 3:12-13 (emphasis mine)

When John and Peter were arrested and questioned by the priests, the captain of the temple, and the Sadducees, they stood their ground. They were asked, *'By what power, or by what name, have you done this?'* (Acts 4:7) Peter squared off and responded:

Then Peter, filled with the Holy Spirit, said to them, 'Rulers of the people and elders of Israel:

If we this day are judged for a good deed done to a helpless man, by what means he has been made well,

let it be known to you all, and to all the people of Israel, that by the name of Jesus Christ of Nazareth, whom you crucified, whom God raised from the dead, by Him this man stands here before you whole.'

Acts 4:8-10

Peter capped it with:

> Neither is there salvation in any other: for **there is none other name under heaven** given among men, **whereby we must be saved**.
>
> Acts 4:12 (emphasis mine)

This Revelation Empowers

Notice the next verse. These religious men who adamantly opposed the Gospel saw the Gospel. They saw it on Peter and John.

> Now when they saw **the boldness of Peter and John**, and perceived that they were uneducated and untrained men, they marveled. And **they realized** that **they had been with Jesus**.
>
> Acts 4:13 (emphasis mine)

That is what we want. We want others to see our boldness and perceive that we have been with Jesus. And that *HE IS ALIVE!*

He Asked Me 'Why Did You Change?'

Just this afternoon, a man asked me, *'How and why did you change from being an atheist to becoming a Christian?'*

After a medical appointment, I asked the man who had assisted my wife and me for over an hour a question. *'I want to ask you* (calling him by name), *have you asked Jesus to be your Lord and Savior?'* He responded, *'No. And I prefer not to talk about religion. It is a private matter.'* I nodded; I understood. And made a final statement, *'I ask that because I was once an atheist.'*

This kind man then asked me *how that could happen*. Intently, he listened as I passionately shared my story of how I came to know God was real (read a fuller account in Chapter 12 *I Do Not Believe in Atheists*). I then gave him one of my *The BULLET* tracts.[10] He thanked me and said, *'I will read this.'*

Knowing God will show up to help you share His Gospel empowers. It empowers you.

Non-Apostles Had This Revelation

Some churches and denominations today try to argue that miracles and healings have passed away with the ministry of Jesus and of the Apostles (Jesus' twelve selected disciples). Well, the problem with that is that it is not biblical. Steven, *a man full of faith and the Holy Spirit*, did miracles. He was only a deacon, certainly not one of the twelve. (Acts 6:5)

And Stephen, full of faith and power, did great wonders and signs among the people.

This was *just a regular guy* whose job was to pass out food to the widows who caught heat because he was so full of God. They arrested a waiter.

And they were not able to resist the wisdom and the Spirit by which he spoke.
And all who sat in the council, looking steadfastly at him, saw his face as the face of an angel.

Acts 6:8,10, 15:3

He was just a regular guy doing a mundane job, full of faith and the glory of God, preaching and living Jesus. God endorsed his efforts. He will champion yours. Expect Him to.

Philip Too

Philip was a fellow *waiter on tables*. Persecution happened in Jerusalem, and believers scattered. So, what did Philip do? He went to a neighboring town and started preaching Jesus! And look what happened—God showed up! Remember, preach yourself, no divine intervention. Preach the living Son of God, and *Papa God will be proud*. He will come to your meeting! The Lord did to Philip's! He will go to yours!

> *Then Philip went down to the city of Samaria and* **preached Christ to them.**
>
> *And the multitudes with one accord heeded the things spoken by Philip,* **hearing and seeing the miracles** *which he did.*
>
> *For unclean spirits, crying with a loud voice, came out of many who were possessed; and many who were paralyzed, and lame were healed.*
>
> *And there was great joy in that city.*
>
> Acts 8:5-8 (emphasis mine)

Indeed, I understand they heard what Philip preached, but how did they *see* them? The next phrase explains and answers this question. They were *hearing and seeing the miracles*.

Are you getting this? If you preach Jesus, God the Father will throw a party to honor His Son. And He will attend your party!

And What about Ananias?

Now, this is one gutsy and obedient man. Ananias was given clear direction in a vision to go and pray for *Saul of Tarsus: for, behold, he prayeth* (Acts 9:11). Ananias questions the Lord. Are you sure? *I have heard of this man.* Yeah, he kills Christians, and Ananias is one. But God insisted, and Ananias persisted. He obeyed.

> *And Ananias went his way and entered the house; and **laying his hands on him** he said, 'Brother Saul, the Lord Jesus, who appeared to you on the road as you came, has sent me that you may **receive your sight** and **be filled with the Holy Spirit**,' (also a wonder!).*
>
> *Immediately **there fell from his eyes** something like scales, and **he received his sight** at once; and he arose and was baptized.*
>
> Acts 9:17-18 (emphasis & parenthesis mine)

Ananias risked his life and obeyed God to get a man healed and filled with the Holy Ghost. That man would affect the Western world with his preaching and the entire globe through his writings—the Apostle Paul.

Ananias got it. God confirms His Word. Preach His Word. Expect Him to confirm.

We Must Have This Revelation

This doctrine that God is retired and no longer in the healing and miracle business is errant. The process of growing in this revelation and confidence that Jesus will confirm His Gospel is fine. I had to. We are constantly evolving.

I Did Not Know She was a Lightie

Before I share this last story (of this chapter), let me first talk about race. We all have one. Or maybe several mixed. Upon asking my dad about our ancestry, he would say, *'We are English, Dutch, German, and Great Dane.'* Thanks, Dad! (He was 6 foot 5 inches tall.) On my mother's side, I am Scottish-Irish. Well, this combination produced a red-headed, freckled kid.

While street witnessing, I've had odd occurrences on at least three continents. Deep in conversations, I did not notice at first. But then I felt it—a child was petting my hairy arm! Scots can grow hair! Once, my niece jokingly referred to my freckled arms as 'hairy salami arms.'

God loves the diverse way in which he has made each of us. *We are precious in His sight.*

The Ladies and I Sat on The Patio

Five ladies and I sat in a row outside on the patio in the courtyard of this home. For three weeks before Tommy's arrival, I was hospitably housed by a businesswoman in Cape Coast, Ghana. The woman on the far end was this woman's mother. The woman closest to me was a friend, a nurse, who had stopped by for a visit.

As we visited (the businesswoman interpreting the gist of the conversation), the subject came to her mother's eyesight. She was suffering from glaucoma, and her sight was feeble. I, of course, invited her to attend Tommy's beach crusade (which was to begin in two days). She declined, stating that she lived in another town and *needed to get home to her elderly husband.*

Why Don't You Pray for Me?

Then, according to her daughter's interpretation, she said, *'Why don't you pray for me?'*

Gulp! Now, I was on the spot. But we held hands and prayed. Believing in God's healing, I did my best with the faith I had. (I trusted that others in the group were releasing their faith.) When we said the *Amen*, the mother looked down in my direction. She spoke to her daughter, who interpreted for my benefit, *'Oh, I did not know* (naming the nurse sitting next to me) *was a lightie.'* Among those in the Black community, even as a white guy, I have heard references to how light or dark is a black person's skin. The nurse had a fair complexion, and now the mother could see she did! God had cleared her vision! Praise God!

Get the revelation—God will confirm His Word, especially when reaching the lost!

This is the beautiful little deaf girl. God lovingly opened her ears that day. He is so good.

In this light, evangelism was not interpreted as a human undertaking, but as a divine project which had been going on from the beginning and would continue until God's purpose was fulfilled. It was altogether the Spirit's work. All the disciples were asked to do was to let the Spirit have complete charge of their lives.[1]

—**Robert E. Coleman**

Do you not say, 'There are still four months and then comes the harvest?' Behold, I say to you, lift up your eyes and look at the fields, for they are already white for harvest!

—**John 4:35**

CHAPTER 15

It Is Hard Here

Oh, how I have been waiting to write this chapter! It's as if I've found the cure for cancer. The entire pack of lies the devil has been feeding the Body of Christ about how and why we cannot reach the world, for Christ has been exposed. He is a liar!

When you get this, you will utterly be transformed as you digest and assimilate the truth. The harvest is ripe! People (the fruit on the tree) are ready to fall into the Kingdom of God. Oh, get this, please!

Let us begin with the Word of God, as, of course, we must.

Jesus Said the Harvest Is Ripe

> *Do you not say, 'There are still four months and then comes the harvest?'* **Behold, I say to you, lift up your eyes and look at the fields**, *for they* **are already white for harvest**!
>
> *And he who reaps receives wages, and gathers fruit for eternal life, that both he who sows and he who reaps may rejoice together.*
>
> *For in this the saying is true: 'One sows and another reaps.'*

> **I sent you to reap** that for which that for **which you have not labored**; others have labored, and **you have entered into their labors.**
>
> John 4:35-38 (emphasis mine)

The setting is Samaria. Jesus has just brought the *Samaritan woman* to Himself (she is now a child of God). She has gone back into the city and is telling everyone:

> *Come, see a man, which told me all things that ever I did: is not this the Christ?*
>
> John 4:29 KJV

[This is *her story*. She suffered from rejection and was ostracized. Now she was wonderfully accepted!]

This woman is lit! She has had an incredible weight lifted off her heart. This Samaritan woman has found *The One*, and she knows it. She is telling everyone! Let me say that again, *she is telling everyone!*

When we get this like she got it, we will tell everyone.

The Internet Was Down

I just got off the phone with our internet provider because of an area outage. As is customary, the gal (whose nickname is *May*—like was my mother's middle name) asks, *'Is there anything else I can help you with?'* In response, I said yes. I then asked her,

Have you ever accepted Jesus as your Lord and Savior?

Her response, with a nervous chuckle, was, *Well, yeah.*

It Is Hard Here

I continued. *The reason I asked is because I used to be an atheist. [My story—what is yours?] Someone challenged me to ask if 'God was real.' I was nervous but intrigued. I told them, 'Yes.'*

That night or a few nights later, I was lying in bed and remembered the challenge. Getting out of my bed, I kneeled on the wood floor of my bedroom. I uttered the Lord's Prayer (Matthew 6:9-13), uncertain of the presence of anyone to hear it. I had recited this at church before, but it was more like a dirge. This time, Bill Burgess was 'trying' to communicate—if there was a God listening.

When I spoke, God came in! I did not see a light or hear anything, but I knew His Presence had entered my room. I knew He was real.

I then told May that I did not know how to make Jesus my Lord yet (that occurred 1 ½ years later), *'but I knew God was real!'*

She Was Ecstatic, Happy, and Profoundly Touched

Remember that I am on a company-recorded line talking to the representative. She was captured. This is the Holy Ghost. I then asked her,

Have you ever heard of 'The CHOSEN?' She told me, 'No, I have not.'

I described it to her as a crowd-funded TV series about Jesus. The narrative details a potential backstory for Mary Magdalene and the moment she encounters Jesus in the Bible. It does this for Peter and others. It is amazing. My wife and I have watched Seasons 1 and 2 three times. We can't wait for Season 3, which is coming out soon.

This has led many to return to Jesus, read the Bible, or find solace if the church hurt them. It is amazing, and it is a free app on your phone.

May told me she would download and watch it. She was ecstatic, happy, and profoundly touched, and she thanked me.

And this was a call with the internet company. The world is open and waiting . . .

JESUS Said, the Harvest Is Ripe

But what are you and I saying? It is *'hard here,' 'people don't want to hear about God today,' 'the world is so dark today—if only people would be open.'* But Jesus says,

> *Do you not say, 'There are still four months and then comes the harvest?'* **Behold, I say to you, lift up your eyes and look** at **the fields**, *for they* **are already white for harvest***!*
>
> John 4:35 (emphasis mine)

This reminds me of a Sunday School class I attended in the College and Careers class. The speakers, a woman and a man, taught about *'Hearing the Voice of God.'* They cited things we have all said, *'I wish I knew what God wanted me to do,' 'I wish I could hear His voice,' 'I wish I were like (some minister) and I could hear the voice of God like they could.'* Then the lady spoke words I have never forgotten:

Somebody is mistaken. Is God lying, or is it you? We know it **cannot** *be God.*

Well, I reiterate those words to you here. We say it *'is hard; people don't want to hear the Gospel. It is hard to witness. We cannot penetrate the hard hearts today. It is so dark.'*

Jesus says, **lift up your eyes and look** at **the fields**, for they **are already white for harvest!**

It Is Hard Here

Somebody is lying, who? God? Or is it us? The Lord Jesus, who poured out His life for us, could He be mistaken?

I do not think so.

South Carolina Pastor

It was Saturday afternoon. The pastor had picked me up from the airport, and we drove to his church. The first service for the *GCS (Great Commission Seminar)* was tonight.

I did something I never did—and you should not do as a guest minister. I preached to and at the pastor for the entire drive, over one hour. I shared testimonies and shared my revelation of *Faith for Souls*. The *'preach just came on me.'* (You preachers will understand.) He listened.

The crew that night was the pastor's *Helps Ministry* workers—Sunday School teachers, ushers, greeters, etc. I sensed they were there because it was expected of them. In all honesty, the crowd was hard, including the pastor.

Right after this service, we conducted our first outreach. The pastor and I partnered together. Our first stop was at a house directly opposite the church. The pastor visited an older member who could not attend recent services because of illness.

This Street Is Hard

He and I then walked down the street. As we walked, he turned to me and said, *'It is hard here. This street is hard.'* Keep in mind, this is the street where his church is. I said nothing.

We walked a block or two and then came to a house where a couple sat in their car in the driveway. The woman was wearing medical smocks. On this cool night, the windows were about halfway down.

I greeted them and shared the Gospel with them. Both the man and the woman prayed with us to receive Christ. They remained in their car as we leaned over and prayed through the cracked window.

You Can Go Inside and Talk with Our Sons

The woman then offered, *'You can go inside. Our* (teenage) *sons are inside.'* She was leading us to share the Gospel with her own kids. (Maybe they were sitting in their car in the dark because their teenagers were inside the house.)

Upon knocking and entering, we discovered two additional boys inside with their sons. Maybe their cousins. The pastor and I shared the Gospel with the teens. They all received Christ and prayed with us to make Jesus their Lord and Savior.

The time had come to make our way back. The pastor and I walked toward his church.

But then I will never forget what happened next. As we walked, the pastor turned toward me and said, *'Maybe this street is not so hard after all.'*

It Is All about How You See It

I do not intend to oversimplify, but it all depends on your perspective. If you perceive it as difficult, it will be. If you see it (the neighborhood community) as ripe, and they are waiting to receive the Gospel, they are.

Perception is everything.

Again, I recall a quote by Charles Capps[2] that resonates still,

It Is Hard Here

The man (person) who says, 'He can,' and the man who says, 'He can't,' are both right.

How do you see it? What are you saying? Do you agree with Jesus—or with your natural senses, experiences, or feelings? Are you listening to church statistics about *trends today*? What about the news reports about *decreased church attendance and less interest in religion*? Who wants religion anyway? What people *need* is Jesus!

Who is the authority in your life? Is it Jesus? Is it the Word of God? Or is it something else? Take **Jesus at His Word** if you want to see the **results of Jesus** in your life!

Hong Kong

This was my second trip to India. The route took me through Hong Kong. I was traveling by myself. It was a unique trip—I had no contacts in India but a dinner date in Bombay. Initially, I had been scheduled to speak at a youth conference in India, but about three days before my departure, the event had been canceled because of some violent opposition. I had my tickets and fire in my belly. I was going anyway.

Bombay (Mumbi)

Soon after I delivered a sermon at a church in New Jersey, a woman from India who was a member of that church came up to me in excitement. She asked, *'Where are you going? What part of India are you traveling to?'* I responded, *'I'm going to Bombay (now called Mumbi).'* In exuberance, she exclaimed, *'I knew it! I knew it!'*

She then told me she had been praying and praying for someone to share the Gospel with her sister in Bombay. Traveling almost 10,000

Faith For Souls

miles around the world, my only confirmed ministry event ended up being a dinner date with this lady's sister and her husband.

I met with this wealthy couple three times, twice in their home and once for lunch at the *Polo Club of Bombay (Mumbi)*. With each re-invitation, I told them, *'You know I am going to share the Gospel of Christ with you again.'* They said, *'We know.'*

I saw inroads, especially with the husband, that I believe eventually affected his wife.

[Two nights before I left for this trip to India, I met another Rhema Bible school graduate who had worked with indigenous churches in and around Bombay. I brought the contact information he had given me—though no one knew I was coming. God opened doors with these wonderful brothers. Indian churches were raising leaders, building churches, and reaping souls—especially with the young up-and-coming middle class, without the usual Western sponsorship.]

Bibles to China

Of all the things you dream to do in your life, for me, one of those was to get to bring Bibles into China. Passing through Hong Kong was my chance. I had heard of a church ministry that organized smuggling Bibles into the communist giant. I had planned to do so while in transit to India with this ministry.

Carrying Bibles, I would travel with some men from the *Full Gospel Businessmen's Association*[3] from Hong Kong. I traveled with their leadership team (including the president, vice president, secretary, and treasurer) and three men's wives.

It Is Hard Here

Together, we took a hovercraft[4] up Sham Chun River[5] up to Shenzhen.[6] We each had a backpack, a small suitcase, or a briefcase. Each carried a selection of Bibles and other study aids. Others in our group and I were stopped for inspection when we went through customs. They took most of the Bibles but left me with one copy of each (type of book). Not an immense success, but something.

You Know, It Is Hard in Hong Kong

While we were gliding across the bay in the hovercraft, one of the Full Gospel Businessmen told me those words I had heard before. He said, *'You know it is hard here. It is hard to win people to Christ in Hong Kong.'*

Once we dropped off the Bibles, this group of entrepreneurs (with me tagging along) headed to a beautiful, high-end hotel in Shenzhen. The businessmen had an appointment with a Chinese attorney. They were preparing for a business conference they were sponsoring in this hotel soon. It presented a business opportunity, but for my fellow brothers and sisters in Christ, it offered a chance to influence Chinese businesspeople for Christ.

Completing that meeting, our group of eight went into the ballroom where the conference would occur. The room was grand, with ceilings towering two stories high and adorned with exquisite French décor. Magnificent.

We gathered near the 8-foot-tall stage as a group, held hands, and prayed. We prayed for the coming event that it might open up opportunities for the Gospel with the Chinese.

I Watched and Prayed

I am a *watch-and-pray* type of guy. As we prayed, I noticed the hotel staff in the room. As we finished, I promptly walked toward the event coordinator. I addressed him:

Sir, do you know Jesus as your Lord and Savior? Have you ever been Born Again?

His response was surprising (we were conversing in English). He said, *'I have been wondering about that. I have watched broadcast TV programs from the US that have talked about being Born Again.'* By now, some of my Hong Kong brothers had gathered. I instructed them to pray with the man.

They laid hands, and all prayed for him. They prayed for God's blessing upon him.

I asked, *'Did you lead him in a prayer to receive Christ?'* One said, *'Well, no.'* I told him, *'Do it!'* They did.

All the Hotel Staff in the Ballroom Accepted Christ

While they prayed, I saw that across the large hall, near the far wall, were various wait staff and hotel workers. I waved my arm and motioned for them to join us. They swiftly responded.

I paired up with a waiter, but he could not understand enough English. I asked one of our group to interpret. He accepted Christ and was Born Again. The rest of our Christian businessmen and women followed suit, praying with each staff member. God was blessing us with a harvest.

It Is Hard Here

Friends Store

Afterward, the wives of these Christian businessmen wanted to stop at a particular department store. The name of the large department store had large neon letters above it in English. It read, *Friends Store*. My party told me that the CCP (Chinese Communist Party) had a unique currency of Yen just for foreigners to spend in stores like this. This gave a positive impression to outsiders about the state of their nation. [China has increased by leaps and bounds over the ensuing decades and has become an impressive industrial and economic magnet.]

The ladies enjoyed themselves. The men leisurely strolled along. I found a clerk behind one of the many counters and asked, 'Are you Born Again?' These clerks spoke no English, so I compelled my businessmen friends to interpret. Two clerks received Christ while the ladies shopped.

Through the day's events, I missed my contact to get back to Hong Kong. The Full Gospel Businessman treasurer was very gracious and said I could share a room with him and then return tomorrow. I gladly accepted.

Dinner Entertainment

I was also invited to dinner with the party. We had a wonderful, authentic Chinese-style meal. In the center of the large round table was a huge lazy-Susan (a turntable). Wait staff brought a plethora of exotic Chinese fare. We each had our bowl of rice. They instructed me to reach with my chopsticks, take something from one dish, and eat it over my rice bowl.

Now, the men's wives were having much fun with me. They insisted I try every item, and then they would tell me what I had eaten.

One such item was full of small bones. It was fried until crispy and smothered in a rich sauce. But with each bite, it fell apart in my mouth. I removed one small bone after another. Finally, I completed the task and asked, *'Okay, what is it?'* To this, the women laughed, especially the instigator of this torment. Laughing, she said, *'No, you guess.'* I tried to resist. She insisted. I did not want to guess because of what I thought I had eaten. Still laughing, she pried a response from my lips. I said, *'A monkey's hand. I think I ate a monkey's hand.'*

The women squealed! The men were laughing, too. Then my tormentor declared, *'It is not a monkey's hand. It is a chicken's foot* (of course)*!'* I ate a chicken foot *for Christ*!

The Security Guard Accepted Christ

Leaving the meal, we headed to the hotel. We came to a traffic light. While waiting, I noticed a small-framed man in a security uniform. He was the security guard who worked at that intersection. I strode over and asked, *'Do you know Jesus as Lord and Savior? Are you Born Again?'* He spoke no English, and of course, I knew no Chinese. By now, my companions were learning my ways, and one of the men came to my rescue. This man prayed and gave his heart to Jesus in a few moments.

Others from our group spoke to other people.

A police officer came up to us. He told us we could not do this here. We paused briefly. He left. Then we continued. Several more were born again.

My new friends got me on the train the next day, traveling back to Hong Kong. I sat looking out the train window, noticing how clean and organized everything I saw was along the way, unlike many parts of US cities. I also had deep joy in my heart thinking of these conversions. And this was Communist China. *It was not hard here.*

It Is Hard Here

Returning from India

Sixteen days later, I was again in Hong Kong. I had a one-night layover before flying back to San Francisco for a quick stop to see my mother and then continuing to Oklahoma.

From the hotel, I telephoned the Full Gospel Businessmen treasurer. I thanked him again for sharing his room with me and for how much I enjoyed my time with their group.

My Hong Kong brother then shared:

After you left, we led five more to Christ, including two Hong Kong taxicab drivers. Hong Kong is not so hard after all.

What delight—they got it! Perception is everything.

Did You Sense the Darkness, Brother?

Flying into more than one U.S. city, I have been greeted by people from a church who had agreed to provide transportation and asked this question. More than once, I have heard, *'Oh Brother, did you sense the darkness as you flew into* (naming the airport of their city)*?'*

My response: *'How wonderful! There are many lost sinners here. We will have a wonderful harvest of souls. Even a small light becomes powerful in great darkness.'*

What is your view? To whom are you listening? Who do you believe?

Norwegian Missionary in Nepal

I was in Katmandu, Nepal. Along with a couple from my church, we taught and preached at missionary Deborah Strong's short-term intense

Pastor's School.[6] She was helping to train these men of God who worked in the remote areas of the Himalayas.

One afternoon, our party was joined by a veteran missionary from Norway. He was in his 80s and retired, but here he was. I listened. This dear brother made a statement in conversation that gripped my heart. He said,

> *'Yah, since 1863* (approximate date) *ve, haave had a pray-err meeting every Tursday, praying for Nepal.'* (Excuse my poor attempt to capture his Norwegian accent.)

I was struck. Five years ago, while in India for the first time, I discovered Nepal was a Gospel-resistant monarchy. I prayed, wept, and sought God. Here I was, teaching and preaching. One day, we did an outreach, passing out tracts at a central park in Katmandu. I was overcome as brown hands grabbed the tracts out of my hands before I could even step away from the van.

I knew my prayer had played a part. But here, this dear, seasoned Norwegian man of God said that believers from his community in Norway had been praying for Nepal for 150 years!

Do you see it? Jesus said:

> **I sent you to reap** that for which that for **which you have not labored**; *others have labored, and* **you have entered into their labors**.
>
> John 4:38 (emphasis mine)

I was enjoying reaping because of Norwegian brethren who had prayed a hundred years before I even *thought about* being born! God

It Is Hard Here

is bringing in *HIS HARVEST*! Believe it! Become a part of it. Believe the words of Jesus, for **He said**:

> *Do you not say, 'There are still four months and then comes the harvest?'* **Behold, I say to you, lift up your eyes and look** *at* **the fields**, *for they* **are already white for harvest***!*
>
> John 4:35 (emphasis mine)

Who Are You Going to Believe?

Now, realize that no one can do something exactly the way someone else does it and retain any kind of spontaneity or relaxation. We must trust the Holy Spirit to lead us and not try to create or follow a recipe of how people must witness.[1]

—**Nellie Pickard**

But I promise you this—the Holy Spirit will come upon you, and you will be seized with power. You will be my messengers to Jerusalem, throughout Judea, the distant provinces—even to the remotest places on earth!

—**Acts 1:8 TPT**

CHAPTER 16

Creativity of the Creator

*T*he teams headed out. Pastor Larry did not have a partner but did not need one.

Doing the *GCS (Great Commission Seminar)* was for his church, not for him. The pastor was already lit—a fantastic soul winner.

Pastor Larry knocked on the door. A young man, only about 21 years old, opened the door. He had no shirt and did not have a job. The guy was living with his girlfriend, who was pregnant with his second kid—nothing but attitude.

> This young guy addressed Pastor Larry. *'Yeah, what do you want?'*
>
> With a big smile, the pastor announced, *'Today's your **lucky day**!'*
>
> *'Yeah, why is that?'*
>
> Pastor Larry continued, *'Because **you're going to get saved**!'*
>
> *'Oh yeah, is that right?'*
>
> With exuberant confidence and even more joy, Pastor said, *'That's right!'*

You know he did! Later that afternoon, I returned to visit this guy and his girlfriend with Pastor Larry. We carried them a couple of bags of groceries (since the guy did not work). The guy still had his shirt off. When I met him, this young man told me: *'I don't like preachers. But I like this one!'*

What Happened?

What happened? This man, Pastor Larry, was just himself. I have told this testimony, describing Brother Larry, and have said, *'Pastor Larry is like Santa Claus* (without the belly and the white beard), *full of joy, jolly, and bringing gifts.'* He is a happy soul who loves Jesus. His desire was for others to know Him, too. Beautiful.

The Holy Spirit Upon

Let's look at our wonderful text. Look at what Jesus said and what He did not say.

> But I promise you this—**the Holy Spirit will come upon you, and you will be seized with power**. You will be my messengers to Jerusalem, throughout Judea, the distant provinces—even to the remotest places on earth!
>
> Acts 1:8 TPT (emphasis mine)

What Jesus promised was that we would have the Holy Spirit. In John's Gospel, Jesus said:

> If you love Me, keep My commandments.
> And I will pray the Father, and He will give you another Helper, that He may abide with you forever.
>
> John 14:15-16

Creativity of the Creator

Another in Greek is *allos*, which means another *of the same kind*. Jesus promises He will send the Holy Spirit to be with us and come upon us in a manner that mirrors Himself. He has given *Himself* to us in the Person of the Holy Spirit.

Liberty to Be Yourself in Christ

In our text, Jesus promised the disciples (us) that *'the Holy Spirit will come upon you.'* And when He does, each disciple will be **seized with power**. It's the Dunamis, or miracle-working power of God, manifesting in our lives. The Holy Spirit brings with Him *the miraculous power, might, and strength of God.*[2] This produces liberty—liberty, and freedom to flow with God to be a living, beautiful witness for Christ.

But Not a Copy of Someone Else

Jesus never said that when the Holy Spirit comes upon us, we will become duplicates of Pastor Larry. (Or William Burgess or anyone else.) God does not need you to be, or want you to become, someone you are not. He wants to free you to be *who you are*, but in Christ!

You can be you and still lead many dear souls to Christ. You may have a bold, vibrant personality. Or you may be soft-spoken, maybe even introverted, and still become effective at leading people to Jesus.

Evangelism Explosion

As a very young believer, I was invited to a church visitation program at my Presbyterian Church. Their program was called Evangelism Explosion,[3] founded by Dr. James Kennedy.[4] That everyday people could lead others to Jesus had a sound effect on me.

Years later, when the Lord led me to begin a church, I did not want to do so by immigration from other churches, but by the New Birth of people led to Christ. We used EE (Evangelism Explosion). It is a non-confrontational yet clear, logical, biblical approach to sharing the Gospel. And the crowning jewel of the program is that it is built upon on-the-job training.

On-the-Job Training

As a pastor, I trained two people, a man and a woman. We covered the methods and also did weekly visits. These two saw me lead people to Christ. As they grew, they each became trainers.[5] The three of us prayerfully selected and invited others to become trained using the same method. After each evangelism session, we would all gather at the church to share testimonies, discuss challenges, and encourage one another.

The EE program at my church progressed to offer training sessions in both the morning and evening. Many were won to Christ. However, what was more valuable was that believers were trained to reproduce as Christians and win others.

Even the Quiet Became Trainers

During our training, I observed that the best trainers were not always the most confident and personable individuals—the complete opposite. Witnessing quiet believers transform into successful soul winners, and trainers was a delightful experience. Often, these were very soft, gentlewomen—women who had a hunger to be used by the Lord to bring souls to Christ.

Creativity of the Creator

Jesus promised: *the Holy Spirit will come upon you, and you will be seized with power. You will be my messengers.* He didn't say you must change who God created you to be. The Spirit upon *you*.

Skateboarders

I recently heard this story while attending a Life Group[6] at West Coast Life Church in Southern California. Our Pastors are wonderful. Pastors RayGene and Beth Wilson. Pastor Ray lights up my heart, preaching each Sunday. Pastor Beth brings the church together, connecting hearts with love. The story I heard was of Pastor Beth and some skateboarders.

After a church prayer meeting for the coming election, I stopped Pastor Beth and asked to hear the story firsthand.

She related:

I saw four young people skateboarding in the parking lot near Vonn's Grocery store. I felt the Lord speak to my heart to give them each $20 and tell them how much the Lord loves them. When I went to the ATM, I was impressed to get five $20s. Upon returning to the skaters, their number had increased to five.

I handed each young person a twenty and told them that the Lord had impressed upon my heart to do so and to let them know how precious and dear each of them is to Jesus.

The guy with the most brutal attitude cried. He told of how his dad was on heroin. A girl skater shared of how she had been raped. (Tears must have moistened Pastor Beth's eyes.)

She then prayed for them for God's love, protection, and mercy. What love! Jesus, through my pastor, Pastor Beth, is doing what she does remarkably well—loving people like Jesus does.

Where's the Party?

We were out in a residential area in a town in Pennsylvania doing outreach with a local church. My partner was a man in his twenties, and I was in my thirties. It approached 4:00 p.m. I knocked on the door, and a young lady, 17 years old, answered. I said: *Where's the Party?*

This conservative young lady, a student at a Catholic high school, looked shocked. I then continued,

> *No, we are just kidding. We are here to talk to you about Jesus. I want to ask you, are you Born Again?*
>
> She responded that *my friends at school and I had been discussing that. What is it to be Born Again? We have been talking about whether we would go to heaven.*
>
> With grace, I explained the Gospel and the significance of Jesus' words.
>
> *You must be Born Again.* I read the passage in John chapter 3 as Jesus spoke with Nicodemus. This precious girl prayed with us to receive Christ.

Now, this was not my standard approach. I do not think I have used it before or since. But what was going on? My brother and I were just rejoicing. We were glad to be out sharing the Gospel. I just had *joy in my belly.* Humor and joy came out of my mouth. God used it, and she was saved.

A method you should try—no. Be exuding joy—indeed. Remember, this is Good News!

Seattle, Washington

Up in the Northwest, I had traveled to conduct another *GCS (Great Commission Seminar)*. Before the evening meeting, the church pastor and I walked into an outdoor mall to share the Gospel.

Approaching us was a trio, a young teenage couple holding hands and a woman (who turned out to be the boy's mother). I approached the young love birds and said, *'Are you two engaged?'* They said they were not. I continued,

> *The key to a successful relationship, especially in marriage, is having Jesus Christ at the center.*

At this, the young man's mother spoke. *They* (her son and the young lady) *would like to get married, but my agreement with my son is that she* (the young lady) *must be Born Again. She* (the mom called the girl's name) *is Mormon.*

She Could Not Confess Jesus as Lord

We shared the Gospel. The young lady told us she wanted to become Born Again. But something unusual occurred, unusual to me. When we began praying together, the young girl couldn't utter, *'Jesus is Lord.'* The pastor took the lead. He had dealt with leading Mormons to Christ before. The pastor knew he was dealing with a spirit. He dealt with that spirit. The young woman appeared to be stunned. Then, she was peaceful and could pray. She confessed Jesus as her Lord and was saved.

> *That if you confess with your mouth, 'Jesus is Lord,' and believe in your heart that God raised Him from the dead, you will be saved.*

For with your heart you believe and are justified, and with your mouth you confess and are saved.

Romans 10:9-10 BSB

Consider What Is Taking Place Here

Now consider what has taken place. I greeted a young (teenage) couple with, *'Are you two engaged?'* How bizarre. But as you observe the entire exchange, the Spirit of God must have led me to do so. When we become free of being so self-conscious and become more Jesus conscious—more Holy Spirit aware, we can flow with Him. He can use us in ways we could not imagine.

Consider these verses. Spend a little time pondering. Meditate upon them.

For all who are led by the Spirit of God are sons of God.

For you did not receive a spirit of slavery that returns you to fear, but you received the Spirit of sonship, by whom we cry, 'Abba! Father!'

The Spirit Himself testifies with our spirit that we are God's Children.

Romans 8:14-16 BSB

The Passion Is Wonderful

The Passion Translation is wonderful here:

The mature children of God are those who are moved by the impulses of the Holy Spirit.

That is what we are talking about here: being *moved by the impulses of the Holy Spirit*. Just by being free and happy in God, the Holy Spirit nailed it—twice. I did not know the conservative Catholic girl had been seeking God with her friends. Approaching a young teenage couple and asking if they are engaged is just strange. Odd in our eyes, right on the mark with the Holy Ghost. That is the point: you have the Holy Spirit of God dwelling on the inside of you!

> *And you did **not receive the 'spirit of religious duty,'** leading you back into the fear of never being good enough. But you have received the **'Spirit of full acceptance,'** enfolding you into the family of God. And you will never feel orphaned, for as he rises up within us, **our spirits join him in saying** the words of tender affection, **'Beloved Father!'***
>
> Romans 8:15 TPT (emphasis mine)

Not a Spirit of Religious Duty

The Jehovah's Witness I spent time with at my door yesterday, then again on the phone, has that awful 'spirit of religious duty' upon him. That is not us. The purpose of challenging you to meditate on these beautiful truths is for them to be absorbed into your heart.

Soul winning, my beloved brother and sister, is not a religious duty. It is a blast! It is proclaiming *freedom to the captive*. Liberty to those hurting—like Pastor Beth to those skaters. They were crying and pouring their souls out to a stranger. Why? Because of the love and healing sweetly offered to the poor (in heart). The Spirit will always lead us to preach *Good* News! We must grasp that *the Gospel is Good News!*

I found a great quote by Jonathan Gainsbrugh.

> *When we Christians stay 'loaded' with the Holy Spirit, we will live differently. Our evangelism will be a supernaturally natural overflow from the reservoir that God keeps filled in our hearts. He fills us full of His love and*

joy and concern for others both in this world and in eternity! When we are full to overflowing, the Joy of Evangelism occurs![17]

I Thrive Spiritually When I Am Sharing Jesus

Just this morning, while spending time reading, praying, and sharing with my precious wife, Shirley, I commented to her, *'I am in the best place spiritually, in my own walk with Christ, when actively sharing my faith.'* This is how I expressed this to her.

These things occur when you and I passionately seek to share Jesus with others.

1. *We focus on The Cross.* The cross is not given enough attention in Christian circles these days. The Cross is where it all happened. There, my sins were paid—so were yours. The Blood and Life of Jesus, God's Son, was poured out there for me—and you. The ground is level for all at its foot.

2. *Earnestly seeking God for souls.* I cannot be effective if I do not seek God with all my heart to win others to Christ. The above examples illustrate this. I am not that clever. I do not know how to reach every unique individual—but God does. As I cry to God for souls, it changes my heart.

Ask of Me, and I will give You The nations for Your inheritance, And the ends of the earth for Your possession.

Psalm 2:8

This is a prophetic Word to Christ. Yet, He is in me. As I cry for this inheritance of souls, I am transformed over and again.

3. *You are busy doing God's business.* I see myself like one running along the rapids, trying to save a man being swept towards the falls ahead. Running after souls, you and I are doing the very thing Jesus came to do.

For the Son of Man has come to seek and to save the lost.

Luke 19:10 BSB

It is much harder to get wrapped up in myself (the flesh) when I run to save one about to perish. I think the Lord knows that, too.

4. *Rejoicing over one soul.* The Bible tells us the angels rejoice over just one coming to Christ (Luke 15:7). Every New Birth is a time of exuberant celebration. It invokes praise to God. Do you know what happens when we praise God? God shows up! That is a beautiful way to live; God hangs out with you daily.

But thou art holy, O thou that inhabitest the praises of Israel.

Psalm 22:3 KJV

A Brick Layer on a Snowy Day

I was again with the pastor in Nebraska. Today, he, I, and his grown daughter drove around on a snowy day in Omaha, looking for divine appointments to share the Gospel. We were headed back to the church when we passed a new construction, a two-story brick home. A bricklayer was up on scaffolding.

The pastor's daughter spoke, *Let's talk to him.*

As we got out of the car and walked near the workman, I asked, 'Would you mind if we stood out in the cold with you for a few minutes?'

He was agreeable. We continued as a team, sharing Jesus with the man.

> I then asked him if he *would like to become Born Again. Would you like to receive the gift of Eternal Life?*
>
> The man answered, *Yes, I would.*
>
> He climbed down the scaffolding, removed his glove, and placed his hand in mind. We prayed together—this young man made Jesus His Lord.

A moment later, the foreman drove up, and the man returned to work—*a divine appointment.*

Flow with the Holy Spirit—He Will Make You Look Good

The *Creativity of the Creator* you experience as you seek to be used by Him to reach people is endless. When you think you have heard and seen everything, He will do something else.

Seeing believers gather and share countless times after an outreach, I have developed amusement towards my own life. These people are becoming free. One man (in fact, the head usher) at a church where I conducted a *GCS* in western New Mexico greeted me with, *I have tried that knocking-on-doors stuff. I am not going out* (to the outreach we would have).

That man came for the outreach. And he was a part of a team that led one to Christ. He was beaming. So was I.

Inside, I was musing. *So, I am the expert?* I am helping people everywhere break through their fears and become free to become who they were created to be—*soul winners for Jesus*. Now that is *funny*—not that saints were experiencing success winning the lost. It was amusing that this quiet art student, who had no intent or skill to win the lost, was now traveling the country and the world, showing other believers that they could do it too! God is fun!

He Is Awesome!

The man with Christ in him, the Holy Ghost, is greater than any other power in the world.[1]

—**John G Lake**

Behold, I send the Promise of My Father upon you; but tarry in the city of Jerusalem until you are endued with power from on high.

—**Luke 24:49**

CHAPTER 17

Power from on High

I drove from rural Arkansas to just outside Oklahoma City, Oklahoma, in just over five hours. Still, in my 20s, I was pastoring my first church.

Evangelism Explosion (EE)[2] gave me a positive and highly effective way to share the Gospel without confrontation. I went on this trip to get certified as a trainer and planned to implement the program in my local church.

The event had a large turnout, with 150 to 200 attendees coming for certification. Including EE trainers and instructional staff, our number reached over 250. Most of them were ministers or seminary students. During the day, we participated in workshops and collaborated in small groups. By night, we went in groups of three to visit families in the community and share the Gospel.

I Never Tire of Hearing or Telling of One Coming to Christ

My team had the privilege of leading a dear lady to Christ. The trainer asked me to share the Gospel, and then she led the woman in prayer. Another team member already did the introductory part of the visit. I was selected to testify about our experience back at the church.

What a joy to testify about a soul coming to Christ! I never tire of hearing another testimony of someone accepting Jesus as their Lord and Savior.

What Is It about You?

As the meeting broke up that night, a Baptist pastor stopped me. He said,

> *'What is it about you? I listened to others sharing about their visits. Others also led people to Christ, but you shine! What is it about you?'*

I understood what this man saw. He witnessed God's presence upon me through the Baptism of the Holy Spirit. Just as Jesus spoke:

> *But I promise you this—**the Holy Spirit will come upon you**, and **you will be seized with power. You will be my messengers** to Jerusalem, throughout Judea, the distant provinces—even to the remotest places on earth!*
>
> Acts 1:8 TPT (emphasis mine)

The Spirit *upon* brings a power to be a witness that is more than ourselves. This is for all believers.

You Shall Receive the Gift of The Holy Ghost

Peter preached about Jesus Christ and the Holy Ghost on the Day of Pentecost.

> *Then Peter said to them, 'Repent, and let every one of you be baptized in the name of Jesus Christ for the remission of sins; and you shall receive the gift of the Holy Spirit.*

For the promise is to you and to your children, and to all who are afar off, as many as the Lord our God will call.'

Acts 2:38-39

The Baptism of the Holy Spirit is a gift. This is the baptism of Jesus. John talked about his baptism in water, which symbolized repentance. Then he spoke of Christ:

Those who repent I baptize with water, but there is coming a man (Jesus) after me who is more powerful than I. In fact, I'm not even worthy enough to pick up his sandals. He will submerge you into union with the Spirit of Holiness and with raging fire!

Matthew 3:11 TPT (parenthesis mine)

Jesus commanded the first disciples to *tarry* (wait) *in the city of Jerusalem until you are endued with power from on high* Luke 24:49. From then until now, the Baptism of the Spirit was intended for all Jesus' disciples. This chapter will lay down the biblical groundwork for this statement.

Note: The Baptism Is a Gift for Those Who Ask

Like any gift, we must receive that gift. What the Father is looking for is hungry hearts.

If imperfect parents know how to lovingly take care of their children and give them what they need, how much more will the perfect heavenly Father give the Holy Spirit's fullness when his children ask him?

Luke 11:13 TPT

Please note: a gift is not earned! I have encountered Christians who misunderstood and asked, *'Are you implying that I am not spiritual?'* or *'Do I have to meet certain standards to receive the Holy Spirit Baptism?'* Peter made it clear: *you will receive the gift of the Holy Spirit, for the promise is to you and to your children.*

This Pastor Was Hungry; Others Were Not

This dear Baptist pastor and I sat in the car on that cold December night. I explained the scriptures to him (which I will discuss below). He experienced a magnificent filling of the Holy Ghost and spoke in a new heavenly language (other tongues)! God had Baptized him *with the Holy Ghost and fire.* (Matthew 3:11) His ministry would never be the same.

While sitting alone at a diner the day prior, I noticed others from the EE conference nearby. I overheard three men discussing the Baptism of the Holy Ghost at an adjacent table. One man adamantly objected to the notion that this is meant for today, asserting that anyone who disagrees is a heretic. It brought to mind statements made against Jesus by the Pharisees.

These men were not hungry. I made no interjection and avoided getting into a fight. However, if a believer is searching, I am committed to helping them receive what Jesus called *the Promise of My Father.*

My Baptism of the Holy Ghost

Being a Born-Again believer for less than six months, an opportunity presented itself. My church hosted Bible classes. Specific courses granted college credit. I enrolled in *The Book of Acts* course taught by a professor from my university—the perfect combination. As a new believer, I could earn college credit by studying the Bible.

During the course syllabus review, the professor discussed the required term paper. He went over a list of potential subjects. Before addressing the last topic, he gave a preface. He warned that the upcoming topic, *Glossolalia*—the Gift of Tongues in the early church—could be controversial.

This sparked my interest—*what was this?*

The Gift of Tongues in the Early Church

You got it. The topic I selected for my required term paper was precisely that. What is *Glossolalia*, and what caused the controversy?

I checked out many books from the public university library—many theological works. In addition, there was a paperback written by Dennis J. Bennet, a leader in the Charismatic movement.[3] I took my books to the student union and began with the paperback, *The Holy Spirit and You*.[4] Bennet made impressive statements concerning the baptism of the Holy Spirit. He explained that the Baptism would build you up and make you strong. God would give you a private prayer language from heaven to help you pray, even when you did not know what to pray. I jotted down the scriptural references.

Back in my dorm room, I sat alone on my bed. I examined the scriptures. They were in my Bible. I prayed with a childlike faith and simplicity in my heart.

> *Heavenly Father, I want everything you have for me. I desire nothing else. This Baptism of the Holy Spirit will help me walk with you. It is in my Bible. So, I am asking for the Baptism of the Holy Spirit now.*

My Hands Went Up. Tears Came Down.

No one had told me to lift my hands—they did not do that at my church—but my hands floated up. Tears streamed down my cheeks. No one cried at church. I spoke, but it was more like singing. The sound resembled that of an American Indian language. I worshipped God. I had never worshipped like that before.

After a few moments, I collected myself. My roommate came in. I remained quiet, yet I knew. I had received the Baptism of the Holy Spirit and *this speaking in tongues*.

The next day, full of enthusiasm, I shared my news with a fellow Christian in my dormitory. I described my experience to him. *I had received the Baptism of the Holy Ghost!*

That Is of the Devil!

To my utter shock and horror, the brother told me, *That is of the devil!*

I was terrified and utterly confused. *I wanted nothing of the devil!* It would be over a year and a half before I spoke in tongues again.

Interesting. Something the Bible tells us that Jesus alone would give (Matthew 3:11; Acts 1:8) had flipped and now was *of the devil*. It reminds me of the current political arena today.

New Major, New College

The following year, I changed majors and universities. I was now an Art Education major at San Jose State University. I took many long hours of studio courses but loved it—I was in my element.

Parking became problematic because of the large student population, with most living off campus. I would pay the fee and park in the gravel lots opposite the science department, arriving early and leaving late. As I exited the lot one day, the attendant ran after my old Pontiac convertible. The gal was curious about the individual with the Christian bumper sticker on their car, which stayed parked in her lot all day.

Praying in My Prayer Language

Over the ensuing weeks, we became friends. She always had stories to tell—stories of people receiving help, being healed, and coming to Christ. I noticed another thing peculiar about her stories. This enthusiastic believer frequently mentioned *I was praying in my prayer language, and....* Upon reflecting on the fantastic testimonies, it suddenly occurred to me. This praying in *her prayer language* was undoubtedly what the Bible calls other tongues—Glossolalia.

I Copied Every Scripture about Tongues

Until late, I immersed myself in studying scriptures about the Baptism of the Holy Spirit and speaking in tongues. I wrote each passage in a notebook. As a believer for a couple of years, reading and studying the Bible daily, I had gained more knowledge.

I could not find it. I meticulously reviewed each passage and saw no evidence suggesting that the Baptism of the Spirit or speaking in tongues was demonic. It was not in the Bible.

I prayed for an extended period, confessing any wrongdoing I could think of. I refused to have anything to do with the devil. Then I took a step. I asked again for the Baptism, and from my mouth, it came. Tongues. It differed from before, but it came. This was *my prayer language*. Worshiping and praying in other tongues has been my daily habit for over forty years. I have not stopped.

Srikakulam, India, Pastors' Conference

Before we led pastors' conferences, Melchizedek, my Indian partner, a friend, David from my church, and I explored this region. One city in the northernmost part of the Indian state of Andre Pradesh is Srikakulam. To the north of Srikakulam lies the state of Odisha. Foreign missionaries were brutally murdered earlier that year. We passed through the entire region, including the village where the attack occurred.[5] The Spirit impressed upon me the importance of *walking the land* (Genesis 13:17).

A year later, we conducted a Pastor's conference just below the Odisha border in Srikakulam. Pastors from both states, including ministers from near the village in Odisha where the violence happened, attended the meeting.

Impact leadership, you affect a region—especially men of God.

The Holy Ghost Fell

During one of the morning sessions, the Lord impressed upon me to preach about the Baptism of the Holy Spirit. Just as I finished, I was about to instruct our team to lay hands. According to scripture, the Baptism of the Holy Spirit can be received by laying on hands. (Acts 8:14-17; Acts 9:17-19; Acts 19:6) But I sensed the Holy Spirit moving upon us to wait. A stillness settled over the room. We stayed in anticipation.

Then it happened. A man sitting near the front spoke in other tongues. Then, another pastor. And then another. Soon, the entire room of people worshipped God, speaking in languages they did not know (1 Corinthians 14:2). It was like the Day of Pentecost. Much like in Acts 10:44-46, the Holy Ghost fell to *our astonishment*.

The Biblical Case for the Baptism of the Spirit

This wonderful topic could fill an entire book, and many excellent books have been written on the subject. In this discussion, I will address the fundamental scriptural support for the Baptism of the Holy Spirit, both in the early church and today. I'll keep it short, but my arguments will be rooted in the Bible.

The Baptism Was God's Idea

John the Baptist foretold that Jesus, the Son of God, would baptize. John baptized in water, but Jesus's medium would be the Holy Spirit of God Himself. The word for baptism in the Greek is *baptizo*.[7] It means to immerse, submerge, or make whelmed (i.e., thoroughly wet).

> *I indeed baptize you with water unto repentance, but He who is coming after me is mightier than I, whose sandals I am not worthy to carry. He will **baptize you with the Holy Spirit** and **fire**.*
>
> Matthew 3:11 (emphasis mine)

Jesus commanded the disciples to receive the Baptism of the Spirit. It was not optional, not according to our Lord.

Jesus, in Luke's Gospel, speaks of being endowed with heavenly power. Luke, the physician who wrote the Gospel, also penned the Book of the Acts of The Apostles. In the first verses of the Book of Acts, we find Jesus' definition of this endowment. It is the power of the Spirit of God.

> *Behold, I send the Promise of My Father upon you; but tarry in the city of Jerusalem until you are **endued with power from on high***
>
> Luke 24:49 (emphasis mine)

> But **you shall receive power when the Holy Spirit has come upon you;** and **you shall be witnesses to Me** in Jerusalem, and in all Judea and Samaria, and to the end of the earth.
>
> Acts 1:8 (emphasis mine)

Now, it's crucial to observe several things which are vitally important.

1. We are witnesses *of* Jesus. We do not just go witnessing.
2. The purpose of the power is *to be* a witness of Christ. Crucial today.
3. This is so important to our Lord Jesus that He commanded believers *to wait* to receive this endowment *before* they are to fulfill His Great Commission.

Pentecost—the Initial Outpouring of the Spirit

> *When the Day of Pentecost had fully come, they were all with one accord in one place.*
>
> *And suddenly there came **a sound from heaven**, as of **a rushing mighty wind**, and it **filled the whole house** where they were sitting.*
>
> *Then there appeared to them divided **tongues, as of fire**, and one **sat upon each** of them.*
>
> *And **they were all filled with the Holy Spirit** and **began to speak** with **other tongues**, as **the Spirit gave them utterance**.*
>
> Acts 2:1-4 (emphasis mine)

There's so much to teach within these few verses. However, I will present it with bullet points and concise statements.

1. This event came from heaven. *A sound from heaven. A rushing, mighty wind.* In Munich, Germany, my team led an African man to Christ. We then shared the Baptism of the Spirit. As we read this passage, this man spoke in his rich Nigerian accent, *'I am a music major in college. I am going to write music that are sounds from heaven!'*
2. The entire house was filled. The Spirit Baptism is for all (Acts 2:38-39).
3. These *tongues, as of fire,* came from heaven. Men do not baptize men in the Spirit. God does.
4. Each was filled—every person who was present. *Sat upon each of them—they were all filled with the Holy Spirit.*
5. Each person spoke. Human breath produced the sound, but the words came from the Holy Spirit.
6. What did they speak? *Other tongues.* The Apostle Paul says tongues can be *of men or of angels* (1 Corinthians 13:1). But the tongue is not spoken to men but unto God.

   For he who speaks in a tongue does not speak to men but to God; for no one understands him; however, in the Spirit he speaks mysteries.

   1 Corinthians 14:2

7. Human voices spoke heavenly tongues. *As the Spirit gave them utterance.*

Other Occurrences of the Spirit Baptism

The later occurrences of the Baptism of the Holy Spirit recorded in the Book of Acts didn't have the same impressive display as the initial outpouring. Unlike the event of Pentecost in Acts chapter two, no rushing mighty wind or sound from heaven was recorded, yet the Baptism of the Holy Spirit was still given. We will examine each.

However, Mel Tari's book, *Like a Mighty Wind*,[6] tells of an outpouring in Indonesia; they did experience the same signs that occurred in Acts chapter two:

> *That night, as we were praying together, suddenly the Holy Spirit came just as He did on the day of Pentecost. In Acts, chapter 2, we read that He came from heaven like the mighty rushing wind. And that night, as I was sitting next to my sister, I heard this mighty rushing sound. It sounded like a small tornado in the church.*

He continues,

> *Then I heard the fire bell ringing loud and fast. The man in the police station saw that our church was on fire, so he rang the bell to tell the people of the village to come quickly. There was fire.*
>
> *When they got to the church, they saw the flames, but the church wasn't burning. Instead of a natural fire, it was the fire of God. Because of this, many people received Jesus Christ as their Savior and also the baptism of the Holy Spirit.*

I adamantly refuse to tell God when and how to manifest His glory. Feel free. Not me.

Philip Preaching in Samaria

The church scattered because of persecution. They fled Jerusalem. Philip, one of the initial men selected to distribute food to widows in Acts 6, had journeyed to Samaria. We read:

Power from on High

> *Then Philip went down to the city of Samaria and preached Christ to them.*
>
> *And the multitudes with one accord heeded the things spoken by Philip, hearing and seeing the miracles which he did.*
>
> *For unclean spirits, crying with a loud voice, came out of many who were possessed; and many who were paralyzed and lame were healed.*
>
> *And there was great joy in that city.*
>
> Acts 8:5-8

Outstanding. Many were saved, healed, and delivered. However, the apostles knew these people also needed to be baptized with the Holy Spirit, just like they had received on the Day of Pentecost.

> *Now when the apostles who were at Jerusalem heard that Samaria had received the word of God, they sent Peter and John to them,*
>
> *who, when they had come down, prayed for them that they might receive the Holy Spirit.*
>
> *For as yet He had fallen upon none of them. They had only been baptized in the name of the Lord Jesus.*
>
> *Then they laid hands on them, and they received the Holy Spirit.*
>
> Acts 8:14-17

Same Baptism. Identical Holy Spirit. Did they speak in tongues? No mention is made. Nevertheless, it shows that Simon, the former sorcerer, now offered them money. Why?

> *Saying, 'Give me this power also, that anyone on whom I lay hands may receive the Holy Spirit.'*
>
> Acts 8:19

Of course, he was rebuked for this, but what did he see or hear that made him want to buy this power? I am convinced he witnessed believers be filled with the Spirit and speaking in tongues.

Saul's Conversion

In Acts 9, we witness a great miracle. Saul, who was killing Christians and having them tortured for their faith, met the living Christ. (Never give up praying for powerful enemies of the Cross.) You know the story. Saul was knocked off his horse, blinded, and struck with the fear of God. He cried out, dazed, answering the audible voice,

> *And he said, 'Who are You, Lord?' Then the Lord said, 'I am Jesus, whom you are persecuting. It is hard for you to kick against the goads.'*
>
> Acts 9:5

The fear of God gripped Saul. Blinded, he was led into town by the others in his party. Saul was so stricken that he did *not eat or drink* for three days. God spoke to a man named Ananias and told him to go pray for Saul. However, Ananias was leery. He had knowledge of this man and the devastation he caused.

> *But the Lord said to him* (Ananias), *'Go, for he* (Saul—soon to become Paul the Apostle) *is a chosen vessel of Mine to bear My name before Gentiles, kings, and the children of Israel.*
>
> *For I will show him how many things he must suffer for My name's sake.'*
>
> Acts 9:15-16 (parenthesis mine)

Ananias was one gutsy guy. He obeyed and went to lay hands on Saul.

> *And Ananias went his way and entered the house; and laying his hands on him he said, 'Brother Saul, the Lord Jesus, who appeared to you on the road as you came, has sent me that you may receive your sight, and be filled with the Holy Spirit.'*
>
> Acts 9:17

Once more, the Baptism of the Holy Spirit. Can you explain why he was to *be filled with the Holy Spirit*? It's plain. The Lord Jesus, who is both your Lord and mine, ordained that we become witnesses for Him by the power of the Baptism of the Holy Ghost. *Don't leave home without it!* Yet, many Christians have been misinformed that the Holy Spirit Baptism was only for the first believers. That's not true. The job remains unaltered: *act as witnesses for Me, disseminating My message to all corners of the world, equipped with the same endowment.* The endowment is the Baptism of the Holy Spirit, with the evidence of speaking in a new heavenly language. He alone equips us for this work.

When Did Paul Speak in Tongues?

Did Saul, who later became Paul, possess the ability to speak in tongues? Acts 9 does not specify if he did or did not. But observe Paul's own words. What does he say about his speaking in other tongues as he provides instruction for the proper use of the gifts of the Spirit in the church?

> I thank my God **I speak with tongues more than you all**;
>
> yet in the church I would rather speak five words with my understanding, that I may teach others also, than ten thousand words in a tongue.
>
> 1 Corinthians 14:18-19 (emphasis mine)

Paul was unmatched in speaking in tongues. When did he start? It was when Ananias laid hands on him and declared, *'Be filled with the Holy Spirit!'* When did he do all this *praying in the spirit*, if not predominantly during church meetings? His speaking primarily took place in his own private prayer life. Prayer is essential to do the things Paul did, *especially* praying in the spirit.

Just today, though I wanted to continue writing this chapter, I could not. I was compelled *to pray much in other tongues*. After several hours of *praying in the Spirit*, I received confirmation that some readers will also receive the Baptism of the Holy Spirit because of reading this chapter.

Acts 10—Cornelius the Roman Centurion

This is a beautiful story. I would love to preach it! Please take a moment to read Acts 10 to get the entire account. You need to understand the significance of this event and how it shook up the church (recorded in Acts 11). But for brevity, let me just hit some highlights.

1. Cornelius was a godly man, though a gentile.
2. In a vision, the Lord instructed him to seek Peter.
3. As a Jew, Peter was forbidden from entering a gentile home.
4. However, Peter obeyed God and went—along with his men.
5. Peter arrives at Cornelius's and asks, *'What do you want?'*
6. Cornelius relates his vision, being told to seek Peter.
7. Peter preached. He proclaimed the Gospel of Christ.
8. But before he could finish, the Holy Ghost fell.
9. The entire house was full of people who received the Baptism.
10. The Jewish believers heard them all speak in tongues.

What do we have here? We have *another Pentecost*. Why did they need it? Why do we? Two simple reasons:

- Every believer everywhere for all time is called to be a witness for *Jesus*.
- Jesus Christ wants to Baptize you in the Holy Spirit so that you may be that witness for Him.

I love what one sister at the Life Group fellowship said last week at our meeting:

God is not complicated. We make it difficult.

So true!

Baptism of the Spirit in Katmandu, Nepal

Towards the end of our stay in Katmandu, Nepal, we were invited to minister at another Bible school. This was a young group of students, not the spiritually hungry village pastors at Missionary Strong's[8] Bible School. Yet, if we had an opportunity to minister, we definitely would take it.

A couple from my church had accompanied me on this trip. Kelly was a homemaker. Ron was an architect. They both had a rich spiritual heritage. I felt impressed to have Ron preach. His 'go-to' subject was always the Baptism of the Holy Ghost.

Ron ministered from Acts 10. He expounded upon the virtues and the necessity for each believer to receive the baptism that Jesus gives (Matthew 3:11). He shared that the Baptism of the Holy Ghost came with the evidence of speaking in other tongues (Acts 2:1-4).

Ron finished and then gave his invitation. However, no one moved. Not one of us went to lay hands. A 'holy hush' came over the room. Ron waved for us to wait.

Then He came. The Spirit of God had taken over the service.

First upon one, then another, students sitting at their desks spoke in tongues. More began to pray in a new heavenly language. Lives were changing before our eyes. More spoke.

About six students stayed quiet. These were the ones who seemed more lighthearted than sincere. Then one of them spoke in tongues, then another. When the Spirit descended upon them, He came with tremendous power. As the last guy made utterance, a cacophony of languages erupted that filled the entire room—like a powerful engine.

Windows were open. We were up in a third-story room across a courtyard from another three-story building.

It had the sound of a freight train barreling past. Visible faces emerged. People were hanging out of the windows in the building across from us, watching in wonder.

These students had received the Baptism of the Holy Ghost. By the Spirit, *they declared the wondrous things of God* (Acts 2:11). These young men and women would never again be the same as they had when they arrived.

Have You Received the Holy Ghost?

What was the Apostle Paul's question to a group of disciples? These men must have been from my church (that I attended as a youth)—they did not even know about the Holy Ghost:

> *He* (Paul) *says to them, 'Did you receive the Holy Spirit when you believed?' So they said to him, 'We have not so much as heard whether there is a Holy Spirit.'*
>
> Acts 19:2

Power from on High

You know what I find most interesting? John the Baptist, the Apostles, the early believers, and Paul believed Jesus without question. Jesus directed them to be endowed with power from above. Today, let us be as wise. I've chosen to put my trust in Jesus. How about you?

The Apostle asks, *'Unto what were you baptized?'* (verse 3). They knew of John's baptism of repentance. So Paul preached Christ unto them:

> *Then Paul said, 'John indeed baptized with a baptism of repentance, saying to the people that they should believe on Him who would come after him, that is, on Christ Jesus.'*
>
> *When they heard this, they were baptized in the name of the Lord Jesus.*
>
> Acts 19:4-5

I commend these men. Upon hearing the Gospel of Christ Jesus, they promptly took action.

But then, I commend Paul. He brought them directly into the experience of the Baptism of the Spirit.

> *And when Paul had laid hands on them, the Holy Spirit came upon them, and they spoke with tongues and prophesied.*
>
> *Now the men were about twelve in all.*
>
> Acts 19:6-7

The Pattern

In all cases, the Baptism was ministered. Some by sovereign outpouring. Some by the ministry of the laying of hands of a Believer. All received the Baptism—none were excluded. The evidence of speaking in other tongues—*tongues of men and of angels*—was evident or implied.

Why? Why was the Baptism of the Holy Spirit so important? Is it necessary today?

Yes! Every believer must be filled with the Holy Spirit (and continue to be filled) because:

- Every believer is a witness to the resurrected Christ.
- To effectively be a witness of Christ, we need heaven's outpouring.
- That outpouring is the Baptism of the Holy Spirit- promised to all (Acts 2:39).
- With the Baptism of the Spirit comes the evidence of other tongues.

Ricochet Faith for the Baptism

During the revival in Lagos, Nigeria, I was asked to speak at a Pentecostal church. I knew without questioning what the Lord needed for me to minister—the Baptism of the Holy Ghost.

Two days prior, Brother Moses (his actual name) reached out to my roommate, Pastor Archangel (his name), and me for help. Brother Archangel decisively determined the remedy for this brother's fear and hesitation. He needed to receive the Baptism of the Spirit he preached to others.

Boldly, my roommate laid hands. Filled with the Spirit, the evangelist went out under the power, speaking in a heavenly language.

Limited Time, Even Less Experience

I knew if an evangelist from this church body needed the Baptism, how much the members? But time was limited. The service was a Friday night prayer service. For a few minutes, the congregation prayed at once over a particular need, then a buzzer would sound. Another need was addressed. All prayed aloud. Then, the buzzer.

I thought they would use the buzzer on me if I preached too long!

But I had a bigger problem. I had not ministered to a large group, the Baptism of the Holy Ghost. I was wavering in my faith whether people would receive the Baptism of the Spirit if I were to give an altar call, and people responded.

Then it occurred to me,

There would be no problem if Brother Archangel were here. He would boldly extend an invitation and then more boldly lay hands. They would all receive the Baptism.

I reasoned with myself and to the Lord,

Lord, I know you are not a respecter of persons (Acts 10:34). I know you want me to minister the Baptism of the Holy Spirit. You desire these dear believers to have what they need and what you have promised.

I have little faith that I can do this. But I know Pastor Archangel could believe. So, I will ricochet my faith off him as if he were here.

I Laid Hands in Ricochet Faith—It Worked!

You know the crazy thing is—it worked! I preached (briefly), gave the call, and 72 came forward to receive the Baptism of the Holy Ghost. With borrowed faith, I boldly declared,

When I lay my hands upon you, you will be Baptized in the Holy Spirit, and you will receive and speak in a new heavenly prayer language (other tongues).

Faith For Souls

As I laid hands, seventy of those dear souls started speaking in languages they didn't know. And another one after the meeting. A few days later, I heard that the last person had also received their prayer language! God is perfect, and He's also a blast!

Simple Instruction to Receive the Baptism

Although there is much more to teach, let me end with this. Here are some tips for receiving or helping someone receive the Baptism of the Holy Spirit.

1. The Baptism of the Holy Spirit is for all (Acts 2:38-39).
2. Jesus is the Baptizer of the Holy Spirit (Matthew 3:11).
3. We need the Baptism to be witnesses of Christ (Luke 24:49; Acts 1:8).
4. Three ways to receive.
    a. The Laying on of Hands of a Believer (Acts 9:17; Acts 19:6).
    b. Sovereign Outpouring by the Holy Spirit (Acts 2:1-4; Acts 10:44).
    c. By simply asking (Luke 11:13).
5. Have faith in the promise to receive (Acts 2:39).
6. The person will speak (Acts 2:4; Acts 10:46).
7. But the Holy Spirit gives the utterance (Acts 2:4).
8. Praying in tongues will build you up (1 Corinthians 14:4).
9. Praying in the Spirit allows you to pray mysterious things you do not know how to address (1 Corinthians 14:2).
10. Praying in the Holy Ghost will keep you in the love of God. Perfect love always defeats the enemy (Jude 20-21; 1 John 4:7-19).

T.L. Osborn's Version of Acts 1:8

I love this fantastic version of Acts 1:8 by T.L. Osborn. Let it speak to you:

> *You shall receive virtue, miracle ability, and supernatural energy; after that, the Holy Ghost has come upon you for a unique and specific purpose, to enable you to give absolute evidence and miraculous proof of My resurrection. It is this power working in you that will demonstrate and exhibit the proof of your testimony to verify your claims with documented credentials, and you are to exhibit this supernatural evidence of My resurrection in your own cities and countries and into the inner cities and to the remotest part of the earth.*
>
> Acts 1:8 (as expounded by T.L. Osborn)

Street Witnessing in Guntur, India

One afternoon, we went into the streets of Guntur, India, to share the Gospel. I led a young group of street kids to Christ. They needed everything I could give them. After praying together to receive Jesus as their Lord and Savior, I shared about the Baptism of the Holy Spirit. I instructed that the Spirit of God would come upon them as I laid my hands on their heads. They would experience His Presence. Then, He would baptize them with the Holy Spirit. And the Holy Spirit would give them a new language to pray and to help them.

I laid my hands upon the tallest, a girl. Her hands up, eyes closed, the Spirit of God came upon her so sweetly. She worshipped in a new tongue. Then, her younger brother did the same.

When I got to the littlest one, the little sister, her hands were already up. Her eyes were closed. She had already been baptized in the Holy Spirit. I had not even touched her. Glory to God. He is so good!

Conclusion

It's all about love.

> Those who are loved by God, **let his love continually pour from you to one another**, because God is love.
>
> **Everyone who loves is fathered by God and experiences an intimate knowledge of him.** The one who doesn't love has yet to know God, for **God is love**.
>
> **The light of God's love shined within us** when he sent his matchless Son into the world **so that we might live through him**.
>
> **This is love: He loved us long before we loved him. It was his love, not ours.** He proved it by sending his Son to be the pleasing sacrificial offering to take away our sins.
>
> Delightfully loved ones, if **he loved us with such tremendous love, then 'loving one another' should be our way of life**.
>
> 1 John 4:7-11 TPT (emphasis mine)

The Progression of Loving Others

The Spirit of God urged me to read and reflect on 1 Corinthians 13, the love chapter. This passage beautifully defines the love of God and what it isn't. The Lord compelled me to write it down as a declaration of His love for me. This is my paraphrase taken from a compilation of various Bible translations.

> *God loves me, endures long, and is patient and kind with me.*
>
> *God (love) is never envious nor boils over with jealousy towards me.*
>
> *He (love) is not demanding or irritable towards me and keeps no record of my wrongs.*
>
> *God (love) does not rejoice when I fail but rejoices when I succeed.*
>
> *God never gives up on me. He never loses faith in me. He is ever ready to believe the best of me.*
>
> *His hopes for me are fadeless under all circumstances.*
>
> *Love, God's love for me, never fails. It never fades out, becomes obsolete, or comes to an end. He will always love me.*

As I considered what I had written, what He says and believes of me according to the Word of God, proved by the ultimate sacrifice of His Son, I was undone.

If He Loves Me, I Can Love Me

The next day, God dealt with me again—again about the love chapter of 1 Corinthians 13. But on this day, He put a different emphasis upon the Word. The Lord had me look through the same lens of God's love, but this time towards myself. If He loved me with this depth, I could and should apply the same measure to how I saw myself. I wrote out the verses again:

> *Because God loves me, I can love me. I endure long and am patient and kind toward myself.*
>
> *I never boil over with anger or jealousy because I love myself, because He loves me.*

Conclusion

I am not demanding towards myself or irritable, and I do not keep a record of my failings because my Lord Jesus loves me, and He does not.

I do not say, 'I failed again—I knew I would.' No, I only rejoice in my triumphs in Christ.

I never give up, especially on myself. I never lose faith in myself, and I am always ready to believe in the best of myself because God, in His great love, has redeemed me and valued me.

I am full of hope. My hope is fadeless in all circumstances because God Almighty believes in me enough to crucify His only Son, to make me his son, too!

I will never stop loving (your name), and I will never fail. I will fulfill my call and finish my course. And I will one day hear my Lord Jesus declare, 'Well done thou good and faithful servant.' I know this because His love is absolute and will never end.

I know God loves me. Therefore, I love myself.

Because He Loves Me, and I Love Me, I Can Afford to Love Others

God directed me again on the third day to look at 1 Corinthians 13. He quickened my heart. The Lord showed me a profound truth: *I can love myself because God loves me. Now, I could afford to love others.* [Much of this confession is taken from *Today's Passion Translation*.]

My love, God's love in me, is immense and patient for others. Because of His love pouring through me, I can be consistently kind and gentle—even to the rude.

I refuse to be jealous of someone else's blessing—I am genuinely happy for them.

It is no longer all about me—thinking and talking about my achievements. I want others to succeed as much as or more than me.

Because of Jesus, I do not traffic in shame or disrespect or seek selfish honor. I honor others.

I am not easily irritated or quick to take offense. Christ has set me free—free to love people.

The love of God that fills my heart celebrates honesty, and I find no fault.

I am a safe shelter of the love of God that never stops believing in the best for others.

God's love in me never takes failure as defeat, for it never gives up.

His Love for me will never stop. And because of this love, people are drawn to Christ in me and desire to hear and receive the Gospel on which I stand.

A Christ-Centered Love Changes the Rules

With an understanding of Christ-centered love, the rules change. So many live their lives day in and day out, worrying about what others think about them. Jesus sets us free from this obsession. When we know God loves us, not only can we accept ourselves and stop being *our own worst enemy*, but we can also love other people without regard to whether that love is returned. What they say and do may sting our feelings, but we know the truth. They need Jesus. Without Him, they cannot display His love. So if they are unkind or rude, or even mean towards us—so what?

I will live and show Christ to them. I will proclaim the wonderful Gospel to them. And I will believe. I believe this Gospel can change them as it did me.

Conclusion

The Light Is the Love of God

When believers clam up and do not proclaim the glorious Gospel of the Lord Jesus Christ, they are ripping themselves off. Jesus said clearly.

> *You are the light of the world. A city that is set on a hill cannot be hidden.*
>
> Matthew 5:14

Holding back the light is like holding your breath. It hurts you. When we realize that light is God's love in our hearts, shining His light *becomes life*. According to Jesus,

> *A thief has only one thing in mind—he wants to steal, slaughter, and destroy. But I have come to give you everything in abundance, more than you expect—life in its fullness until your overflow!*
>
> John 10:10 TPT

Stop holding your breath.

What Jesus Said About Love

When asked which was the greatest commandment, Jesus responded:

> *Jesus answered him, 'The most important of all the commandments is this: "The Lord Yahweh, our God, is one!"*
>
> *You are to love the Lord Yahweh, your God, with a passionate heart, from the depths of your soul, with your every thought, and with all your strength. This is the great and supreme commandment.*

> *And the second is this: "You must love your neighbor in the same way you love yourself." You will never find a greater commandment than these.'*
>
> Mark 12:29-31 TPT

Loving God and loving our neighbor *in the same way you love yourself*.

In Luke's account, the man who had asked wanted to justify himself. He asked further, *And who is my neighbor?* Luke 10:29

Jesus responds with the famous illustration of the Good Samaritan. We know it well. The Master concludes with a telling question:

> *'What do you think? Which of the three became a neighbor to the man attacked by robbers?'*

The lawyer responded,

> *'The one who treated him kindly,' the religion scholar responded. Jesus said, 'Go and do the same.'*
>
> Luke 10:36-37 MSG

The Good Samaritan crossed the street. His heart was moved with compassion toward this hurting soul. Unlike the priest or the Levite, he did not *look on him* and passed on by.

According to Jesus, to fulfill these two commandments requires action. Not just ascent.

What Are You Going To Do?

This all sounds very similar to what the Lord asked of me as I walked out of the SJSU Student Union those many years ago.

Conclusion

What are you going to do to reach people for Christ in your last semester of college?

Jesus asks you today the same question:

So which of these three do you think was neighbor to him who fell among the thieves?

Please know I am not the one asking the question.

Let me say it more plainly: Are you the *Good Samaritan* to the lost, or just a religious Christian? Will you *cross the street*—will you approach the lost? We cannot just pass by.

An Anecdote

When I attended Bible college, an insurance company had set up a multilevel marketing program. Needing to make money, I considered signing up. But before I made that decision, I needed to find out whether I had the courage to approach strangers with the product.

After my Bible college classes, I changed into a suit and went on foot to a beautiful residential area over the hill from my apartment.

[At this time, I had no car, and my small motorcycle had been stolen. I believed God for the *sevenfold restoration*, according to Proverbs 6:31. God blessed me with a motorcycle that was almost brand new and seven times more powerful. But at this time, I was still *on foot*.]

I walked up to the first home and rang the bell. A man answered. I introduced myself and spoke of the opportunity to purchase insurance coverage. He was polite but uninterested—which was good, as I was not a registered agent (I did not sign up to be).

Faith For Souls

Then I realized. If I can find the courage to sell an insurance product, then why can't I do the same for sharing the Gospel? *Selling* the Gospel was of more significant benefit—it has *eternal coverage*.

Timothy

Opportunities present to us all, all the time.

One irritable opportunity can be a telemarketing call. When I would get *'these scam calls,'* I used to goof around. I might say something off the wall like *'In n Out Burger, may I take your order, please?'* or make a crazy sound or even scream!

Then, I thought I ought to do something more productive and preach the Gospel. Now, if I take the time to answer the call, I respond,

> *Hello?* (After a brief pause, I continue.) *Jesus said you must be Born Again to see the Kingdom of God. That means to go to heaven, to have Heaven in your heart.*
>
> *Are you Born Again?*
>
> *The Bible says, 'If you confess Jesus as your Lord, and believe He has risen from the dead, you shall be saved.' Do you want to be saved?*

Usually, after the first couple of sentences, the call hangs up. But I know that there is a human on the other end of the call, even if it is computer-generated, in the event they connect with someone willing to engage in conversation. As I have done this dozens of times, I grew in my faith. I declared, *'Someone is going to answer me.'*

I had a couple of calls where the operator kept the line open for over a minute. They were listening. One of those was the same number—they listened to me twice sharing the Gospel. So then I began to declare, *'Someone is going to get saved!'*

Conclusion

One woman with a strong Asian accent responded. We conversed as I shared the Good News of Christ. She told me she wanted to receive Christ and become Born Again. But when I told her we would pray right now, she became nervous and responded, *'I can't pray now. There are twenty other coworkers here. And my supervisor is in the room.'* Unfortunately, she hung up.

But I persisted.

One afternoon, I had just gotten home. I was standing in our kitchen with my wife sitting across the counter when the phone rang. I began . . . *Jesus said you must be Born Again.*

This young man opened up to me and said what I told him was encouraging. Before we got off the call, I offered for him to take down my phone number and contact me. As soon as we hung up, I received a text. It was from this young man (I will call him Timothy).

I responded with a text with the promise from John 1:12.

But to all who believed him and accepted him, he gave the right to become children of God.

John 1:12 NLT

A week later, I received a text from Timothy. He said he was *having a tough time and did not know if he could go on.* I texted him back. *We needed to talk.* Would he receive a call in about 30 minutes? He said *yes*.

In our previous conversation, I knew Timothy was an aviation student and lived somewhere in Southern California. He was apparently the oldest child of a single parent and *the only man in the house*. He was struggling in school, dealing with family needs, and trying to find a job.

Thirty minutes later, I called him, and he answered my call. I explained that what he needed more than anything else was to receive

Faith For Souls

Jesus as His Lord and Savior. Timothy prayed with me over the line and made Jesus Lord.

Six months have passed. Timothy and I are still texting. He is doing much better—*more at peace.* He has a job and is still plugging away in school.

What a blessing to help this young man find Christ.

Timothys and Ruths are waiting . . . *for you to cross the street.*

I Believe Better Things of You

The writer of Hebrews, likely the Apostle Paul, stated:

But, beloved, we are persuaded better things of you, and things that accompany salvation, though we thus speak.

Hebrews 6:9 KJV

Thank you for being so gracious in reading this revelation that Jesus gave me. I believe *Faith For Souls* is growing in your heart. Therefore, I also believe you will hear the Lord speak those immortal words,

Well done, thou good and faithful servant.

Matthew 25:21 KJV

My Prayer for You

Precious Heavenly Father,

I pray for this dear saint who has read my book. They have opened their heart to me, but more importantly, to You, Lord Jesus, to this **Faith For Souls** *revelation you gave me.*

I now release my faith for an impartation to win souls for Christ, not by might, or cunning, or by even much learning, but by the Great Helper, the Holy Ghost Himself.

(Zechariah 4:6; John 14:16-17)

Blow their minds! Let them see you open doors to people's hearts supernaturally everywhere they go. People thirsting and hungering for life—for the true Gospel of the Lord Jesus Christ.

(Luke 5:10; Corinthians 16:9)

I ask for the gifts and the operations of the Spirit of God to operate, such as is needed in any situation.

(1 Corinthians 12:7-11; John 14:12-14)

I ask that this brother or sister not be self-conscious but God-conscious. That they would know that they walk with the Lord Jesus Himself, and He with them, through the Person of the Holy Ghost.

(1 Corinthians 4:3-4; John 15:4-5)

Faith For Souls

Quicken the Word of God to them. May they see 'soul winning' revelation truths throughout the Bible.

(Proverbs 11:30: 1 Peter 3:15)

Speak to them in the night seasons. Awake them with a sense of destiny that:

(Psalm 16:7; Isaiah 50:4)

Today, someone is coming to Christ! I am led by the Spirit of God, and even in the busyness of my day, Lord, you will have me to be at the right place at the right time. I will recognize an 'open door for the Gospel' with that person whose heart is open to receive the living Christ and to make Him the Lord and Master of their lives today.

(Romans 8:14; John 4:35-38; Ephesians 6:19-20)

Empower me with love and courage. Fill my mouth, leading me to say what may be the simplest thing, but the right thing, which will open the door for a conversation with a lost man or woman, boy or girl, teen, or older person.

(Proverbs 14:26-27:1 John 4:16-18: John 4:7-10)

Give me ears to hear what your Spirit is saying to me.

(Revelations 2:7)

Today, I renounce fear or worry that I would not know what to do or would not know what to say because, by your Spirit, I do know, and I will know.

(2 Timothy 1:7; Philippians 4:6-8; Matthew 10:19-20)

My Prayer for You

Let your love and compassion flow through me towards another, so much so that they cannot resist the Spirit by which I speak.

(Romans 5:5; Matthew 14:14; Acts 6:10)

Today, give me the boldness to be the light!

(Proverbs 28:1; Acts 4:29-30; Matthew 5:14)

Lord Jesus, give me souls. With all that is within me, I ask that you give me souls for the Kingdom of God.

(Psalm 2:8; Genesis 30:1; 1 Corinthians 9:19-22)

And Lord, I covenant with you now that I will give you all the glory. Not diminishing that you are in me and using my life, but not being deceived by false vanity that I have done this by my great talent and skill. You have done this- and it is glorious!

(2 Corinthians 3:5-6; Acts 3:12-16)

Thank you, Lord, for allowing me to partner with you to bring your other sons and daughters home to you!

(2 Corinthians 5:18-20; 1 Timothy 2:3-4)

And Lord, I make it my aim to yield to you, obey you, and be fruitful in you, that you will say to me when I look into your eyes, 'Well done, though, good and faithful servant!'

(Matthew 25:21; 2 Timothy 4:7-8)

In Jesus' Glorious Name. AMEN!

Prayer of Salvation

This prayer of salvation and explanation was transcribed from Greg Laurie's Testimony.[1] Greg is a wonderful pastor and evangelist who came to Christ during the *Jesus Movement*[2] in the 1960s-1970s. The story was recently released in a movie called *Jesus Revolution*.

Greg Laurie first shares his story. Then he explains how and why we must receive Jesus.

Greg's Story

One of the privileges I had was to go to my father, who adopted me, and pray with him to come to Christ. He then lived 15 more years before he went to heaven. I was able to pray with my mother a month before she died and went to heaven. And I was able to pray with my son when he was just a little boy, to make a commitment to Jesus Christ. And now he, too, is in heaven.

I would like to pray with you as well because I'd like you to go to heaven. And I believe deep down inside, you want to go to heaven. You see, you were made for another world. You are a living soul. You were made in the image of God. And there is nothing that this world offers that is going to satisfy the deepest desire inside of you.

We Are on a Quest

C.S. Lewis called this, *'The inconsolable longing: the secret signature of every soul.'* Meaning that deep down, we long for something more. That is why, from the moment you were born, you have been on a quest. You have been searching. I was searching as a young boy. And I even looked into drugs, drinking, and partying, thinking I'd find the answer there. But I didn't.

Then I heard the message of Jesus Christ, and I believed. It was when I heard the statement (that Jesus had said), *'You are for Me. Or you are against Me.'* And I thought, *'Am I against God? I don't want to be. I want to be for Him.'* And I believed in Jesus on that day. I have never regretted it. And you won't either.

Would You Like to Go to Heaven?

Would you like to go to heaven when you die? Would you like your sins forgiven? Would you like the void deep inside of you filled? If so, there are just a few things you need to know really quickly.

1. RECOGNIZE YOU ARE A SINNER.

    Do not take that personally. We're all sinners. The Bible says we've all sinned and fallen short of God's glory.

    For all have sinned, and come short of the glory of God.

    Romans 3:23

    Every one of us has broken God's commandments. And every one of us has fallen short of God's standards. There are no exceptions.

2. REALIZE JESUS CHRIST DIED FOR YOUR SINS.

    Realize that Jesus Christ, the Son of God, voluntarily went to a cross and died there in *your place*. He came to pay a debt He did not owe because you owed a debt you could not pay. Jesus took hold of a Holy God with one hand and unholy man with the other, and they drove spikes through His hands. He died for the sins of the world. Jesus Himself said,

For God so loved the world, that He gave His only begotten Son, that whoever believes in Him should not perish but have everlasting life.

John 3:16

You need to realize you are a sinner. Recognize Christ died for you. Then you need to repent for your sins.

3. REPENT FOR YOUR SINS.

What does that mean? Well, the word *repent* means *'to change your direction.'* It means to be sorry for what you have done. But sorry enough to stop. Because the Bible says, 'godly sorrow will produce repentance.'

For godly sorrow produces repentance leading to salvation, not to be regretted; but the sorrow of the world produces death.

2 Corinthians 7:10

The Bible also tells us that 'God has commanded people everywhere to repent.'

In the past God tolerated our ignorance of these things, but now the time of deception has passed away. He commands us all to repent and turn to God.

Acts 17:30 [TPT]

What does that mean? It means repenting from all known sins. Make a U-turn on the road of life. And start following Jesus Christ.

Prayer of Salvation

4. RECEIVE JESUS CHRIST INTO YOUR LIFE.

   You must receive Jesus into your life. What does that mean? It means there must come a moment in your life, when you say, *'Jesus Christ, come into my life.'* I cannot do that for you. Only you can do it for yourself. The Bible says,

   But to all who did receive Him, to those who believed in His name, He gave the right to become children of God.

   John 1:12 [BSB]

   Jesus Himself says, 'Behold, I stand at the door and knock. And if you will hear My voice and open the door, I will come in.'

   Behold, I stand at the door, and knock. If anyone hears My voice and opens the door, I will come in to him, and dine with him, and he with Me.

   Revelation 3:20

To be a Christian is not just to follow a creed. It is having Christ Himself live in you.

Would You Like to Be Forgiven of Your Sins?

Would you like Christ to live in you now? Would you like to be forgiven of your sins? Would you like to find the meaning and purpose for your life? Would you like to go to heaven when you die? If so, would you pray this prayer with me right now?

This is a prayer where you are asking Jesus to come into your life. Again, pray this prayer. Right now. After me.

Let's Pray

Lord Jesus.

I know that I am a sinner. But I believe that you died on the cross, and shed your blood for every sin I have ever committed.

I turn now from my sin and choose to follow you from this moment forward.

Be my Savior. Be my Lord. Be my God. And my friend.

Thank you for calling me, loving me, and accepting me.

In Jesus' Name, I pray. Amen.

This Is about What God Has Done for You

If you just prayed that prayer, maybe you felt something different, like an emotional experience: a deep peace, great joy, or maybe sorrow for the things that you have done.

The again, you may be more like I was, on that day I prayed that prayer. And you felt absolutely nothing.

You Have Eternal Life

Well, listen. This is not about what you felt. This is about what God has done for you. And the Bible says, 'We write these things to you, that you might know you have eternal life.'

These things I have written to you who believe in the name of the Son of God, that you may know that you have eternal life, and that you may continue to believe in the name of the Son of God.

1 John 5:13

Prayer of Salvation

If you prayed and meant it, I want you to know that, on the authority of God's Word, you have eternal life. You will go to heaven when you die. You have made the right decision to follow Jesus Christ.

God Bless You

Bibliography

Preface

1. Burgess, W. (1999) *The Bullet.* Gospel tract. Broken Arrow, OK: His Harvest Ministries.

Introduction

1. History.com Editors. 'Columbine Shooting.' (November 9, 2009) A&E Television Networks.
2. Discussion with a Walmart District Manager. (1987)

Chapter 1

1. Copeland, G. (1994) *John G. Lake: His Life, His Sermons, His Boldness of Faith.* Fort Worth, TX: Kenneth Copeland Publications. (p. 120).
2. Christianity Today, 'Martin Luther: Passionate Reformer.' (October 17, 2017) https://www.christianitytoday.com/history/people/theologians/martin-luther.html
3. Bible Verse Study.com https://www.bibleversestudy.com/johngospel/john6-fear-not.htm
4. Church on the Move. Tulsa, OK. https://churchonthemove.com/locations/tulsa/
5. Wikipedia. 'Willie George.' https://en.wikipedia.org/wiki/Willie_George
6. Capps, C. (1993) Broken Arrow, OK. Live sermon.
7. (Capps, 1993).
8. Bible Tools. 'Witnessing.' https://www.bibletools.org/index.cfm/fuseaction/Lexicon.show/ID/G3140/martureo.htm
9. The Bible Hub. 'Faith.' https://biblehub.com/greek/4102.htm

Chapter 2

1. Dorsett, L. (1997) *A Passion for Souls: The Life of D. L. Moody.* Chicago, IL: Moody Press.
2. Graham, B. 'What did Jesus mean when he said, Let the dead bury the dead?' (October 5, 2004) Billy Graham Evangelistic Association.

Bibliography

3. Got Questions. 'What does the Bible say about repentance?'
   https://www.gotquestions.org/Bible-repentance.html
4. Men's Night June 17, 2022, Lakewood Church. Darryl Strawberry.
   https://www.youtube.com/watch?v=HF0Rr5PzG60

Chapter 3

1. O'Dell, M. (1994) *Diary of a Soldier*. Naperville, IL: O'Dell Ministries. (p. 58).
2. O'Dell, J & M. (1990) 'India Harvest Plan.' O'Dell Ministries.
   http://www.odellministries.org/index-0.html
3. Osborn, T.L., and D. (1985) *The Gospel According to TL & Daisy: Classic Documentary*. Tulsa, OK: Osfo Books.
4. (Osborn & Osborn, 1985).

Chapter 4

1. Storey, T. (1989) *Dare to be Bold: God Needs Forceful Men*. Tulsa, OK: Harrison House. (p. 43).
2. Christianity Today. 'Charles Finney: Father of American revival.'
   https://www.christianitytoday.com/history/people/evangelistsandapologists/charles-finney.html
3. Betty Crocker's Cookbook: New and Revised Edition. (January 1, 1978)
   Betty Crocker's Cookbook: New and Revised Edition: Betty Crocker: 9780307098221: Amazon.com: Books
4. Dallas, J. (2019) The Chosen: Jesus Calls Peter. Season 1, Episode 4.
   (33) The Chosen: Jesus Calls Peter - YouTube

Chapter 5

1. (Storey, 1989) (p. 122).

Chapter 6

1. Coleman, R. (1993) *The Master Plan of Evangelism: with Study Guide*. Grand Rapids, MI: Fleming H. Revell. (p. 24)
2. Cox, I., Hartman, M., Owens, M., & Passalacua, T. 'Sea Otters as Keystone Species.' Ohio State University. A World Unseen: The Diversity of Life. (April 27, 2022) https://u.osu.edu/worldunseen/2022/04/27/sea-otters-as-keystone-species/
3. Fraser, S. Life of Faith Bible Church. https://lofbc.org/

4. Pickard, N. (1988) *What Do You Say When: An Inspirational Guide to Witnessing.* Grand Rapids, MI: Baker Book House. (p. 88)
5. Dictionary of African Christian Biography. 'Idahosa, Benson Andrew.' (1995) https://dacb.org/stories/nigeria/idahosa-bensona/
6. Osborn, T.L. (1981) *Kenneth E. Hagin Camp Meeting.* Tulsa, OK. Live sermon.
7. (Osborn, 1981).

Chapter 7

1. (Pickard, 1988) (p. 13)
2. (Osborn, 1981).

Chapter 8

1. (Story, 1989). (p. 48).
2. Burgess, W. (1992) *Tongue and Interpretation.* Ponca City, OK.
3. Bells Amusement Park. https://en.wikipedia.org/wiki/Bell%27s_Amusement_Park
4. Roberts, O. (1976) *A Daily Guide to Miracles: And Successful Living Through SEED-FAITH.* Tulsa, OK: Pinoak Publications. (p.8)
5. Lindsey, H. (1978) *Late Great Planet Earth (movie).* Pacific International Enterprises.
6. Allbritton, D. (1989) *Soulwinning Seminar.* Church On The Move. Tulsa, OK. Live sermon.
7. Biblestudytools.com. 'Eyes Are Windows to the Soul Bible Verses.' (February 25, 2021) https://www.biblestudytools.com/topical-verses/eyes-are-windows-to-the-soul-bible-verses/
8. Tommy, M. *Created to Thrive: Matt Tommy Mentoring.* Online mentorship by subscription.
9. Evans, J. *Power Sales University.* Online mentorship by subscription.
10. Peter Paul Rubens. *Elevation of the Cross.* (1610-1611) [Book cover art.]

Chapter 9

1. Frodsham, S. (1948) *Smith Wigglesworth: Apostle of Faith.* Spring Field, MO: Gospel Publishing House.
2. Alcoholics Anonymous. https://www.aa.org/
3. Greek Word Studies. *Sanctify.* http://greekwordstudies.blogspot.com/2007/03/sanctify.html

Bibliography

4. Lowery, R. (1876). *Nothing But the Blood.* https://hymnary.org/text/what_can_wash_away_my_sin
5. Bible Hub. *Perfected* John 17:23. https://biblehub.com/text/john/17-23.htm
6. Strong's Concordance. *Teleioo.* https://biblehub.com/greek/5048.htm
7. White, T. (2020) *The Todd White Story: Life is Short- Leave a Legacy.* Orlando, FL: Christ for all Nations.
8. Switzer, J. ACCUWORD Translation. *Unpublished.*
9. Daugherty, B. (1998) *Living in God's Abundance.* Tulsa, OK: Victory Christian Center.
10. Provance, J & K. (2021) *I AM: Who the Bible Says I Am.* Tulsa, OK: Word and Spirit Publishing.

Chapter 10

1. Capps, C. (1984) Little Rock, AR. Live sermon.
2. Emerson, R. (1865) American essayist, lecturer, philosopher, and poet. Source: https://quotepark.com/authors/ralph-waldo-emerson/
3. George, W. (1989) *Men's Advance.* Church On the Move. Tulsa, OK. Live sermon.
4. Sumrall, L. (1981) *Rhema Bible Training Center.* Broken Arrow, OK. Live sermon.
5. Hagin, K. (1980) *Rhema Bible Training Center.* Broken Arrow, OK. Live sermon.
6. (Coleman, 1993). (p. 67)
7. (Burgess, 1999).
8. Capps, C. (1992) Broken Arrow, OK. Live sermon.
9. Lang, Chelsea. *Alla Prima Bootcamp.* Mentorship for representational art. Online mentorship by subscription.

Chapter 11

1. (Osborn & Osborn, 1985). (p. 132)
2. Tobener, J. 'Landlords Are Prohibited By Law From Entering Tenants' Units Without Proper Notice And Without A Permissible Purpose' (June 10, 2021) https://www.tobenerlaw.com/landlords-prohibited-from-entering-without-notice/
3. Dictionary.com. 'Reconciliation'. https://www.dictionary.com/browse/reconciliation

Faith For Souls

4. Bible Hub. *Reconciling.* 2 Corinthians 5:19. https://biblehub.com/greek/2644.htm
5. Merriam-Webster.com. 'Jurisdiction'. https://www.merriam-webster.com/dictionary/jurisdiction
6. (Capps, 1992).
7. Stephens. (1550) Elzevir, Griesbach, Lachmann, Tischendorf, Tregelles, Alford, & Wordsworth. (1624). *The Englishman's Greek New Testament: An Interlinear Literal Translation.* Grand Rapids, MI: Zondervan Publishing House.
8. Melchizedek, K. (2023) *Grace Realities: Where Sin Has No Dominion.* Andhra Pradesh, India. (p. 93)
9. Gainsbrugh, J. (1986) *The Joy of Evangelism.* Felton, CA: Delta Lithograph. (p. 1)
10. (Gainsbrugh, 1986) (p. 2)

Chapter 12

1. Sumrall, L. (1984) *Fishers of Men: A Handbook For Soulwinners.* South Bend, IN: LESEA Publication. (p. 53)
2. Yugoslavia. https://en.wikipedia.org/wiki/Yugoslavia
3. Campus Crusade. *Four Spiritual Laws* tract. https://campusministry.org/docs/tools/FourSpiritualLaws.pdf
4. Microsoft Bing. 'Religion.' definition of religion - Search (bing.com)
5. BBC News. 'Fall of the Berlin Wall: How 1989 reshaped the modern world.' (November 5, 2019) https://www.bbc.com/news/world-europe-50013048
6. Merriam-Webster.com. 'Conscious'. https://www.merriam-webster.com/dictionary/conscious
7. Merriam-Webster.com. 'Conscience'. https://www.merriam-webster.com/dictionary/conscience
8. Edwards, B. (2012) *Drawing From the Right Side of the Brian: The Definitive 4th Edition.* New York City, NY: TarcherPerigee.
9. Mayo Clinic. 'Reactive Attachment Disorder.' https://www.mayoclinic.org/diseases-conditions/reactive-attachment-disorder/symptoms-causes/syc-20352939
10. God Is Not Dead (movie 2014) https://www.amazon.com/Gods-Not-Dead-Kevin-Sorbo/dp/B00KD5HFJG

Bibliography

11. VisitNorway.com 'The Most Famous Fjords.' https://www.visitnorway.com/things-to-do/nature-attractions/fjords/the-fjords-explained/
12. Hapnes, A. 'National Forest Heritage in Norway.' (March 2003) WWF-Norway.
13. Strong, D. 'The Mission Field'-video. (June 11, 2011) https://www.youtube.com/watch?v=enjNRKhTP9Y
14. Strong, D. CBN News. 'US Missionary in Nepal: The Needs are Staggering.' (April 26, 2015) https://www1.cbn.com/cbnnews/world/2015/april/exclusive-us-missionary-in-nepal-the-needs-are-staggering
15. Britannica. 'Himalayas mountains, Asia.' (August 25, 2022) https://www.britannica.com/place/Himalayas
16. O'Dell, T. Frontier Evangelism. https://www.tommyodell.org/
17. Wikipedia. 'Sarah Desert.' https://en.wikipedia.org/wiki/Sahara
18. Rhodes, J. Inquiries Journal. 'Intelligent Design in the Complexity of the Human Body.' (2015, Vol 7 No. 03). http://www.inquiriesjournal.com/articles/1010/intelligent-design-in-the-complexity-of-the-human-body
19. (Sumrall, 1984) (p. 54)
20. University of Cincinnati: Online. Master of Educational Leadership Courses. https://online.uc.edu/masters-programs/med-educational-leadership/curriculum/
21. Melugin, B. (2022) *The 15 Core Tenets of Orthodox Atheism*. Creation Today blog. https://creationtoday.org/the-15-core-tenets-of-orthodox-atheism/
22. Brim, B. (1995) *The Blood and the Glory*. Tulsa, OK: Harrison House, Inc.
23. (Brim, 1995). (p. 67)

Chapter 13

1. Price, F. (1979) *Faith, Foolishness, or Presumption?* Tulsa, OK: Harrison House, Inc. (p. 146)
2. Francen, M. (1996) *A Quest for Souls*. Tulsa, OK: Francen World Outreach Publications.
3. Mitropoulos, A. (1994) *As You Go . . . Preach: The Power of Literature Evangelism*. Broken Arrow, OK: Mitropoulos Ministries, Inc.
4. (Mitropoulos, 1994) (p. 6)
5. Hagin, K. (1978) *Ministering to the Oppressed: Volume III of Satan, Demons, and Demon Possession Series*. Tulsa, OK: Faith Library Publications.

Faith For Souls

Chapter 14

1. Osborn, TL. (1981) *Miracles: Proof of God's Power.* Tulsa, OK: Osfo Books. (p. 46)
2. Bible Hub. Mark 16:20. https://biblehub.com/blb/mark/16.htm
3. O'Dell, J & M. (1990) 'India Harvest Plan.' O'Dell Ministries. http://www.odellministries.org/index-0.html
4. (O'Dell. 1990).
5. Sappenfield, M. 'Tear up the maps: Indian cities shed colonial names. The Christian Science Monitor.' (September 7, 2006).
6. 'Emancipation Proclamation.' National Archives. (January 28, 2022).
7. 'Cape Coast Castle.' Slavery and Remembrance: A Guide to Sites, Museums, and Memories. https://slaveryandremembrance.org/articles/article/?id=A0103
8. 'Voices for Human Rights.' Youth for Human Rights: Making Human Rights a Global Reality. https://www.youthforhumanrights.org/voices-for-human-rights/champions/martin-luther-king-jr.html
9. Bosworth, F.F. (1974, 9th edition) *Christ the Healer.* Old Tappan, NJ: Fleming H. Revell Company.
10. (Burgess, 1999).

Chapter 15

1. (Coleman, 1993) (p. 65)
2. (Capps, 1984).
3. Full Gospel Businessmen's Association. (established 1952) Home | FGBMFI
4. Hovercraft- Hong Kong Yaumati Ferry Co. Ltd. (43) Hovercraft - Hong Kong Yaumati Ferry Co. Ltd. - YouTube
5. Shan Chun River. https://en.wikipedia.org/wiki/Sham_Chun_River
6. Shenzhen. Shenzhen - Wikipedia
7. (Strong, 2011).

Chapter 16

1. (Pickard, 1988)
2. Bible Hub. (2004-2022) Strong's Greek: 1411. δύναμις (dunamis) -- (miraculous) power, might, strength (biblehub.com)

Bibliography

3. Evangelism Explosion. (1962) Training. https://evangelismexplosion.org/training/
4. Evangelism Explosion. Founder Dr. D James Kennedy. https://evangelismexplosion.org/about-us/history/
5. Evangelism Explosion. Classic EE – the Original. https://evangelismexplosion.org/ministries/classic-ee/
6. West Coast Life Church. Life Groups. https://www.westcoastlife.tv/lifegroups
7. (Gainsbrugh, 1986) (p.38)

Chapter 17

1. (Copeland, 1994) (p. 11)
2. (Evangelism Explosions, 1962) https://evangelismexplosion.org/
3. Wikipedia. 'Dennis Bennet (priest).' https://en.wikipedia.org/wiki/Dennis_Bennett_%28priest%29
4. Bennet, D. (1971) *The Holy Spirit and You: A Guide to the Spirit Filled Life*. Newberry, FL: Bridge-Logos.
5. Babu, S. '23 Years Since the Ghastly Killings of Graham Staines and His Sons'. Madhyaman Technologies. (January 22, 2022) https://english.madhyamam.com/india/22-years-since-the-ghastly-killings-of-graham-staines-and-his-sons-which-shook-the-nation-753505
6. Tari, M. (1971) *Like a Might Wind*. Carol Stream, IL: Creation House. (p.24-25)
7. Blue Letter Bible. *Baptizo*. https://www.blueletterbible.org/lexicon/g907/kjv/tr/0-1/
8. (Strong, 2011).

THE BULLET

This Gospel tract the Lord gave to me in an instant the moment I heard of the Columbine shooting[1]. I was overseas on the Isle of Man, which is situated between England and Ireland. As the broadcast told of the tragedy, my heart was immediately pulled to make a tract called *THE BULLET*.

I did not begin writing the tract right away. But a couple of months later, as I was attempting to visit a prisoner at the jail in Tulsa, OK, sitting waiting, for the chain gang of prisoners to be processed, I decided *'I might as well use my time and begin'* to pen the tract. Below is a reproduction of the content. I have passed out thousands of these tracts.

Note: The cover is solid black with a computerized image that looks like a bullet or a meteor shooting across, and the name is *THE BULLET*. As I began to write it came out with a rhythm.

BANG!

You're **DEAD!**

If the moment you touched this paper a bullet pierced your brain or your heart, where would you be right now?

Just 'dead...''dead like a dog...''when you're dead, you're dead...'

Is that so? Many people talk tough when they're not 'under the gun.'

A highly intelligent retired nurse once told me, 'I have seen many an atheist flat on his back, with his dying breath cry, **'OH GOD!!'**

Funny, isn't it. We all seem to know all about things we know nothing about. Let's just suppose you are the smartest human being alive...even the most intelligent man or woman the world has ever seen. You would know so much more than everyone else. You're the genius of geniuses. Smarts you've got!

Do you suppose that if you were that intelligent you would be smart enough to admit **YOU DON'T KNOW EVERYTHING?**

What if the thing you don't know is **GOD**? What if...? 'The fool says in his heart there is no God' (Psalm 14:1)

'who exchanged the truth of God for the lie, and worshipped and served the creature rather than the creator...' (Romans 1:25)

If you were that person who knew so much but did not know God...

YOU WOULD NOT KNOW

- That God loves the human race.

- That He made you unique, different from all others, made in His own image.

- That He created you on His level, not to be God, but to be of His own family, His own kind, His own child.

- That He loves you personally!

- That if there were no one else in the entire would that had 'missed the mark (sin)' and earned the 'wages of sin (death),' He still would have sacrificed His only Son to die in payment for you.

- That if you call upon Jesus Christ acknowledging His rightful LORDSHIP, God's saving LIFE will enter into you NOW.

- That peace, acceptance and self-worth will flood your heart . . . your innermost being, the moment you make Jesus Lord, **BECAUSE** . . .

JESUS TOOK YOUR BULLET!

The shot was aimed for you- but He 'stepped in front' . . . on the cross He cried in those last moments, 'Father, forgive them, they **KNOW NOT** what they do!'

The thing about Jesus though, is HE ONLY STAYED DEAD THREE DAYS! The grave could not hold Him. Hell was forced to release Him (Ezekiel 18:5-9). At daybreak that third day, Jesus Christ rose from the dead! Now He offers you a choice.

He declares to you, 'I AM the resurrection and the life: He who believes in Me, though he may die, he shall live! 'And whoever lives and believes in Me shall never die. Do you believe this?' (John 11:25-26)

When a person opens his heart to Jesus as Savior, as Lord, as his best friend- they WILL NEVER KNOW DEATH BECAUSE . . .

'He tasted death for every man,' (Hebrews 2:1)

The life that enters your soul is indescribable! More than twenty years ago I received that life. All the words to fill enough books to fill the earth cannot describe what I have.

You can have it, too. Just ask for it. Pray to your Creator.

'God, who made the heaven and the earth if You are real, I want You. I am **blown away** by Your sacrificial love for me- to give Your only Son as a human sacrifice, that I might have life! I believe Jesus rose from the dead. Now I have a choice.

I could accept Him, or I could reject Him. I make my decision: Jesus, come into my heart. Jesus, be my Savior, my Lord, my very best friend. In Jesus' Name, Amen.'

Congratulations! I am so happy about your decision! Please write me and tell me about your decision to receive the living Son of God into your heart.

HE will never leave you. HE will never forsake you. (Hebrews 13:5)

Press into His Word (the Bible) . . . it is your INHERITANCE! (Ephesians 1:17-19). Include JESUS in everything you do . . . PRAY (converse with God) (John 16:23-24). THIRST for His Presence, let Him fill you full with the Holy Spirit of God (Luke 11:13; Acts 2:1-4). **LIFE** . . . has just begun! (1 John 5:11-12)

Write me:
William Burgess
Po Box 682
Nuevo, CA 92567
Email:
pastorbill49ers@gmail.com

About the Author

William **Burgess** is a pastor and evangelist. He has pastored for more than twenty years. As an evangelist, he has served churches across the United States, teaching and demonstrating personal soul winning, working with the local pastors and congregations. In addition, William has ministered seventy trips worldwide, conducting pastors' conferences, street evangelism, and an open-air crusade with 3,500 decisions for Christ. His heart is to see believers become free to express their faith and that all men will be saved.

William has a BA in Art Education from San Jose State University, California; a Master of Educational Leadership-Administration from the University of Cincinnati, Ohio; and is a graduate of Rhema Bible Training College, with a concentration in pastoral studies.

William is married to Shirley Burgess, his partner in ministry and the love of his life.

New book coming soon!

FAITH FOR SOULS: *Supernatural Fruitfulness*

Jesus Promised Fruitfulness

> *I am the vine, you are the branches.* **He who abides in Me**, *and I in him,* **bears much fruit**; *for without Me you can do nothing.*
>
> John 15:5 (emphasis mine)

There is no believer alive who does not desire to hear the Lord speak these words: *Well done, good and faithful servant!* (Matthew 25:21 BSB). Can you imagine seeing our precious Lord Jesus face to face and for Him to greet you, pleased with a well-lived life?

All else will pass. Lives we touch with His grace and love will have eternal fruit.

He Gave Us Supernatural Tools for the Job

Jesus gave us what we need to experience a supernatural life. No person can restore a soul to God, but in Christ, we can. This is our role on the earth.

> *Now all things are of God, who has reconciled us to Himself through Jesus Christ, and* **has given us the ministry of reconciliation**.
>
> *That is, that God was in Christ reconciling the world to Himself, not imputing their trespasses to them, and* **has committed to us the word of reconciliation**.
>
> 2 Corinthians 5:18-19 (emphasis mine)

Can you imagine? Our job is to go around and tell people that God is not mad at them. He loves them, accepts them, and holds nothing against them. What a glorious gospel!

The next book in this series, **Faith For Souls: Supernatural Fruitfulness**, provides examples and teaches simple truths that will lead you to an extraordinary life of much fruit.

Sign Up for Notice of Publication

www.ingramcontent.com/pod-product-compliance
Lightning Source LLC
Chambersburg PA
CBHW072146070526
44585CB00015B/1012